VOICES  PENRITH AR

VOICES AGAINST WAR

A Century of Protest

LYN SMITH

ISIS

LARGE PRINT

Oxford

Copyright © Lyn Smith and the Imperial War Museum, 2009

First published in Great Britain 2009
by
Mainstream Publishing Company (Edinburgh) Ltd.

Published in Large Print 2010 by ISIS Publishing Ltd.,
7 Centremead, Osney Mead, Oxford OX2 0ES
by arrangement with
Mainstream Publishing Company (Edinburgh) Ltd.

British Library Cataloguing in Publication Data
Smith, Lyn, 1934–
    Voices against war.
    1. Anti-war demonstrations - - History.
    2. Pacifists - - History.
    3. Large type books.
    I. Title
    303.6'6'09–dc22

ISBN 978–0–7531–5243–0 (hb)
ISBN 978–0–7531–5244–7 (pb)

Printed and bound in Great Britain by
T. J. International Ltd., Padstow, Cornwall.

To kill one man is to be guilty of a capital crime, to kill ten men is to increase the guilt ten-fold. This the rulers of the earth all recognise, and yet when it comes to the greatest crime — the waging of war on another state — they praise it! . . . So those who recognise a small crime as such, but do not recognise the wickedness of the greatest crime of all — the waging of war on another state — cannot distinguish right and wrong. So as to right and wrong, the rulers of the world are in confusion.

Mozi, China, circa 470–391 BC

Acknowledgements

Eyebrows have often been raised at the thought of the Imperial War Museum, of all places, housing one of the largest sound archives of an anti-war movement in the world, not least by those invited by the Museum to record their testimonies on the topic. But this should not be too surprising as the Museum's writ has always been much wider than the sharp end of war. As its 21st Annual Report, published on the eve of the Second World War, explained, as well as providing a lasting memorial to common effort and sacrifice, it also aimed to demonstrate the futility of war and stated that its task was to make a historical record of war 'that was to end war'. But it is true to say that, although all the main collections contain material relating to conscientious objection, anti-war protest and peace campaigning, the issue was not given much prominence by the Museum until the 1970s, the focus being very much on the combatants and accoutrements of both world wars and other twentieth-century conflicts. The Sound Archive has been paramount in bringing this important topic to the fore. In the mid-1970s, a large collection of testimonies of First World War conscientious objects was recorded, and over the past 30 years, the archive has expanded to include the development of the movement throughout the twentieth century and beyond, up to the very moment this book goes to print.

It is on this vast and rich archive that Voices Against War is mainly based. My thanks to those within the Sound Archive: Peter Hart, Richard McDonough, Richard Hughes and James Atkinson, with a special tribute to the Keeper of the Sound Archive, Margaret Brooks, who pioneered the anti-war project and who has supported my interviewing work on the subject as well as this book. I am very appreciative of the help given by Roderick Suddaby, Tony Richards, Sabrina Rowlatt and the staff of the Documents Department, and those in the Reading andf Listening rooms who have provided tapes and other materials so willingly and efficiently. Hilary Roberts and Ian Carter of the Photograph Archive also deserve my thanks. I would like to make special acknowledgement to Abbie Ratcliffe, who has guided this book through to publication, and also to Madeleine James and Sarah Paterson for their assistance. The enthusiasm of Elizabeth Bowers for this project is also much appreciated. Terry Charman's expertise as the Museum's senior Historian is greatly valued; I am very grateful for his helpful criticisms and suggestions. At Mainsteam Publishing I thank Bill Campbell and Graeme Blaikie for their support, I also wish to express my appreciation to Karyn Millar for her patience and fine editing skills, and to thank Sharon Campbell and Kate McClelland for their valued assistance. I am indebted to my agent Barbara Levy for her advice and assistance throughout. Roderick Bailey, Fran Whittle and Debbie Locke have given their own special help, for which I am grateful. My thanks to all the members of my family and friends, whose encouragement has been so vital, with particular thanks to my husband, Peter, who has lived with anti-war protesters for many years, always interested, ever supportive.

Especially, I must thank Robert Fisk for his characteristically thought-provoking foreword; and Don McCullin for permission to use extracts from his IWM filmed interview of 2009.

Finally, my thanks to copyright holders for granting permission for the use of records, documents and photographs, with particular thanks to Mr Wilfrid Hayler and Kazuyo Yamane. My apologies to any copyright holder I have been unable to trace. This book would not have been possible without the cooperation of those who have given of their time and effort to record their testimonies, and I gladly acknowledge that my greatest debt is to them.

Contents

Foreword

My father used to call them "conchies". After dozens of postcards from his old Birkenhead schoolmates — all of which I have, all of whom died in the 1914–18 war — he headed off to Ireland and then to do his duty in the Third Battle of the Somme in 1918. He was an old-fashioned patriot and wasn't interested in men who wouldn't fight for their country. He gave me A.E.W. Mason's *The Four Feathers* to read and insisted I watch the old Zoltan Korda movie of the 1902 book in which young Harry Feversham leaves his regiment before the Sudanese campaign and receives three white feathers from his friends and one from his fiancée.

Bill Fisk wasn't trying to teach me lessons about cowardice. He just didn't want his son to be a Benjamin Britten or a W. H. Auden or a D. H. Lawrence, skiving off to America or the English countryside when the enemy was at the gates. In 1940, when the Nazis planned to invade Britain, MI5 asked Bill to lead the resistance movement in his home town of Maidstone — I long ago gave the Imperial War Museum his plans for blowing up Maidstone East railway bridge when a German troop train was passing over it — and Bill said yes, but of course the Germans would quickly have captured him and Bill would have been shot as a "terrorist". In which case there might one day — after the liberation of the United Kingdom — have been a nice little memorial stone to his memory in All Saints Church, Maidstone. But I wouldn't exist.

I don't think Bill realised that Harry Feversham wasn't a coward, but I certainly didn't want any white feathers, and I ended up witnessing more wars than Bill could ever have imagined. Given my abject fear in battle zones, I deserved a hundred white feathers, but that wasn't the point. "Tell me, Fellah," Bill would say to me. "If the Nazis were coming for your mum and dad, wouldn't you fight for them?" And of course, 1939 — when Auden really was pondering the fate of Europe from a dive on 52nd Street — was almost as critical as 1940, when Operation Sealion was about to be launched. One of Karsh's massive photographs of an ebullient Churchill hung in our dining room for decades until Bill died and my mother Peggy gently asked me if I thought it would be all right to replace it with a watercolour of All Saints Church and the River Medway.

I used to take the view that there was a middle way; that a conscientious objector — however much he hated war — could be a stretcher bearer, a padre, a front-line doctor. Thus you helped to save life while others destroyed it. In a way, I guess that's why I go to wars — to write about those who suffer — but I would never carry a rifle. But wait — I did carry a rifle in Afghanistan, in 1980, when the Soviet convoy upon which I was travelling was ambushed by the Mujahedin and when I feared that the Afghan guerrillas, if they reached our Russian army lorry, were not going to say, "Hands up, members of the National Union of Journalists, and step aside," before slaughtering the occupants of the truck. So in the end, Bill's son *was* prepared to hold a rifle, a big Kalashnikov AK-47, which a Soviet officer called Yuri handed to me. I wanted to defend myself. Would I have opened fire? I doubt it, though at school, in the Combined Cadet Force, I was quite a good shot and was even recommended for Bisley. All the targets we shot at there looked like Germans and my old Lee-Enfield .303 was, of course, Great War vintage. It was Dad's generation of rifle.

I suspect the whole thing revolves around the idea of equal sacrifice. Why should Bill prepare to join the resistance while Auden sat safe in New York? I can rage against our false wars — Where are the weapons of massive destruction? Why are we bombing the villages of Afghanistan? — but when Hitler's legions are on their way, it might be a different story. Once you start fighting in a war, of course, you are immediately complicit in a form of mass murder. I know there are rules of war — most soldiers, in my experience, don't obey them — but at the end of the day, I can only quote Tolstoy on Napoleon's invasion of Russia in *War and Peace*:

war began, that is, an event took place opposed to human reason and to human nature. Millions of men perpetrated against one another such innumerable crimes, frauds, treacheries, thefts . . . incendiarisms and murders, as in whole centuries are not recorded in the annals of all the law courts of the world, but which those who committed them did not at the time regard as being crimes.[1]

Of course, there's the comforting "they-are-worse-than-us" argument for participation in war. How can you compare the Allies to Hitler (I notice this doesn't usually contain any comparisons of Stalin to Hitler) when we know about the inhuman crimes of Nazi Germany? But that's a dodgy one, which George W. Bush and the insufferable Blair tried to mimic after the revelations of US torture at Abu Ghraib in Iraq. It was awful — but we're not as bad as Saddam. Yet if we're going to use Saddam as the base-plate for our conscience, where does that leave us? And does that square with Hamburg and Dresden and Hiroshima? Again, I know, *they* started it, in Rotterdam and London and Coventry and in the revolting behaviour of Japanese troops in South East Asia. But I was very struck in Canada recently by the words of an ex-Lancaster navigator, John Ladbrooke, who turned up in Toronto to meet his old Second World War Canadian rear-gunner, Donald Bowman. As the *Toronto Star* reported:

---

[1] Leo Tolstoy, *War and Peace*, tr. Louis and Almyer Maude (Oxford: Oxford University Press 1954).

4

One of those missions — the bombing of Darmstadt, Germany — left its mark on Ladbrooke. When he recounted it for Bowman, tears welled up in his eyes. He told Bowman how he had read a book about the damage their mission did to the city and he found it terribly upsetting. Still, it was war, he said as he tried to regain his composure and blinked back his tears. "We were engaged in something that was bigger than us."[1]

And that's one way of responding to participation in war: that it is bigger than us, that we cannot be held responsible for our part in causing pain when this titanic conflict has overwhelmed mankind. Again, that doesn't answer the conscientious objector who takes Tolstoy's view. The moment you start shooting, you are a war criminal, a murderer, outside the law. Or are you?

It's certainly easier to make this argument if you're on the side of the good guys. In two world wars, Britain did not shoot or hang those who refused to fight. Desertion, yes, on the Western Front. Not in the Second World War. But the Soviets did and — in my part of the world — the Iraqis did, the Syrians did . . . It's a lot easier to say no in Britain than it was in Saddam's Iraq, where drumhead courts decided on death for deserters during the eight-year war with Iran. I've met a man who witnessed these executions and

---

[1] "Wartime Pals Together Again", *Toronto Star* (14 April 2009).

whose friend pleaded, hopelessly, for the lives of his comrades.

And what of those who refused to serve in the *Webrmacht?* That needed fortitude of unthinkable proportions. On my wall at home in Beirut, I have a painting on a silk screen by the German artist Wolfgang Correns. It shows a pastoral scene of farm buildings and pale mountains, perhaps in Bavaria, painted in 1935, when Hitler was already two years in power. Correns's son Robert was drafted into the German army but deserted because he refused to fight for Hitler. He hid in the basement of his grandfather's home in Berlin until the end of hostilities. That took courage. Then, two days after the fall of Berlin, Soviet soldiers saw the twenty-two year old in the garden of his grandfather's home. And shot him dead.

Robert Fisk
Beirut, 2009

Introduction

On 15 February 2003, an estimated two million people took to the streets of London to protest against the build-up to the war against Iraq — a record number for any British protest. Not all of the protesters would consider themselves pacifists, but whatever the basis of objection to that war, their protest was part of one of the most enduring movements in British history. Based on 200 testimonies from the Imperial War Museum's vast collection of anti-war recordings, and a small selection of documents, this book will tell the story of a diverse range of British men and women who have participated in anti-war protests from the First World War to the present day, and others who have a point to make. Their experiences are complemented with those from other countries wherever this has been possible, or relevant. It is hoped that gathered together they will contribute to an understanding of some of the critical stages of the anti-war movement during a century of conflict and provide insights into some of the ethical and practical problems surrounding the issues of war, peace and conflict resolution in today's troubled world.

The all-embracing term "anti-war" is used in this book. It covers pacifism in all its shades, as well as those who eschew the concept as applying to themselves but for a variety of reasons have resisted war and militarism and worked for peace. Pacifism in its basic sense is the belief that all war and violence is wrong and should be rejected; its historical roots go back almost 2,000 years, a significant, more recent, stage being the Peace Testimony of the Quakers in 1661. Pacifists have always been central to the anti-war movement. The term "pacificist" is used for those who disapprove of war and realise that its prevention must always be attempted, but accept that it is sometimes necessary. Pacificism developed in the eighteenth century from the twin roots of Christianity and political Radicalism. Other protesters take the view that war itself is not wrong but some part of it is unacceptable, or perhaps a particular conflict may be considered unjustified. The distinction between these various positions may seem straightforward enough, but when looking at how witnesses in this book perceive and justify their own anti-war stances and obligations to society, a large range of different, often confused, positions are revealed, illustrating the sheer complexity of the issue.

Another source of confusion concerns the relationship between pacifism and conscientious objection, terms that are often used synonymously. Conscientious objection is a status granted by the state to an individual who refuses to participate in a war into which he or she has been conscripted; such a person is a conscientious objector (CO), not necessarily a pacifist. Logically, in time of war pacifists should be COs, but not all COs need be pacifists. Conscientious objection, as with pacifism, is of a highly individual nature. COs have objected to very different aspects of wars and have submitted a wide range of reasons for their objections, including religious, moral, humanitarian and political grounds, and often a mix of these. It is no wonder that tribunals, when attempting to test the sincerity of would-be COs, found the task so daunting.

Developments in the anti-war movement have always been connected with international events. It was the First World War that led to the emergence of the modern anti-war movement, when, in January 1916, national conscription for military service was introduced for the first time in British history, and a new group, conscientious objectors — the "conchies" — came into being. In all, 16,000 COs faced tribunals during the war. They were branded as cowards, reviled and persecuted. Many endured repeated prison sentences; some, like Howard Marten, faced the death penalty; a number ended the war with impaired health; and 69 died. Yet by 1919 it was accepted that a man had a right to follow his conscience in time of war, and the foundations had been laid for all subsequent protests against war until the present day.

The story continues through the interwar period of peace, covering the expansion of the movement when it gained public legitimacy. Some notable personalities became very influential to the cause of peace at this time, not least Mahatma Gandhi, whose policy of non-violence (satyagraha) took a strong hold that has lasted to the present day — the young Tony Benn, for instance, who sat at Gandhi's feet, being strongly impressed. Influential peace organisations were founded: War Resisters' International (WRI) and the Peace Pledge Union (PPU), for example. The PPU, under the leadership of the charismatic and socially acceptable parson Dick Sheppard, became particularly important, attracting a vast following of signed-up supporters by 1938. But with the rise of Hitler and the spread of other forms of totalitarianism during the 1930s, a crisis occurred that led to much painful heart-searching within the anti-war ranks, causing many to leave the movement, arguing, as A. A. Milne did, that the Fascist advance had to be stopped. Even so, during the Second World War sixty thousand men successfully claimed conscientious objection, almost four times as many as in the First World War. After women were conscripted in December 1941, there were 1,074 who faced tribunals.

Voices from the Second World War reveal important changes in treatment: there was a concern to fit objectors into work that they could conscientiously perform and find satisfying, unlike the boring, menial nature of alternative work offered to the conchies of the earlier war. They also had a relatively easier time with the authorities and the public, although brutality (albeit more random) did occur, and many suffered physical and mental abuse. There was no real movement in this war to fight against conscription — that struggle had already been won; also, being more dispersed and less liable to repeated prison sentences, the camaraderie that had been so vital for the 1914–18 COs was not so strongly developed in their Second World War counterparts. This resulted in feelings of loneliness and isolation, which many describe. The exceptions were members of tight-knit units like the Friends Ambulance Unit (FAU) and the Parachute Field Ambulance (PFA), who performed their humanitarian service alongside fighting troops, bonding together as they shared the risks and dangers of war zones. Excruciating dilemmas also confronted many conchies in this war, especially when the full horror of Nazism emerged. This led many to revise their stance and enter the forces. Conversely, many combatants, witnessing the reality of a Total War of epic proportions, opted to leave, claiming CO status.

Conscription continued into the post-war period with the introduction of National Service for young men between the ages of 18 and 20. Just over 9,000 registered as COs, a much smaller proportion than in the Second World War — this was in line with the declining support for the anti-war movement in the early post-war period. With the emergence of the anti-nuclear protest in 1958 the movement began to recover, but not quickly enough to have much impact on the attitudes of conscripts, as National Service ended in 1960, the last conscripts discharged in 1963. This meant that Britain was never to experience anything like the anti-draft movement that erupted in the United States with the Vietnam War in the 1960s.

During the Cold War, it was the growing awareness of the nature of atomic weapons and the developing nuclear-arms race between the two superpowers — the United States and the Soviet Union — that gave rise to a new kind of protest, which related more to the moral issue of the survival of mankind rather than war. From the 1950s, this led to the formation of a range of anti-nuclear organisations, the Campaign for Nuclear Disarmament (CND) and the Greenham Women's Peace Camp the most well known. Testimonies from this period chart the successes and failures of the so-called "nuclear pacifists", as well as the splits and schisms within the anti-nuclear movement and between this and the more traditional pacifist organisations such as the PPU and WRI.

The end of the Cold War and initial hopes of a more peaceful world led to a lull in anti-war and peace activity. But the failure of the "peace dividend", which resulted in a new range of regional and intrastate conflicts, fed a resurgence. The First Gulf War of 1990–1, the Balkan wars of 1991–5, the Afghanistan war of 2001 and continuing conflict in the Middle East had great impact on the movement, not least because of the vast numbers of civilian deaths in these conflicts graphically portrayed in the press and on TV. Images of devastation, streams of refugees and horrendous human suffering resulted in a widespread gut reaction against war. This was a factor that, together with a growing suspicion of the fraudulent basis of another conflict building up in Iraq, fed the huge public outcry against that war in 2003 and the mass mobilisation of a wave of protesters to the ranks of new anti-war organisations such as the Stop the War Coalition (STWC), the Muslim Association of Britain (MAB) and, later, after the war had started, support for Military Families Against the [Iraq] War (MFAW). Much of the revulsion against war in the twenty-first century has a very different basis from the ideological and philosophical bases of earlier protesters, although the pacifist stance is a continuing thread.

Given the nature of oral history and the dependence on individual testimony, inevitably there are gaps in this book. There is, for example, a paucity of voices from service personnel who, since the end of conscription in 1960, as volunteers to the Armed Services, have refused to serve in certain wars for various reasons, many facing court martial, dishonourable discharge and prison sentences. This is particularly regretted, but, given the terms of the Official Secrets Act, it has not been possible to interview these people or publish written accounts.

The twentieth century is regarded as the most bloody in history, claiming 187 million deaths in war. As the century progressed, a far higher percentage of war fatalities were civilian than in any previous century: during the First World War, one-fifth of casualties were civilian; the figure rose to two-thirds in the Second World War; in twenty-first-century warfare, such as Iraq, the estimated figure is as high as 90 per cent. But, as I hope the voices in this book reveal, these turbulent years are also notable for a robust resistance to warfare and a vigorous struggle for peace as well as continuing non-violent activism, which started with Mahatma Gandhi.

Pacifism, in all its variants, is often identified with eccentricity, truculence, self-righteousness, even with a lack of moral fibre, but the voices that echo throughout this century of strife should indicate a different, more positive, perspective: that of human endurance, sacrifice, fortitude and high moral purpose. It is hoped that their testimonies will provide insights into the complexity of the anti-war issue, as well as offering a counterbalance and complement to the vast range of military accounts of conflicts. For my part, it has been a pleasure and great privilege to have met so many people in the movement and to have recorded their experiences. I dedicate this book to them and their fellow campaigners, who, each in their own way, have struggled against war and tried to push the world along the path of peace.

Lyn Smith
June 2009

CHAPTER
ONE

1914–18: First World War

Having the death sentence read out gave you the sort of feeling of being outside yourself. It was very curious. A sort of impersonal feeling, something that wasn't affecting you personally, that you were almost looking on at the proceedings. Very strange . . .

At the outbreak of war in August 1914, Britain had not within living memory been involved in a European war. Few had any conception of what such a war entailed, least of all the generals who had fought in the Boer War, which had ended just over a decade ago. The response, in the main, was enthusiastic, and young men, many underage, flocked to the recruitment centres eager to join the fight before it was over. Eighteen months later, 2,675,149 Britons had volunteered, but by January 1916 numbers had drastically declined. From November 1914, the stalemate of trench warfare had set in on the Western Front and, given the high death toll and injury rate, there was no escaping the fact that a long war of attrition lay ahead and many more soldiers were going to be required than in any previous war.

In August 1915, a new Act had been passed whereby the Local Government Board was empowered to register all men between 15 and 65 years of age. When the register revealed that 2,179,231 single men of military age were still not in the forces, the Earl of Derby, in his new role as Director General of Recruiting, launched the so-called "Derby Scheme" in the push for volunteers. Many rallied to the call, but not enough. The Dardanelles disaster had raised the casualty rate to 528,227 killed, wounded or missing, and conscription had become unavoidable.

Among all the Great Powers involved, Britain alone did not have conscription at the outbreak of war. On 5 January 1916, a Military Service Bill was put forward by Herbert Asquith, the British prime minister, which introduced national conscription for the first time in British history. The Bill was approved on 24 January by 383 votes to 36, after heated and bitter debate. Opposition to the Bill came not only from pacifists but also from those arguing on political, moral, legal and humanitarian grounds. In effect, from 2 March 1916, under the Military Service Act (MSA), single British male citizens aged 18 to 41 were liable for call-up; after a few months, it was extended to include married men. Exemptions were granted for those doing work of national importance, recognised demands of business and for those with a conscientious objection to bearing arms. Tribunals were established to test the sincerity of those who refused to fight. This is when a new concept, the "conchies", came into being: men who were prepared to go to great lengths to stand up for their beliefs, forming a movement that, in effect, challenged the authority of the state.

Conscientious objectors came from very different social, political and educational backgrounds, and their objection stemmed from a variety of roots that supported the legality and morality of their position. They included socialists, Christians of different denominations, Jehovah's Witnesses, Christadelphians, Plymouth Brothers, Muggletonians, Quakers and intellectual gatherings such as the Bloomsbury Group. There were great differences in the way these individuals and groups reacted to the war and how much compromise they were prepared to make.

The Labour Party, being the most internationally minded political party, opposed the war in principle, but once war started divisions emerged, with many members swept along by the patriotic fervour of the time, particularly after the German invasion of Belgium on 4 August 1914. The group of parliamentary pacifists was led by Ramsay MacDonald. The Union of Democratic Control, a pressure group that called for a negotiated peace, was founded in 1914. Keir Hardie and George Lansbury, both members of the Independent Labour Party (ILP), continued to passionately denounce the war.

During the war, two organisations were formed for pacifists and other war-resisters. The No-Conscription Fellowship (NCF) was set up in November 1914. Fenner Brockway was the honorary secretary and Clifford Allen its chairman. Its membership was open to men of all political and religious opinions liable for call-up who would refuse to bear arms from conscientious motives. Another organisation, the Fellowship of Reconciliation (FOR), had been founded in December 1914. This was an association of Christian pacifists of all denominations.

Very soon after the Military Service Bill was passed, a two-day meeting organised by the NCF was held in Devonshire House, the Quaker headquarters in Bishopsgate. Two thousand young men from one hundred and ninety-eight

17

branches across the country attended. During the meeting, the framework of resistance to bearing arms was laid down. The men voted to reject service as stated in the Bill and refuse to engage in all alternative work likely to help organise the country for war. The exact form of protest was left to the individual. On the second day of the meeting, the names of 15 COs already arrested were announced. At the end of the meeting, the agreed pledge was read out by Clifford Allen, vowing "whatever the penalties awaiting us, to undertake no service which for us is wrong . . ." As members emerged from the meeting, pro-conscription hecklers outside gave a taste of the vitriol and hostility that was to increase during the next three years of war.

Military conscription for women was not considered in the First World War, but women played an important role on the home front, working either to persuade men into the war, or to oppose it. The women's Suffragette movement had gained in strength by 1914. At first it opted for peace, but soon the mood shifted and the agreement was made to halt pacifist activity until the end of the war. In fact, with Mrs Pankhurst in the lead it was active in the recruitment of women munition workers, and its members were busy handing out white feathers, the traditional symbol of cowardice, to "shirkers". The "Peacettes", many of whom were Suffragettes, continued to oppose the war. They had their roots in the Hague Conferences of 1899 and 1907. Overcoming the huge problems of wartime travel, just three British delegates out of the one hundred and eighty who aimed to get there managed to attend the Hague Conference in April 1915. In all, 2,000 women of 12 countries attended the conference, their main demands being cooperation in place of conflict, an end to the bloodshed, the establishment of a just and lasting peace, and women's participation in the post-war peace settlement. Once conscription was introduced in 1916, women played a vital role in providing practical and psychological support for COs, serving on committees, attending tribunals, speaking at public meetings against the war and keeping homes and businesses going. By 1918, when most of the leadership of the NCF was in gaol, it was their women supporters who kept the organisation alive, Catherine Marshall taking over Clifford Allen's role as chairman while he was in prison. Other pacifist women, mainly from the upper and middle classes, opted for humanitarian service in the Voluntary Aid Detachments (VADs), or drove ambulances with the First Aid Nursing Yeomanry (FANY).

Bert Brocklesby, alternativist (later absolutist) CO, Conisbrough, South Yorkshire

I got what was perhaps my earliest lesson in international pacifism from a young German, Walter, who had left his own country to avoid being conscripted and had settled in Conisbrough as a pork butcher. He became unpopular during the Boer War because he was able to see the issues with an unbiased mind. One day — I was about eleven years old — I saw him working in the yard below a room where we played. I called out "pro-Boer!" and dodged out of sight. He came upstairs to where we were playing and asked me if the Methodists were praying for victory. I said they were. He then told me that Paul Kruger was a

Christian; did I suppose *he* was praying for victory? I supposed so. "Well," he remarked, "that puts God into a fix, doesn't it?" And he left me to think it over. I remembered that simple wordplay when 14 years later we were again praying for victory . . .

Howard Marten, alternativist CO, London

Even as far back as the Boer War, I felt that war was inconsistent with our Christian beliefs. I was at school at the time and enjoyed a certain amount of unpopularity because of my pacifist views, and there was a good deal of violence in London towards what they called the "pro-Boers" — the epithet which was flung at pacifists. The old Queen's Hall was the scene of many meetings held against the Boer War. That, I think, was my first experience of being personally involved in peace work . . . But between the Boer War and the war of 1914 was a more or less quiescent period, although I think many people, with hindsight, realised that there was a certain inevitability about the way things were going — the building up of the German fleet as a challenge to the Royal Navy, and the attitudes of both ourselves and the Germans were becoming increasingly difficult to meet with.

Harold Bing, absolutist CO, London

When I heard that a big anti-war demonstration was to be held in Trafalgar Square on Sunday, 2nd August 1914, and that Keir Hardie was to be one of the speakers, I walked up from my home to Trafalgar Square — about eleven miles — took part in that demonstration, listened to Keir Hardie and of course walked home again afterwards, which perhaps showed a certain amount of boyish enthusiasm for the anti-war cause. It was quite a thrilling meeting with about 10,000 people there and certainly very definitely anti-war. But at the very same time, while we were demonstrating in Trafalgar Square, the Cabinet was sitting at Downing Street deciding on the ultimatum which brought the country into the war two days later, on 4th August.

Fenner Brockway, absolutist CO, London

The whole ILP was anti-militarist, internationalist. We could never think in terms of taking up arms against our fellow workers, and as the war of 1914–18 approached, we became very strongly against the danger of war . . . Almost on the eve of war, a great conference was held in the Cathedral of Basel, Switzerland, where Keir Hardie and others spoke from the pulpit. *Thousands* were against the war and yet, nevertheless, war *was* declared . . . And I remember that day and how

21

our banner heading on the *Labour Leader* was: "The German workers are still our brothers." And we were encouraged by the fact that in Germany, socialists were opposed to the war: Karl Liebknecht, and Rosa Luxemburg — my political heroine.

Bert Brocklesby, alternativist (later absolutist) CO, Conisbrough, South Yorkshire

On August Bank Holiday, a group of us set off on our cycles making for Castleton in the Peak District, where our choir was having its annual outing. Just before we left them, we all sang hymns together in the Winnats gorge. There seemed something very solemn and impressive about this, and we could not at the time realise that we were singing goodbye to peace and indeed the funeral song of a whole era. The next day saw us as far away as Wolverhampton. The whole country was seething with excitement as the Germans had invaded Belgium and Britain might be at war at any time. People seeing us with our camping equipment asked if we were joining up. Heading for Kidderminster the next morning, we passed a newsagent by the roadside, where we saw a placard: "Britain declares war on Germany." We were *stunned*. War with Germany! How could such a thing be? The ruling houses of Britain and Germany were linked by the closest ties of blood. Queen Victoria had seen to that, thinking it was a sure way to preserve peace. So that is how we received the most fateful news, and from that time, the world became a quite different place.

Sybil Morrison, Suffragette, London

What I chiefly remember about London then was the excitement. People were excited, they weren't horrified by it as they were in the Second World War — it was *completely* different. They rushed out in the street, followed the soldiers as they marched through the streets and kissed them, threw flowers and seemed to think it was something to be thrilled about because we were told it was all going to be over by Christmas . . . We were conned. We were made to believe this was a war to end all wars and there'd never be another war. I don't know how I could have been so foolish because my intelligence, not my experience, tells me that you can't end wars by using wars. But we certainly believed it then.

Bert Brocklesby, alternativist (later absolutist) CO, Conisbrough, South Yorkshire

The first signs of madness soon appeared. We saw details of the army mobilising and the papers reporting thousands of recruits volunteering for service at every recruiting station in the country . . . It seemed *monstrous* to me that men should sell their souls to wicked commanders who might order them to commit the foulest crimes . . . to start hating millions of people I had never seen.

Rose Kerrigan (Klasko), schoolgirl, Glasgow

The war started when I was 11. At school, we were told that we went to war to save little Belgium because it had been attacked. And there was all this propaganda about the German soldiers bayoneting babies and everything . . . My dad said this wasn't true, that really the war was for markets, that Germany wanted to expand their colonies like Britain and France, and this is why we'd gone to war.

Fenner Brockway, absolutist CO, London

In 1915, with the prospect of conscription, the opposition to the war took a new form. It was my wife who suggested that those of us who would refuse military service should get together . . . I got my wife to write a letter to the *Labour Leader* advocating that. As a result of that, the names poured in of young men who would refuse to fight in the war . . . As all these names poured in, we formed ourselves into a committee under the chairmanship of Clifford Allen. I wouldn't say that we had any common philosophy then — all the implications of pacifism. But the statement of principles, which those who joined the

No-Conscription Fellowship signed, spoke of the sanctity of human life, and its essence was pacifist.

Howard Marten, alternativist CO, London

You found the ranks of the No-Conscription Fellowship were made up of men from every conceivable angle of life. You had all sorts of religious groups, from the Salvation Army to the Seventh-Day Adventists, Church of England, Roman Catholics; there was no limit. It was a sort of cross section of every type. Then you had in addition to that the more politically minded: the Independent Labour Party, and different degrees of socialists, and the ordinary political parties. Then a very curious group of what I used to call "artistically minded". There were a lot of men who were not in any way organised or attached, but I should call them the "aesthetic group": artists, musicians, all that. They had a terrific repugnance at war, which could only express itself individually . . . There were of course splits within the NCF and within the pacifist movement. They were some of the most argumentative people. You found so many points of view; it seemed inherent among pacifists. The thing that brings them to that point is that they're all men of strong individuality, and when you get that clash of personality coming along, you almost inevitably strike strong differences of opinion.

Wilfred Littleboy, absolutist CO, Birmingham

Well then, "Will you March too, or wait till March 2?" as the posters went in 1916 — that was the date when the conscription Act first came in, and special tribunals were set up to which people might apply [as conscientious objectors]. Their first duty was to be quite sure that the conviction that was claimed by applicants was really genuine, and there was very little difficulty for most members of the Society of Friends: it was recognised and accepted that would be the case. But those whose claims were on political or moral grounds, rather than religious, had a much more difficult time in proving their conviction before tribunals.

By the end of March 1916, 2,000 tribunals had been established. These were under the aegis of the War Office until 1917, when the Ministry of Labour and National Service took control of all recruiting matters. Tribunals were to be composed of members of "impartial and balanced judgement", but in fact the system seldom achieved this aim. Hearings were held in public and were usually of about five minutes' duration. Applicants were allowed to be represented by a friend or a solicitor. Tribunal panels were composed of eight or nine members who were appointed by the Borough or District Council concerned. They were local dignitaries who generally had very little legal experience, with many strongly supporting the war, except for a small number of Quakers who were appointed. A uniformed military representative also served on the panel. Although a few women were appointed, members were mainly men. Both the applicant and the military representative had the right of appeal to an appeal tribunal whose members were appointed by the Crown. The justice of the system depended largely on the way in which tribunals interpreted and used their powers.

A CO applied to his local tribunal for exemption to military service. The panel attempted to judge the sincerity of the young men standing before it with probing questions that it hoped would reveal the depth and degree of objection. Religious objectors found it easier to convince tribunals of their sincerity than those who objected on moral, humanitarian or political grounds. The tribunal was given four options: refusal of exemption, exemption from combatant duty only, exemption conditional on undertaking work of national importance, and absolute exemption. If the CO was rejected by the local tribunal or offered an unacceptable position, he could then attend an appeal tribunal, and if he was refused again, he could then appear before a central tribunal in London.

Two main categories of COs went before tribunals. "Alternativists" were those COs who rejected military service but were prepared to accept alternative forms of service. COs who accepted alternative forms of service at their tribunal were in three main groups: men performing non-combatant duties in the army, including those serving in the Royal Army Medical Corps (RAMC); those who undertook various forms of civilian work; and those engaged in humanitarian relief work. Tribunals would receive a list of occupations identified as being work of national importance. The recommendations included agriculture, market gardening, forestry, food supply, shipping, transport, mining, education, civilian hospitals, asylums and infirmaries. They also included those working with the Friends Relief Service (FRS) and the Friends Ambulance Unit (FAU), the former organisation working with civilians only, the latter willing to work alongside the fighting troops.

"Absolutists", on the other hand, were men who were unwilling to accept anything short of the absolute exemption that tribunals were empowered to give under the MSA. They were determined to oppose conscription uncompromisingly and thus to end it, and rejected any negotiation with the authorities. Very few COs were given this exemption; this meant that just over 6,000 were arrested and taken to the army barracks or camp to which they had been assigned and put in the guardroom. How long a man was detained there depended on how willing he was to obey military orders. Sooner or later he would disobey an order — refuse to don an army uniform, for instance — and then be subject to a court martial followed by a prison term. At first this would be in a military prison, then, from mid-1916, in a civilian prison. A standard sentence was 112 days' hard labour, fewer with good-conduct remission. After serving his sentence and being freed, the CO was then rearrested as a deserter, court-martialled once more and returned to prison — the so-called "cat-and-mouse" system. It is calculated that some 655 objectors were court-martialled twice, 521 three times, 319 four times, 50 five times and 3 six times. As the war dragged on, sentences were increased to up to two years' hard labour.

Concerns had been expressed during the passage of the MSA that an objector might become liable to the death penalty. These seemed justified when 35 COs were shipped with their regiments to France in May and June 1916, when it was rumoured that the death sentence — permitted under army law — had been imposed on them. It was confirmed on 29 June by the Under-Secretary for War, H. J. Tennant. However, it proved to be an exercise in intimidation, as it was soon announced that in all cases the sentence had been commuted to penal servitude.

Howard Marten, alternativist CO, London

My first, local tribunal was pretty hostile. They were men of not very great depth of vision or understanding, and although I wouldn't say that I was a complete absolutist, a do-nothing, I wasn't prepared to do anything under military direction, or to be exempted in a very restricted way. I think people get the impression that it was only that people wouldn't fight. It was something more than that; it was an objection to having one's life directed by an outside authority . . .

After I had been rejected by the tribunals, I was committed to a magistrate's court to await a military escort. And then I was handed over to a military escort and taken to Mill Hill Barracks. Then the first thing you had to face was putting on a [army] uniform. You see, you either had to accept uniform and take it or you had to sit on or lay on the floor and kick. Well, I wasn't prepared to do undignified things. I said to the NCOs in charge, "Look here. I suppose you've got orders to dress me forcibly. I have no objection to putting on a uniform, but it won't alter my attitude." And I compromised in that way.

Stephen Winsten, alternativist CO, London

When I had to go before my tribunal, I found that I couldn't say, "I'm a political conscientious objector or a religious conscientious objector . . ." I just couldn't label myself. So I was told by Fenner Brockway, "Look here, if you're going before a tribunal, get a letter of some kind." So I asked Aylmer Maude, the chief biographer of Tolstoy, who wrote a letter saying: "Pacifism to him is native even if he can't justify it or explain it, and you'll never get him to fight. He'll be useless to you and, in fact, he may be a nuisance by talking to others, preventing soldiers doing their bit." So the military representative simply said, "Don't you think, Mr Winsten, that this country that's provided you with work, given you a good job as a teacher, don't you think you *owe* something to such a country?" That letter didn't influence him in the least because he thought it was one conchie supporting another conchie — the same old story everywhere . . . He meant that I was a dirty cad and that I wasn't going to get away with this kind of plea. I was then teaching in the roughest school in London and teaching according to my principles all the time. So I said to him, "It is because I *love* England, sir, that I'm willing to serve in any position and do a service which I don't think you would ever do." "Well," he said, "I think we'll put you down as a political objector. And therefore you can't get exemption. We can only give it to religious [objectors]." There it was. So he did.

Wilfred Littleboy, absolutist CO, Birmingham

I went before the tribunal here in Birmingham. Neville Chamberlain, then Lord Mayor of Birmingham, was in the chair . . . he was, within limits, entirely considerate: "Couldn't you do so and so?" and "You're an accountant, couldn't you go into the office of a munitions factory? You'd be paid as an accountant." Well, I was surprised that a person of his intelligence asked a question of that kind because the answer, to me at any rate, seemed so obvious. In the end he said, "Well, I'm proposing to adjourn this case for a month to give you time to think it over, to come back with a further suggestion in a month's time." I said, "I can't give to you the slightest expectation that I shall make any change." "Well," he said, "nevertheless I'm going to give you that opportunity." . . .

Next time I came up, there was another chairman, and he was much more rigid and started immediately telling me off because I'd not accepted the opportunity of finding a way out. And I discovered that it's much easier to say "no" to a person who's losing his temper than to go on saying "no" to a person who's entirely considerate of you.

George Dutch, absolutist CO, Maxton Camp, 1916

The major was very unpleasant, hectoring. "Well," he said when he'd read my statement, "all I can say is that in my opinion conscientious objection is just another name for cowardice" — very insulting and unpleasant . . . Then he said, "Take him away! Take him away and don't put a rag on him, he's got to dress himself [in army uniform]." And of course the NCOs did as they were told. I was taken back, and they stripped me of my own clothing and put the uniform down beside me and said, "Now you've got to put it on." I said, "I will *not* put it on." They said, "All right, you've got to sit there." I sat there . . .

After a day or two, suddenly my tent was taken up and put right up on top of the cliff overlooking the sea. This was November and it was pretty cold, misty weather. My uniform was put beside me again by the tent pole, and just to make things worse than ever, they rolled the tent walls up so that the wind came right into the tent, all round, and I could just sit there and freeze, which I did. The orders were that no one was to come near me until I dressed and came down. Well I didn't dress and didn't go down. I stayed there, I'm not quite sure how long it was, but I think it must have been at least ten days — and nights — in just my singlet and pants. Before I'd been there many hours, I was frozen right through with exposure. So frozen that I didn't feel a lot, I was just insensitive. I just sat there and set my teeth to stick whatever came . . .

(Sir) Francis Meynell, absolutist CO, imprisoned in Hounslow Barracks, London, 1917

I decided to do the strike very early on. I had a good friend, a socialist and a doctor, who advised that a hunger strike by itself would never succeed, but thirst striking would very quickly bring one to the point of death. The idea of hunger striking came from the Suffragettes. I had my call-up, and instead of waiting to be arrested, I surrendered to a police station. Then, in Hounslow Barracks, I was taken before a sergeant major with a strong face and tender eye, and we had a real argument. I told him that I refused to do active service and why I had done so . . .

The first few days I put water in my mouth and spat it out, thinking that it wouldn't affect things. But then my doctor friend visited and said not at all, that I would be absorbing it, so I had to give that up. The painful thing was the drying up of my tongue; it was really like a little piece of wood in the decaying barrel of my mouth. That was highly unpleasant and that developed late in the strike — on the ninth or tenth day . . . Throughout my hunger strike, I had fantasies of flying to heaven and also of walking home; I was certainly not in an ordinary frame of mind. Psychologically, from one's physical condition, one did get into a state of euphoria. I used to have a bath and would lie in the water, but the doctor advised me to give that up as I was absorbing water. There was a danger of brain damage, although I didn't know much about that at the time. I don't think that I ever felt that I had to give my hunger strike up; I think that my absolute set of mind became even firmer the more infirm I became. I thought it would be a quick thing — release from the barracks or death . . . My doctor friend came to see me one day and told me that I would last two days, no longer, so I knew that I was about to collapse . . .

After my release, I had to have elaborate treatment to my stomach. This was the early days of radiotherapy and I had a lot of that. It was some weeks before I returned to a normal state and back to work. My action was decisive and over more quickly. I thought going to prison would be more horrifying. I hope martyrs felt the same, but ridiculous, really, to think of me as a martyr!

Fenner Brockway, absolutist CO, repeated prison sentences 1916–19

I was in prison when 39 [sic] boys were condemned to death in France. It was really the activity of Catherine Marshall, secretary of the National Union of Women's Suffrage Societies; Sir

John Simon; Asquith [the prime minister]; and others who saved them from being shot. There was a deputation to Asquith very late at night, and he gave instructions that although they had been sentenced they were not to be shot . . . They were taken to France because they couldn't be sentenced to death here.

Howard Marten, alternativist CO, imprisoned in Rouen Camp, France, 1916

I think there was a very definite movement that they would break our resistance by sending us to France. If they could get us into the firing line, then they could pass the death sentence, and that was that. Well, they got us, the first party, about 17 of us. As it happened, a message got out because somebody in the train crossing London threw a note which landed on the platform, which reached somebody he knew in the headquarters of the No-Conscription Fellowship. That was the first word that got around that we were on our way to France. It enabled the NCF and others to realise our whereabouts. Of course, there was a tremendous fight going on in Parliament during all this period . . .

The first punishment in Cinder City Camp was stopping three days' pay, but as we refused pay under any circumstances, that amounted to nothing. Then we were given 28 days' field punishment. Now field punishment can be a very nasty thing. In its most extreme form, a man can be tied up to a gun carriage, which isn't at all a pleasant thing. But normally he's sent to what is known as a field punishment barracks, and there the prisoners are tied up for three nights out of four. They're tied up maybe on a fence, or to ropes, with their arms extended and their feet tied together, or they may be tied back to back. It varies in form, and that's done for two hours. Not exactly a pleasant experience and it happened to me . . .

Then we were forever being threatened with the death sentence. Over and over again we'd be marched out and read a notice: some man being sentenced to death through disobedience at the front. It was all done with the idea of intimidating us . . .

Finally, after our second court martial, we were taken out to the parade ground, where a big concourse of men was lined up in an immense square. We were taken to the side of it, and then under escort taken out one by one to the middle of the square. I was the first . . . Then an officer in charge of the proceedings read out the various crimes and misdemeanours — refusing to obey a lawful command, disobedience at Boulogne and so on and so forth — and then: "The sentence of the court is to suffer death by being shot." Then there was a pause, and one thought, "Well, that's that." And then, "Confirmed by the Commander-in-Chief." That's double-sealed it now. Then another long pause, and, "But subsequently commuted to penal servitude for ten years." . . . Having the death sentence read out gave you the sort of feeling of being outside yourself. It was very curious. A sort of impersonal feeling, something that wasn't affecting you personally, that you were almost looking on at the proceedings. Very strange . . .

Bert Brocklesby, alternativist (later absolutist) CO, repeated prison sentences, including Henriville and Rouen camps, France, 1916

Ten years held no terrors for us. We would only be held in prison till the end of the war, and we should be saved from all the cat-and-mouse business that some thousands of COs were steadfastly enduring.

We were moved in stages: first to the field punishment barracks, then to Rouen Military Prison. Then we were marched down to the quayside to await transport to England. Our appearance, as British soldiers under guard, aroused much speculation amongst the townsfolk, who gathered in a crowd of perhaps a hundred or more. Among them were the ordinary British Tommies, who, when they heard we were conchies on our way back to England instead of being shot, became very indignant, and one who could speak French tried to incite the crowd to throw us in the river. But he had no success and we got safely aboard the steamer when it arrived . . . When we were at sea, we hugged each other and rejoiced at leaving that land of death behind. How much a land of death we were to learn later: about the time we were in Rouen Military Prison, one of the bloodiest battles of all history, the Battle of the Somme, was being fought.

Howard Marten, alternativist CO, imprisoned in Rouen Camp, France, 1916

I know one lady, she was the acting secretary of the NCF, and she was very much of the opinion that it would have been much better if we *had* been shot, that the movement would have gained considerably by our deaths. But I never heard any of our men expressing that point of view — that it would have been marvellous propaganda.

Harold Bing, absolutist CO, repeated prison sentences 1916–19

Under a hard-labour sentence, third-division hard labour, which was the severest kind of imprisonment known to the English law at the time, the first month was spent in solitary confinement in the cell, out for the half-hour or so exercise each day. Of course, we were not allowed to talk to anyone else; we marched round the exercise yard at least a yard apart.

Mark Hayler, absolutist CO, repeated prison sentences 1916–19, from his notes

What the silence system means is known only to those who have experienced it. To see all around you human beings like yourself and not to be able to speak to them is the most inhuman punishment that can be meted out to any person. It is cruel and heartless.

Joseph Hoare, alternativist (later absolutist) CO, repeated prison sentences 1916–19

The first night in Pentonville was my first in prison, and a very uncomfortable one too. You weren't allowed a mattress on the bed in those days. There was a zeppelin raid when the first zeppelin was brought down in flames in Potters Bar. I remember the terrific anti-aircraft fire, which created a panic in prison — mainly ordinary prisoners then. They were picking up their stools and banging on the iron doors and standing and screaming, and some were obviously being lugged down the iron steps to the basement like sacks; you could hear it. And then the terrific flare as the zeppelin caught fire. On each of the two wings I can remember the white faces of people looking out of the little windows of the prison . . .

George Dutch, absolutist CO, repeated prison sentences 1916–18

Later, I was put in a solitary-punishment cell in Wandsworth detention barracks. It was an underground cell, regulation size, very dirty and, being in the basement, the only light was through a skylight in the roof — a dirty skylight. The only piece of furniture was a round piece of wood, which was clamped with iron bands into the wall so that if you sat you had to sit upright. And a bed-board, which was clamped down into the floor, which couldn't be moved. There was no bedding at all. You were under punishment and you were on a bread-and-water diet. There were two little wooden pots, one for toilet purposes and the other for drinking water. I'm afraid they used to get them mixed up, but they didn't care. You never got out of the cell for anything and there was nothing to do in the cell whatsoever, apart from a Bible. It was a *dreary* time; all I could do was sit on the stool until my back couldn't stand any more, and get up and walk up and down, or lie on the bare bed-board, which wasn't very comfortable. Night was the same as day. You had no kind of rest at all. After three days — the time of the punishment — I was taken to the commanding officer and given another three days . . .

Actually it went on and on, and after, it would be about 26, 27 days, nearly to the end of my sentence, when the commanding officer came down with his guards. "Well, Private Dutch, I have to inform you that His Majesty has been graciously pleased to grant you a free pardon." It sounds lovely, but it only meant that I was to be handed over to an escort and that I was free to be a soldier, which of course I continued to refuse to be. But that particular punishment was over.

Harold Bing, absolutist CO, repeated prison sentences 1916–19

I saw a couple of warders drag this CO down several iron staircases feet first, with his head banging on each iron step as he came down. I suppose he'd been ordered to come down to interview the governor or something, and he refused to move and they just dragged him down.

Philip Radley, absolutist CO, repeated prison sentences 1916–19

There was this particular warder in Winchester who was always very friendly with us. He'd come across the "ten-year men", as they were called — the men who had been sentenced to death in France. When they came back, he'd been so impressed by them that he had thereafter said that he would do all he could to help us, and for some time he was the liaison between the NCF and the men in our prison, always doing this at risk to himself.

41

Bert Brocklesby, alternativist (later absolutist) CO, repeated prison sentences, including Henriville and Rouen camps, France, 1916

Alf Myers and I were the only COs in the convict section designated as Methodist, and we were visited regularly by a Methodist minister called Wardell, for whom I shall ever feel deep gratitude. His first words were the same as the Winchester chaplain's, but two more different men one could hardly imagine. "Well, young man, what are you here for?" "I am here because my conscience will not allow me to take part in the war." I shall never forget his reply. It gave me something to wrestle with for months . . . "It is very difficult to understand," he said very gravely, "how conscience drives men in exactly opposite directions. Both my boys joined the army as a matter of conscience, and one has paid with his life." . . . Poor bereaved Mr Wardell. Before he left Maidstone, he had to tell me that his remaining son had followed his brother. Yet never did he by word, look or gesture express any condemnation of my attitude.

Donald Grant, alternativist CO, imprisoned in Wormwood Scrubs and Dartmoor Prison

It was severe to be in solitary confinement. I was, if I may say so, less affected than most others because I knew what I was doing. I had a way of life, a philosophy of life. I had a pretty well-filled mind. I could sing. I could recite poetry. I could pray. I could meditate. If I stood on the stool to look out of the window, that was a crime. But I did it. I tried to do it unobserved. When the zeppelins came to London, I stood on the stool to see.

Fenner Brockway, absolutist CO, repeated prison sentences 1916–19

We had a heating pipe going right through our cells, going up to the next floor. We had a complete telephone system. We learned the Morse code in reverse, and by tapping on the pipe we had a prisoner at the end who acted as a kind of switchboard; he could actually put our message through on the pipe to the floor above. I played chess with a boy in the next cell. We only had a slate and a slate pencil, but we could rub out the moves and the whole game would take a week.

Joseph Hoare, alternativist (later absolutist) CO, repeated prison sentences 1916–19

My exercise, apart from doing physical jerks on the floor, was that I used to go on walks. I would walk criss-cross up and down the cell, going on these imaginary walks of places I knew.

Fenner Brockway, absolutist CO, repeated prison sentences 1916–19

The point arose [in Walton Prison, Liverpool] when many of us thought that it was wrong, undignified and humiliating to accept this absolutely inhuman system, and we decided openly to resist it. For ten glorious days, sixty of us ran our own hall in prison. Speaking openly on the exercise ground instead of marching five steps behind each other and not saying a word — round and round. We took arms, we played games, we organised concerts every night. We were shut in our cells, but the Welsh boys would sing at their windows and everyone down the side could hear. But the effect became disastrous because not only did our boys hear, but the ordinary prisoners as well. And so the five leaders were isolated and then transferred to other prisons. I went to Lincoln Prison. I had eight months of solitary confinement there. Three months of bread-and-water treatment until the doctor wouldn't allow more. And yet one had a sense of freedom which I can't describe . . .

The Sinn Fein leaders were detained in Lincoln Prison at the time — de Valera and others — they got to know I was there in a hall alone, a cell alone, 23 hours and 20 minutes out of 24 hours shut in the cell, 40 minutes exercising alone. One day, there was a step outside my cell. I got up on my stool and looked outside, and there was a red-band prisoner there (who's allowed to go about without warders). He signalled me to get down, and through the open panel came a message from the Sinn Feiners: "Just heard you're here. We can do anything except get you out. Let's know what you want." I ordered the *Manchester Guardian* every day, the weekly papers, the *Labour Leader* — then being edited in my absence — and what was then the *New Statesman*, and the *Economist* and the *Observer*. The red-band man used to put them in a drain . . . I think the Sinn Feiners saved my mind in that period of long solitary confinement. I was there the day when de Valera escaped.

Dorothy Bing, civilian pacifist and sister of CO Harold Bing, Croydon

While Harold was in Wormwood Scrubs, on Christmas Eve a whole band of us from Croydon went up and sang carols outside the prison. I remember that was a cold night, but we were all muffled up. We sang carols and they waved their blinds out of the cell windows, so we knew they heard.

Harold Bing, absolutist CO, repeated prison sentences 1916–19

Some died in prison, some went mad, some broke down in health completely and never really recovered, some were discharged because they were on the point of death, some suffered terribly

45

from insomnia — it was almost unbearable for them. This depended partly on one's physical constitution, I think. It depended upon one's temperament. The very sociable type found the silence rule and solitary confinement almost unbearable and almost a strain under which they broke. Those who had more resources within themselves, or had more the monastic temperament, adapted to it very easily. The greater the mental and spiritual resources an individual has, the more he can stand those conditions. So physical and mental conditions would affect whether one suffered much or didn't.

Walter Manthorpe, alternativist CO, repeated prison sentences

I had not a single visitor: my father was very busy, my mother's and sister's time taken up with war. But letters made all the difference. My wife and family kept me well informed with what was going on . . . Your own problem: well, you had made a choice, and with the action you took, you knew the problems that would arise and had to make the best of it. But the most difficult part, the things that went on and on in your mind, were the kinds of problems that your wife and children had . . .

In the summer of 1916, a new policy for absolutists came into force known as the Home Office Scheme (HOS). It was devised for those who had been forcibly enlisted in the army, had disobeyed orders and were in prison and subjected to the cat-and-mouse treatment. It offered them work of "national importance", which consisted of agriculture, land reclamation, quarrying and road-making. It took place in prisons that had been cleared of their regular inmates and in special camps, some tented, such as the infamous settlement at Dyce, near Aberdeen, for work in granite quarries.

Philip Radley, absolutist CO, repeated prison sentences 1916–19

Then they offered us the Home Office Scheme in Lewes [prison]. I felt very doubtful about it. I had a word with one of my older friends at the time during the meeting for worship and he said, "No, this isn't for us, this isn't for us at all." I said "Good," that was the sort of final note that I wanted. We felt it was just giving up the principle, that you would virtually have been under prison conditions doing the same kind of work, but you'd given away your principle on the matter. I refused it. But a lot took the opportunity, and I remember arguing about this. People said, "Well, this is just what we want. I didn't get exemption, but now here they're giving us the alternative that we want." But eleven hundred of us dug our toes in, and this meant, among other things, that when the second war came, they weren't prepared to put people in that position again and were prepared to be more understanding. In all humility, one can say that it was a stand and it had an effect.

Mark Hayler, absolutist CO, HOS, Princetown, Dartmoor, from his notes

The work we did there was worse than futile. About 200 of us were engaged on work within the prison walls, the rest were outside on the moor. I spent ten months on the moor and nearly a year on hospital work within the walls. The agricultural work was absolutely penal and organised on lines as for convicts. If we had been murderers and gangsters, the authorities could not have discovered a worse way of treating us. Of course, the object was to *make* work. The harder it was and the more tiring it was, the better. Let me give you a few examples . . . There was a hand-roller, to which eight men were harnessed, engaged in rolling a field. I have been one of those human horses. The work we did could have been done by one man and one horse in a third of the time. And this, mind you, in a time of the country's [food] crisis. I once worked on digging in a field with about 50 others. It took us three weeks to dig what could have been ploughed easily in three days . . . All spades, shovels, barrows etc. were prodigiously heavy, weighted with lead probably. Everything was purposely out of date to make the job more irksome. All the coke for the gasworks and furnaces was carted by hand, teams of ten men being harnessed to a cart. What was the result of such a policy? This — the men revolted . . .

But when we were working on the moor, you could really chat and that was such a relief . . . I remember once when we went out to work on the moor, this chap said, "Isn't it odd that I'm here in Dartmoor because I won't kill anybody, and my father-in-law had been here because he had killed someone!"

Donald Grant, alternativist CO, HOS, Princetown, Dartmoor

I went off to Dartmoor . . . I first worked on the agricultural group, hot weather, very tiring. However, I was offered a job as an orderly in hospital after a fortnight. I then had a cell to myself in hospital, could have a bath any time. There were five of us . . . You could go out of prison. I galloped over the moors, the tors, read a lot, ran about a lot, played soccer even.

Mark Hayler, absolutist CO, HOS, Princetown, Dartmoor

In Dartmoor we had one young fellow who died there [name unknown]. He was only a boy. I was an orderly in the hospital and I attended him. His wife came down from Yorkshire. I can see her now, sitting outside his cell near the door. He had pneumonia. He had been badly treated in Dartmoor, should never have been sent out on the moor to work in all that weather. He should have

49

had an indoor job. The doctor doubted that he'd live through the night. I said, "I'm on duty and this man is not going to die tonight." I stayed with him all that night, and when I went off duty at 8a.m., he was still alive. But he was not alive the next morning . . .

All the COs followed his coffin down to the little station — they couldn't prevent this. It was put on a train at Princetown and taken to Plymouth. We got to the station. It was all arranged by the COs; some of them got some fog signals and they put them on the line as the little train left and they went off as it went by — a sort of farewell. I remember the men singing "Abide with Me".

Bert Brocklesby, alternativist (later absolutist) CO, HOS, Dyce Camp, Aberdeen

I was driven to the absolute position by the Home Office Scheme. The managers had assured us that our work in the granite quarry was for the repairing of civil roads, but we found that the main objective was a piece of new road up to a new naval aerodrome.

Harold Bing, absolutist CO, repeated prison sentences 1916–19

In all, I think there was a very good spirit of comradeship, and even with those who took the Home Office Scheme, although some were

50

inclined to think, "Well, they've let us down a bit," I don't think there was any hostile feeling towards them. There was a recognition that we were all in the same boat, and for those with family responsibilities or whose wives were unsympathetic, it was always a terrific pressure on them to get out in order that they could keep in touch with their wives instead of being completely isolated from them. In some cases, it was necessary to save a marriage and therefore we were not critical, although those of us who were absolutists felt that ours was the right position and wished that everybody could take it.

It wasn't only within the confines of prison that COs experienced hostility and brutality. Those awaiting arrest, or experiencing a brief respite from the cat-and-mouse system, and COs engaged in various forms of alternative service in the community, often found themselves despised and ostracised. A particularly distressing aspect for these men was that their families also suffered social exclusion.

Percy Leonard, alternativist CO, repeated prison sentences

A [Quaker] family invited me to spend an evening with them in their home. After that, I spent quite a few evenings with them. Once there was a riot outside the house and rioters threatened to burn it down because they had COs inside. We were about six or seven COs there, and they packed us down in the cellar.

Joseph Hoare, alternativist CO, HOS, Princetown, Dartmoor

I remember some of the COs from Princetown going up to the church for a service and being stoned on the way. The parson was standing on a flat tombstone, I won't say *cheering* them on, but any rate encouraging them. I remember myself going to the cathedral at Wakefield [when on the Home Office Scheme there] dressed in corduroys as a gardener. People drew away, you were liable to hear all kinds of remarks, but on the whole they didn't make much of an impression, provided you were lucky enough to have a fair number of people on your side. I never got a white feather.

Dorothy Bing, civilian pacifist and sister of CO Harold Bing, Croydon

It did have a very bad effect on my mother. You see, she came from a very united family. During my childhood, we were constantly taken to see her sisters and their families . . . As soon as they realised that Harold wasn't going to fight for his country, they just cut us dead. It was never healed. After the war was over, they wouldn't have any more to do with us. It was a clean cut, true . . . After the war was over, I went to see them and tried to heal the breach, did my very best. Two sisters who were nearest to her just wouldn't have anything to do with her, or any of us for that matter. And they didn't come to the funeral when she died. She never said much about it, but I'm quite sure it was a dreadful blow that she was cut off from her family. I was never quite sure to what extent she really agreed [with Harold]. She was a housewife, pure and simple.

Harold Bing, absolutist CO, repeated prison sentences 1916–19

On the whole, apart from a few friends and sympathisers, people's attitudes towards me were distinctly hostile. This would be the ostracism of neighbours who knew I was going to appeal to be a CO; a critical attitude of my employers, who terminated my employment after my tribunal and who afterwards refused to reinstate me. Then there was a neighbour full of righteous indignation who chased me a long distance with a heavy stick because I'd put a pacifist leaflet through his door. There were cases of people speaking at public meetings who were torn from their rostrums and thrown into the pond at Peckham Rye or wherever it might be. And of course the press was hostile. In some cases, the clergy were hostile . . .

Elizabeth Lee (Dowland), Red Cross driver, London

I knew plenty of conscientious objectors. They had a right to their own opinion and they did a useful job. They were stretcher-bearers and some of them were doing different jobs in hospitals, they were given jobs that fitted in with their conscience. There was this business of sending white feathers to people. I had one brother who was working as the manager of the aircraft factory. His was a highly responsible job. He often had white feathers sent to him . . . He was quite satisfied that he was doing a job that he was fully qualified to do and he was working more hours than any soldier, and men's lives depended on the quality of the planes that went out of the shop. He was the final one to pass everything out before the test pilot took it up, and a lot of them he tested himself.

A. H. Wallace, wounded soldier home from the front

I was home from France and I got on a bus and, much to my amazement, when I sat down, a woman sitting opposite me opened her bag and took out a white feather, which she gave to me. I was much surprised and said, "What is this for?" She said, "You're a coward." I said, "Excuse me, I'm not a bloody coward, if you'd like to look at my leg, you can find the other piece which is lying in the Fricourt battlefield on the Somme." With that, a gentleman who was sitting nearby said, "Hit the bitch!" I said, "I can't do that," and told her, "The best thing you can do, madam, is to get off or you might find yourself in trouble." She stopped the bus and got off.

Phylis Goodlif, Red Cross worker, in France, 1917–19

My cousin was killed before he was 18. Gradually it weighed on you, we prayed for them all. White feathers? That was rather cruel. We heard about people doing that and they always hit on the wrong people to give them to . . . The Ambulance Service conchies were all very nice people who worked very hard, they faced the dangers like everybody else.

Rose Kerrigan (Klasko), schoolgirl, Glasgow

People jeered at those who weren't in uniform, and women went around offering white feathers to men if they saw they weren't in uniform, and girls boasted about it, you know . . . But that stopped after the second or third year because by then people saw through a lot of it, especially in Glasgow, where the feeling was desperately against the war because it was the home of men like [James] Maxton and Tommy Bell and Helen

Crawford, who all spoke in the Metropole Theatre, and I used to go to these meetings . . .

Cathleen Nesbitt, civilian actress, London

Two of my brothers were killed and the third died of a heart attack, having been damaged by a fall he'd had from a plane. There was this horrible feeling, it seemed that every young man I knew had gone, the casualty lists were *appalling* . . . it all seemed so useless and pointless. I never believed it when people said, "Oh, it's wonderful for the morale and people will be kinder to each other when the war stops." But when war stops, everyone and everything goes back to the same norm . . . There were pacifists, of course: the whole Bloomsbury Group, Lytton Strachey and so many others, all idealists. I think it took more courage to be a pacifist than a soldier, particularly in those days, when pacifists were so scorned . . .

Sybil Morrison, Suffragette and ambulance driver, London

The zeppelin made a big noise; its engines were pretty powerful. And we all heard the shouts. My friends had a balcony in their house in Harrow, and we all went out and saw this awful sight. It was like a big cigar and all of the back part, the gas part, had caught fire. It was roaring flames — blue, red, purple. And it seemed to come floating slowly down instead of falling with a "bang!" And we knew there were about 16 people in it and that they were being roasted to death. Of course, you weren't supposed to feel any pity for your enemies; nevertheless, I was appalled to see the kind, good-hearted British people dancing about in the street at the sight of 16 people being burned alive — clapping and singing and cheering. And my own friends delighted! When I said that I was appalled that anyone could be pleased to see such a terrible sight, they said, "But they're *Germans*; they're the enemy." They're Germans, yes, Germans — not human beings. And it was like a flash to me that this is what war did: it created utter inhumanity in perfectly nice, gentle, kindly people. I felt, "It's not right, it is wrong, and I can't have any further part in it." . . . I also think there's a difference between having a conscientious objection to a war and being a complete objector to all wars. I'm against taking part in *any* war at all; I'm quite sure that wars don't settle anything.

John McCauley, Private, Border Regiment, 7th Division, France, from his diary, *A Manx Soldier's War Diary*

I was destined to see war from another angle. I was attached to a company of about 150 men, and our task was to search for dead bodies and bury them . . . It was a ghastly job, and more than ever I learned what war meant . . . I gradually became hardened, and for three months I continued the job. We worked in pairs and our most important duty was to find the identity discs. After our morning's work was over, a pile of rifles and barbed wire stakes would mark the place where we had buried our gruesome discoveries. There they lay, English, German, Australians, South Africans, Canadians, all mingled together in their last great sleep. Often I have picked up the remains of a fine, brave man on a shovel. Just a little heap of bones and maggots . . . Numerous bodies were found lying submerged in water in shell-holes and mine-craters; bodies that seemed quite whole, but which became like huge masses of white, slimy chalk when we handled them. I shuddered as my hands, covered in soft flesh and slime, moved about in search of the disc, not to be buried unknown . . . In those three months I assisted in the burial of over ten thousand dead — known and unknown . . . If only such scenes as we saw on the abandoned battle-grounds could be brought before the eyes of the peoples of the world, how nearer we would be brought to perpetual peace. But the world quickly forgets. I shall never forget.

J. R. Skirth, NCO, 239 Siege Battery, Royal Garrison Artillery, Battle of Messines, June 1917, from his memoir

What I saw might have been a life-size wax model of a German soldier. He was in a posture I can only describe as half sitting and half reclining. Resting his body on the edge of a smaller shell-hole he had leaned back against a mound of thrown-up earth. But for his complete immobility you would have thought he had assumed that position quite deliberately and, overcome by tiredness, had fallen asleep. Everything about his posture looked perfectly natural and normal, except that there was a something you don't see, you feel. An aura of death . . . It was the deathly pallor of that face which shocked me beyond my powers of description. Part of a lock of blond hair was resting on his forehead above the two closed eyes. There was a suggestion of a smile on the pale lips, a smile of contentment . . . This figure was my enemy. He *had been* my enemy, perhaps, but he wasn't *now*. For this man I should feel hatred not compassion. This man! He was, or had been, no man. He was a *boy* who, but for the colour of his hair and uniform, must have looked very like me. I was nineteen, he probably younger still. What could he possibly have done to deserve *this*? . . . In his wallet there were two mica windows with photographs behind them. One must have been of his parents. The other had "Mein Hans" written diagonally across one of the lower corners. It was the picture of a young girl, who could have been taken for Ella's [Skirth's girlfriend] sister. I was sick with shame and pity . . . Hans had died as uselessly as Bill and Geordie [Skirth's pals recently killed]. That it *might* have been from the blast from one of our shells, one of *my* shells which killed young Hans, I felt a sense of guilt almost overshadowing my pity and sorrow . . .

The Friends Ambulance Unit was formed soon after war started, in the autumn of 1914. Its membership was not confined to Quakers. They were men who had decided that although their religious and humanitarian beliefs prevented them from entering the war in a fighting capacity, they could not stand aside in the midst of conflict. What distinguished FAU members from the FRS and other COs engaged on alternative service was that they offered to serve alongside troops, alleviating the suffering caused by war wherever possible. The FAU began with 43 and ended with over 1,000 men. As it increased in numbers, the more diverse its work became. As well as working in education and agriculture on the home front, it performed civilian relief work at home and abroad. It also entered the heart of the conflict, sharing risks and dangers with front-line services when engaged in ambulance and emergency medical services with the French and British armies in Belgium and France, and serving in hospital ships in the English Channel and in the Mediterranean.

John Harvey, alternativist CO, FAU, Ypres and Poperinghe area, Belgium, April 1915

On Monday, the 19th, the bombardment on the town of Ypres lasted nearly all day long . . . This evening there were several horribly mutilated civilians brought up to the hospital for treatment.

Tuesday 20th: the civil population — already many had left — were streaming out of the doomed town. Very pathetic little groups they made; most had nothing but what they could carry in the hands, and each member of the household, from oldest to youngest, had his little bundle . . .

At our hospital, the Sacré Coeur, the patients were, as far as possible, evacuated today and during the evening to Poperinghe or La Panne . . . Nine of us with our kits were thus packed into an ambulance car and stole off into the dead of night to Poperinghe . . . We were soon busy setting up our newly conceived Casualty Clearing Station [29 Rue d'Ypres], for the temporary reception of wounded British . . . Wounded began to come in about eight hours after we had got going at the place . . . Sunday 25th: today we were at work in our Clearing Station. It now held a second batch of 41 patients in all. Quite a number were Canadians. The men on the whole were gloomy, and savagely resentful of the gas barbarity . . .

Rachel Cadbury (Wilson), Quaker, VAD, Dunkirk, 1917–19

One of the accusations was that the young Quakers went into the FAU to patch men up to become soldiers again. That was the *last* thing they wanted. The first thing they thought of was: there is a man suffering, he must be helped, he must not die . . . I was trained for nursing — to help, to relieve pain and help people to recover, to walk again — that was the object of my training. It wasn't to get them back to the war . . .

I was very keen to go to France as a VAD. I worked in the Queen Alexandra Hospital where the FAU worked — it was the only hospital in Dunkirk . . . I nursed there from October 1917 until 1 January 1919, after the Armistice. Dunkirk was a naval as well as army base, we also had Royal Flying Corps. Our army patients were men coming back from the Belgian front. We had patients in from the Zeebrugge attacks and a lot of the Fourth Army when they were up there. We also had a detachment of Cameron Highlanders in their kilts, which were absolutely alive with lice . . . The operating theatre was good. Each ward had a sister and two VADs, and we worked in shifts. I worked mainly on the surgical war, helped Sister with her dressings, made beds, served meals, cleared up, washed up.

Lloyd Fox, Quaker alternativist CO, FAU, Dunkirk and Courtrai, Belgium, 1917–19

The Ambulance Service in Dunkirk was done entirely by the FAU. I worked in the Dunkirk area, head of a convoy of six, just what I wanted. We lived in a derelict house in the village. We had very good relations with the military, never had any trouble, not even in the sergeants' mess.

Rachel Cadbury (Wilson), Quaker, VAD, Dunkirk, 1917–19

We had masses of shelling from land, air and sea. The bombardment from the sea was *shattering*, so noisy and so sudden. Red Crosses didn't make a difference; the docks were bombarded and we were in the way. We had to stay in the wards with the men, who were terrified. I wasn't, and I found that I couldn't hold more hands than two. We did have two dugouts — fragile things dug into the dunes — and we'd take out the walking cases. There were lots of head wounds, a lot of flying accidents from untrained pilots caught by propellers as they whisked them around. There were cases of gassing, mostly civilians who were gassed when Germans evacuated the villages. They would hide in their cellars and the gas seeped down into the cellars.

Lloyd Fox, British Quaker alternativist CO, FAU, Dunkirk and Courtrai, Belgium, 1917–19

I drove alone across the Ypres battlefield to Courtrai, no sign of life except rats. It looked appalling: a vast sea of shell holes and creased-up shattered vehicles and military equipment. Everything was waterlogged and the road was in a shocking state . . . At Courtrai, five FAU men and a doctor

63

were installed in a large convent. The problem was that the Germans were using a large amount of mustard and phosphine gas . . .

One afternoon, soon after I had arrived, army lorries started to arrive full of gassed women and children from a valley I had previously looked down into on my way there. The Germans had soaked the place with mustard gas to hold up the British advance. Unfortunately, civilians had gone down into their cellars: the worst place if gas is about. Over a period of two or three hours, we had twenty lorry-loads of women and children, about a thousand altogether.

We spent a good deal of time dealing with those who had died, particularly children, taking them down to the convent's mortuary. Most of those alive were lying in blankets on the floor, there were no beds, and just to make things a little worse for everybody, the Germans staged an air raid on the bridgehead at the bottom of the convent's garden. The convent fortunately wasn't hit, but the casualties were pretty miserable hearing bombs coming down. The following day, I was taken by an army doctor to a large hall in Courtrai where we found over a hundred gassed women and children. There was only one old woman caring for them, trying to give them drinks. They were terribly affected by the mustard gas and phosphine, which had practically destroyed the sight of most. Their eyes were swollen and their breathing was beginning to get very bad as the phosphine particularly affected their lungs. The object of our visit was to pick out 20 suitable cases for treatment at the convent. The army captain who took me round said, "I can do nothing, it's up to you, you pick out the 20 that may have some chance of living and take them up to the convent." And there was I, this youngster, given what seemed to be the chance of saving the lives of 20 of these people. All I could do was pick 20 of the toughest-looking children — I thought they might have some chance of survival. I took them to the convent, where they had a special gas unit to try to give them suitable treatment. I don't think it was effective at all.

The following day, I remember seeing a gas orderly coming out in tears. He said, "I just can't stand it any longer, they're choking to death and most of them are the children you brought in two days ago." I went in and the unfortunate children were black in the face, absolutely nothing could be done for them. We washed their eyes out with bicarbonate of soda. The Special Squad were bleeding them, but I think it was a waste of time and effort; they were too badly gassed to be saved. In all, about 800 were killed by gas at that time. It passed more or less unnoticed. It was just at the end of the front. The war news was more concerned with the falling-back of the Germans, but it was one of the worst episodes of civilian gassing in the war.

Rachel Cadbury (Wilson), Quaker, VAD, Dunkirk, 1917–19

Much later, after we were married, Paul and I visited the nuns in this hospital in Courtrai. He had been so impressed with their devotion to the gas victims that he commissioned a picture entitled "Blessed are the Peacemakers"; we took this with us and presented it to the convent. Sadly, during the Second World War it disappeared.

Lloyd Fox, Quaker alternativist CO, FAU, Dunkirk and Courtrai, Belgium, 1917–19

The colonel was much appreciative of our work and was determined that I and one other unit member were presented with a Military Medal for bravery. But that came unstuck. The men at HQ weren't going to give a medal to the FAU and excused themselves by saying that they weren't going to give any more medals to workers in base areas. Well, we were technically in the front-line area and doing a lot of work on the front as well as back at base. Three months later, the sergeant got a medal. He was well known for being the first to dive in the dugout the moment any trouble arose, and doing only desk work at the base. This showed that we were not fairly dealt with by British Army HQ.

When the Armistice was signed on 11 November 1918, after over four years of fighting, three-quarters of a million men were dead. In the elections that followed the Armistice, all the pacifist Members of Parliament who had opposed the war, including Ramsay MacDonald, lost their seats. Despite going to the country on ending conscription, it wasn't until 1919 that it was actually abolished. The NCF was dissolved in the same year. There were variations in the ways COs were treated after the war ended: those in the Non-Combatant Corps (NCC) came under the general demobilisation scheme; by the end of April 1919, all those employed under the Home Office Scheme had been released. But for those who had been imprisoned, the Home Office only started a general commuting of their sentences in June 1919. It wasn't until the end of July of that year that all objectors were released. By early August, they had all been discharged from the army — the "cat and mouse" that had caused so much resentment and dread had finally ended. The Representation of the People Act, 6 February 1918, had disenfranchised nearly all those COs sentenced by court martial to imprisonment or detention, including those who had opted for release under the Home Office Scheme. Few found it easy to return to old jobs or gain new employment.

Perhaps the true figure of the men who opposed the First World War will never be known. No figures are known for those who were reluctant to fight and who successfully evaded call-up or worked in reserved occupations such as mining, or for those who were refused exemption and entered the services when called up, or for those who had become pacifists during the war but continued their service. Anti-war women are also missing from the figures, so too are those above the age limits of conscription and the medically unfit. But, of the 16,000 who faced tribunals, just over 9,000 accepted some form of alternative service, including the Home Office Scheme, and 3,300 served in the NCC of the army. Just over 6,000 had served varying prison sentences, with 819 COs incarcerated for 20 months or more. One thousand three hundred absolutists refused to compromise in any way with the state. Sixty-nine COs were confirmed dead. Thirty-nine had gone mad.

John McCauley, Private, Border Regiment, 7th Division, France, from his diary, *A Manx Soldier's War Diary*

It was November 1918. The Dove of Peace was on the wing. Whether it would be shot down or not was another thing . . . We wanted peace; the Germans wanted it. The whole world was crying out for it . . . Eleven o'clock on the 11th November, 1918, arrived. But the front line was minus some of its stalwarts. Only minutes before that fateful hour, the enemy had meted out death right up to the fateful minute. And the British guns had done the same . . . Eleven o'clock. Cease Fire! A stillness. A hush. A mysterious absence of something. The roar of battle had ceased. A stillness that France had not known for over four years descended on all. Killing had ended. Was it true? We couldn't believe our own eyes and ears. Front line men were afraid to put their heads over the top. It all seemed so strange this sudden peace;

as though the earth was hesitating a minute or two before taking a final plunge to destruction.

Rachel Cadbury (Wilson), Quaker, VAD, Birmingham and Dunkirk

I was on night duty at the time of the Armistice. The hospital had a conservatory on top and we could get there by a little ladder. We knew it was coming and had two hours off. We went up on top, and to our delight it was all quiet on the Western Front! No shells. So we said, "It's come!" Before it would have been flashes and bangs all the time. We had a dance to celebrate and everybody was very gay and happy.

Sybil Morrison, Suffragette and ambulance driver, London

Armistice Day was *insane*. People crowded into the streets, gathered around Buckingham Palace, stood up on top of the buses — traffic was at a standstill. You couldn't *move*, everybody was cheering, singing, shouting and of course immensely, *enormously* relieved. But the awful thing is that there were some people who were killed on that very day when we were rejoicing. If you had anybody at the front, you couldn't really celebrate yet. I went out, yes. I was only too thankful to think that it was over.

69

Helen Pease (Wedgewood), British civilian pacifist organiser of women's trade unions in Britain 1910–22

I was actually at my home in the Potteries that morning when we heard the war had ended . . . everybody went out into the streets, quite unlike what they describe in London. Everybody seemed to be walking up and down the streets saying, "Is it really over? Is it really *over*? Perhaps he'll come back after all." But none of this shouting, no celebrations. And then, of course, the pieces were picked up. And I can remember the men coming back, higgledy-piggledy.

Bert Brocklesby, alternativist (later absolutist) CO, repeated prison sentences, including Henriville and Rouen camps, France, 1916

Then on the eleventh day of the eleventh month at the eleventh hour, suddenly all the buzzers in Maidstone began hooting and we could hear, far away, frantic cheering. Fred was working at a table about two yards from me and he smiled across and uttered a fervent, "Thank God!" But six more months were to pass before we were released. April 1919 was our day of liberation, to the great annoyance of those who were still waiting to see their boys demobbed from the army: why should skunks and shirkers get free before men who have been fighting for their country?

We were taken to our prison cells to gather our personal possessions such as books and photos. As we marched back up "A" Hall, the men were standing at their doors waiting the order to proceed to work. They saw us "on our way out" and a low muffled cheer began, swelling higher and rolling along that house of pain. It was against all the rules, and I doubt if such a thing ever happened before or since. It gripped my heart and made me weep.

Wilfred Littleboy, absolutist CO, repeated prison sentences 1917–19

But November the eleventh . . . Ah, we shall be home for Christmas! In point of fact it was just about six months, because it was early in April 1919 that I was released [from prison] . . . I have this document, "Discharged for misconduct", and printed over it in red ink that if I tried to enlist again I was liable to two years' imprisonment — which always causes me a measure of amusement when I look at it! And of course we were disenfranchised for a period of five years.

Donald Grant, alternativist CO, repeated prison sentences

The war is over. The Armistice is signed. The bugles are blown. And the American and British Quaker Mission to build up France was already at work, and I applied for leave, not only to leave Dartmoor, but to leave Britain to join the *Mission des Amis* in France, which I did at the beginning of 1919 . . . It was very versatile work in France, restoring and finding stock for returning peasants who couldn't even find where their houses had been. We were working where the fronts of Verdun and the Argonne had been . . .

William Harrison, absolutist CO, from his memoir

On November 20th 1918 came the end of my two years' sentence, but not release . . . [Back in the camp at North Shields] for three weeks it was a dreary round of being ordered to put on a uniform to be medically examined, to make a statement for the court martial, and finally the C.M. itself . . . The result was the same: two years' imprisonment with hard labour . . . We were taken by train — this time in handcuffs — to Newcastle prison. Four soldiers for two prisoners. All the soldiers were very glum and afraid of being friendly. Newcastle Prison was a very old one. We stood before the big gates. The bell push caused a jangle somewhere inside. I glanced at the soldier nearest to me. Tears were running down his face and he said "Bloody Hell". But to me it was a sort of Home. I knew that behind that forbidding door I should find true comrades — lads who were engaged in the same struggle against conscription and war as I was.

Harold Bing, absolutist CO, repeated prison sentences 1916–19

After the war, if you looked through the advertisement pages of, say, the *Times Educational Supplement* where you get all the jobs advertised, very frequently at the head of the advert was, "No conscientious objector need apply." Advert after advert said that . . . Another discrimination we faced was that included in the Representation of the People Act, 1918, which first gave the vote to women and extended the vote of other sectors of the male population, was a disenfranchisement of COs for five years after the war, interpreted by the courts as being five years after the signature of the last peace treaty.

Bert Brocklesby, alternativist (later absolutist) CO, repeated prison sentences, including Henriville and Rouen camps, France, 1916

I found myself with a peculiar mental defect which was a direct result of the silent system in prison. In conversation I would suddenly become tongue-tied. I was fully aware of the idea I wished to express, but the word would not come. The prison authorities allowed us to exercise our legs, also our digestive faculties at meal time, but the silent rule meant the faculty of communicating with one's fellows, his most vital mental faculty, is made to rust away. Then he is turned adrift into a fiercely competitive world with his faculties impaired. No wonder so many ex-prisoners reverted to crime . . .

I was surprised to find how bitter local feeling was against me; it seemed much worse than in 1916. I had thought that having proved myself sincere they would give me credit for it. But no, they had suffered the poisoning effects of nearly three more years of war. Possibly they thought that the British Army, the only God that many of them trusted, would certainly break such resistance. But we had beaten the military and they hated us for it. I could feel it as I walked in the streets. And I saw it in the faces of people who at one time pretended to be friends . . . Under such circumstances I preferred to find work away from Conisbrough.

Lewis Maclachlan, alternativist CO, working for the Society of Friends in internment camps, the Netherlands

I had some confrontation once with Lloyd George, who said, "Do you mean to say that if your home was being attacked you wouldn't fight back?" I said, "Well, I hope not, because I think that would be un-Christian." And he just lay back in his chair and looked at me with disgust . . . There is always something in the pacifist case which is imperfect, I think. And when you realise this, you can think up a situation in which pacifism would be revolting where force is being used in a horrible way. Are you just going to do nothing — just stand and do nothing at all? That's very difficult and I don't think there's ever been a complete popular answer. Lots of answers theologically, politically and otherwise, but I think it's still difficult. I would find it difficult to debate, to assert the practical rightness of pacifism in certain instances . . .

Harold Bing, absolutist CO, repeated prison sentences 1916–19

Undoubtedly the experience of COs in prison brought about prison reform. Because when we came out of prison, Fenner Brockway and Stephen Hobhouse together edited that big volume *English Prisons Today*, in which they collected a lot of information both from COs and from other types of prisoners and produced a large volume of evidence which was very condemnatory of the English prison system as it was, and this was a big factor in bringing about prison reform . . . This undoubtedly contributed to the many really remarkable reforms we have had since then. Many who'd been in prison as COs became active in the Howard League or the penal-reform movement. I myself have been a member of the Howard League since 1920, soon after I came out of prison.

John McCauley, Private, Border Regiment, 7th Division, France, from his diary, *A Manx Soldier's War Diary*

Last week Armisticetide crept upon us, and slipped away into history once again. A grim, yet solemn, reminder of that awful era of world war . . . I had known three years and six months' close contact with war. I wanted to feel and know the experience of war in those early days of 1914 . . . I have had my fill of knowledge and the experience of what war is really like . . . I, like millions of young men the world over, plunged into something I did not, could not, understand. But we understand it today. Its folly, futility and unspeakable horrors are too vividly impressed on our minds to be ever erased . . .

Nancy Tennant, British civilian, Ugley, Essex

Nobody wants to glorify war, but on the other hand you don't want to forget what the young men did. Armistice remembrance for me should emphasise the horror as well as the futility of war. On all the village memorials there are endless names for the First World War, and few for the Second World War. They have learnt something, I suppose, if only to kill from a distance.

J. R. Skirth, NCO, 239 Siege Battery, Royal Garrison Artillery, Battle of Messines, June 1917, from his memoir

At nineteen, I found my standards of conduct obsolete, my ideals shattered. I had lost faith in all institutionalised religion. My church had authorised me to break the sixth commandment in the name of patriotism. The "Love Thy Neighbour as Thyself" part didn't fit in; "Blessed are the Peacemakers"? No! Not in 1917. Blessed are the War Winners, Yes. Blessed are the Munition Makers, Yes. Twice blessed, for they lined their pockets and kept their skins intact at one and the same time. These are the thoughts that I couldn't dismiss from my mind during those dreadful months. I wouldn't have stuck a label on myself as belonging to any category — then. But I know what I had become now. It's a word that is distasteful to many. Pacifist.

George Dutch, British absolutist CO, repeated prison sentences 1916–18 and relief work in Poland, 1919

What did we COs achieve in the First World War? Well, first of all we proved that any decent modern government could not coerce man's conscience . . . it was quite plain in the last year of war that they had learnt the lesson, because then it was easy to get exemption. If you were a CO, and they accepted you were, they would give you some kind of service. If it wasn't absolute exemption it was *something* you could do rather than send you to prison, which was a terrible waste of time. We were nothing but sand in the machine, sources of dissatisfaction really . . . It was *utter* folly to put us in the army and we proved that. Also, we set the notion of conscientious objection really going. There's no doubt that in any future war, small or large, you'll have conscientious objectors. Even in countries where they don't recognise it, it will happen. We started a movement which means that no war can be fought in the future without conscientious objection coming up.

Rev. Kenneth Greet, Bristol

My father was a man of peace. He was in the army in the First World War but in the Medical Corps because he refused to contemplate killing anyone. I remember my mother telling me that they prayed that I would be a "peace baby", by which they meant that by the time I was born, the Armistice would have been signed. That happened on 11th November; I was born on the 18th. So at least that prayer was answered. But one prayer that was *not* answered — the prayer offered by thousands of people — that the First World War might be the war to end wars, was certainly not answered. So I grew up, like so many of my contemporaries, with the shadow of war, yet again . . .

CHAPTER
TWO

1919–39: Peace

You had to think, what did victory mean? And so victory is a winged lady on a pedestal, maybe, but not much more than that. Victory ultimately must be the victory of ideas, I think.

The carnage and waste of the First World War and the perceived injustice of the peace led to a widespread revulsion against war and militarism during the interwar period, 1919–39. This resulted in the formation of a mass anti-war movement that took shape and flourished during the 1920s, with combatants as well as conscientious objectors from the First World War playing an important role in its development. The newly founded League of Nations, which promised cooperation rather than strife between nations, was regarded with great enthusiasm, and there was huge support for the League of Nations Union, whose membership peaked at 406,868 in 1931. The Kellogg — Briand Pact of August 1928 was signed by 15 countries and was viewed as a major landmark for peace, with its renunciation of war and pledge that all disputes and conflicts were to be settled by peaceful means rather than force. Issues of international relations, disarmament, peace and war were earnestly and widely discussed, and a whole range of new peace organisations was formed, accommodating a diversity of anti-war and pacifist opinion, which supported the great peace rallies and gatherings that were held at home and abroad. Until the setbacks of the early 1930s, with the rise of Fascism, whatever differences of opinion existed within the movement, there was little friction between the different groups and hopes were high for a new dawn of international peace.

In 1921 the No More War Movement (NMWM) was founded, an anti-capitalist, anti-militarist international peace organisation, a direct successor to the No-Conscription Fellowship, which had been disbanded in 1919. It became the British section of the War Resisters' International, founded in 1921, and later merged with the Peace Pledge Union. Harold Bing, a CO from the First World War, became an active member of the WRI, travelling all over Europe collecting testimonies from those who had been persecuted for not fighting in the war. The Fellowship of Reconciliation, which had proved its mettle with the support it had provided for COs in the war, expanded in 1919 into the International FOR and was notable for its youth work in Europe in the 1920s. The Peace Pledge Union was founded in 1935 after the charismatic Rev. Dick Sheppard appealed in the press for men willing to "outlaw war from their personal lives" to contact him. Thousands did, each pledging "I renounce war and I will never support or sanction another." Women were admitted in 1936. By the late 1930s, the PPU had 113,000 supporters. Organisations such as the Kibbo Kift ("proof of great strength") — a pacifist breakaway group from the Boy Scouts and open to girls — gave opportunities for thousands of young people to engage in open-air activities for world peace.

A large range of religious peace groups of all denominations was also formed. Many of these peace groups were to play an important supportive role for COs in the Second World War by providing advice and assistance as well as representatives to sit on the board of the Central Board for Conscientious Objectors (CBCO), which was established in 1939.

Personalities of the day were very influential. Mahatma Gandhi, for instance, was given great publicity in the media when he visited the East End of London in 1931. His theory of satyagraha (non-violence) struck a chord with pacifists and non-pacifists alike, which continues to this day. The Quaker preacher Richard Gregg promoted Gandhi's ideas in his book *The Power of Non-Violence*. The Wesleyan Rev. Donald Soper, speaking at open-air meetings on Tower Hill and in Hyde Park, was enormously influential, always ready with his argument of the need to harness pacifism to solve many of the world's problems, relishing hecklers and treating them with humour and panache that won many over to the cause. Another was the anarchist Bart de Ligt, a Dutch former pastor, who devised an elaborate anti-war plan of action that was widely circulated and won him vast numbers of supporters.

Fenner Brockway, absolutist CO, First World War

The war ends, we all meet. There are two views: one is that we should continue an organisation which should seek to serve the cause of peace all over the world — a No More War organisation — a view which I held. Clifford Allen and others felt that we should go into our political parties, our

81

organisations, our churches, and within those seek to influence them towards peace. I became secretary of the No More War Movement. We had marvellous demonstrations all over the world, but it fizzled out because it was just an assertion of hope and of the principle of peace rather than any practical proposals for influencing governments towards peace.

Leslie Hardie, factory worker, East End, London

Relatives and friends would tell stories about the First World War; a lot were funny, but one got the anguish behind it all. My favourite uncle was Uncle George, and he had lost a leg and walked very badly with an artificial leg. We lived in the East End of London and one of my abiding memories was seeing groups of ex-soldiers parading around the streets, some of them blind, begging for pennies. There was a man who affected me deeply who had a row of rather tatty pictures, he sat there and he had only half a face. Another sailor that my mother and I used to chat to when we passed had no legs and spent his time turning a little portable organ. Another man, who was always on the railway bridge, had an accordion. I began to think, "These were the heroes that a country should have been grateful to."

Reginald Bottini, shipping clerk, London

I was the only child. My mother was widowed at the age of 23, my father having died on active service in France, in 1918, at the age of 25. I was brought up thereafter by a widowed mother, very conscious of the fact that my father was buried near Boulogne. I remember my mother sobbing quite often when I was a child. She never remarried. I think that influenced, perhaps unconsciously, my thinking about society.

Kenneth Lee, London

The promise was that England would be a land fit for heroes to live in. The 1920s and '30s certainly didn't give that impression. I remember the Jarrow March, the hunger march, and the legislation that applied to the means test. All this was very far from being a country fit for heroes, and this also influenced one's attitude that victory was a rather meaningless term . . . And you had to think, what did victory mean? And so victory is a winged lady on a pedestal, maybe, but not much more than that. Victory ultimately must be the victory of ideas, I think. If you accept the Christian concept that the creative force in life is love — not a soft idea of love but one that people have to struggle in order to develop, that gives them just enough support to enable them to fulfil themselves —

well, then war becomes an absurdity and a total negation.

Kathleen Wigham (Derbyshire), Blackburn, Lancashire

My parents were very, very convinced pacifists, very much against war. Some of my earliest stories have been about the work they did for COs in the First World War, helping them at tribunals . . . Many, many times people have come to the home, and we've seen them crying because their [pacifist] sons had been called up, and I think they were very good at being able to help the young men as they made their stand. We do know of two young COs of the First World War who died through their imprisonment . . . And Harry Holden [another CO] was punished and suffered so much that he had injuries to his voice box, and he came out of prison unable to speak and suffered for many, many years until he died . . . I think this, with my Sunday school training, influenced what I felt about war. My father and mother wouldn't allow war toys in the home.

Donald Soper, undergraduate, Cambridge University

The First World War was the catalyst of my growing thinking and experiences. The existence of the war mentality and the immediate post-war mentality had a great effect on me, because it was when I went to Cambridge as a youngster of 18 that these impressions and experiences crystallised, and it was then that I became a socialist and a pacifist. It was the recognition that for me pacifism was the practical interpretation of the way of Christ, that it represented the Way of the Cross and his teaching and his experience, and, above all, his example represented the heart of the Christian gospel. The problem was how to activate this pacifism in the world in which I was growing up and which was of course looking towards the Second World War.

Paul Eddington, schoolboy, Sibford Quaker School, Banbury, Oxfordshire

A lot of the male staff had been conscientious objectors in the First War. I know that the senior master, Frank Parkin, was in Oxford Gaol. He was in the army, actually wearing a uniform at the time he decided that he was a pacifist and wasn't going to fight any longer. He was thrown into Oxford Gaol and an attempt was made to certify him insane. Mr Herbert, our woodwork master, had been in the Friends Ambulance Unit. Lively stories were remembered with glee, in the cruel way children have, of having a severe thunderstorm once while he was taking woodwork class, and he'd shouted to the boys to put their guns down and get under the benches. They were holding

T-squares — rather sad . . . The headmaster was actually breaking stones in Dartmoor during the First World War, so you can see how completely non-conformist the school was.

Peter Sharp, schoolboy, Bermondsey, London

I went to the Central School, Bermondsey. The headmaster, Dr Jones — commonly known as "Doggerbones" — was a pacifist. He wrote an opera against war. We were known as a "singing family"; every Sunday we'd sing all the old songs around the old coke fire. I remember one from his anti-war opera: "And when you pass from us / Will the world be safe for us / Or must we rise some other day / Sword in hand, to seek and slay other children . . ."

Vic Newcomb, office boy, Stoke Newington, London

In the 1930s, people seemed to be suffering in so many different ways: there were lots of unemployed, which was not relieved as it is today with a welfare system. There were also atrocities associated with small regional wars: Manchuria, Abyssinia and Spain. I was affected by all this. The tales in the press gave me the feeling that all the things tried by our predecessors and politicians were simply not producing the right answers, therefore some kind of dramatic attitude had to evolve from the people themselves. And it seemed to me that harming people must be avoided, so I was very attracted to non-violence as a way of achieving something, that taking the example of Gandhi with his non-violent approach to political problems could achieve results. I was evolving into non-violence as a political tactic rather than a religious or moral aversion to war itself, although I certainly had a moral aversion to causing suffering.

Tony Benn, Westminster schoolboy, London

My father was a very strong influence on me, he had been elected to Parliament in 1906, he fought in the First World War, and he *loathed* the war, and his great interests throughout his life were first of all the League of Nations and then the UN — he was a passionate believer in that. My mother was a very religious woman and she passionately believed in justice. As a child I realised the importance of justice . . . I met Mr Gandhi in 1931 when I was six. He was sitting on the floor and although I can't remember much, he said, "Come and sit next to me." And I sat with my brother and he talked, and the *power* of the man and the power of non-violence got into my mind.

Arun Gandhi, grandson of Mahatma Gandhi

I think the 18 months I spent with Grandfather in India between the ages of 12 and 14 really laid the foundations of my philosophy. Grandfather had a way of teaching, he would not make it a lesson, wouldn't sit you down and say "learn this", but he would use everyday instances and stories to give you the lesson he was trying to teach. That's why it stuck so much. It was a very disciplined lifestyle . . . he allotted an hour for me every day, and he'd tell me stories and ask me what I'd done that day . . . He taught me what anger really is. He said it is not evil, something to be ashamed of. It is a very powerful energy, a motivating factor in our lives, and the problem is that most of us are ashamed of it and are unwilling to learn about it, and so most of us deal with our anger mainly in a negative way and try to get it out of our system as quickly as possible. And so we learn to respond immediately, we blow up and say things and do things that destroy ourselves and our relationships with people. He said that we must avoid that, we must not abuse our anger, and he used the analogy of electricity and said that anger is just like electricity, just as powerful and just as useful if we use it with respect. But if we abuse it, it can be very deadly. That we must be able to channel the anger to use it intelligently, to solve the issues that caused the anger . . .

Grandfather linked this with his philosophy of non-violence. He said the only way to understand non-violence is understanding violence itself. That we tend to look at violence in a physical form and violence is much more widespread than that. The two offsprings of violence are physical and passive violence. Physical violence we know, but passive violence is all the things that we do to one another without using physical force: the way we speak to each other, the way we behave to one another: oppression — economic, political, social, cultural and religious. All the prejudices and hate, all the things we do to one another, are passive violence . . . I began to realise how much violence we practise unconsciously, that we are not violent in the sense that we go out and beat up people, but in the sense that we oppress people in other ways . . . Later, when I heard that Grandfather had been killed, it was such shocking news to me. That flash! — the 18 months I had spent with him flashed through my mind. I couldn't believe that anyone would want to kill someone so kind and gentle. My immediate reaction was that I wanted to throttle that person, but when my dad [Manilal] came back, he reminded me of the lesson that Grandfather had taught me about anger, so I was able to get over it and I forgave the assassin.

Donald Swann, Anglo-Russian schoolboy, Westminster School, London

I hated violence. This was very much related to my parents' experiences in the First World War, where they had served as a doctor and nurse on the Eastern Front, and the Russian Revolution, which they were caught up in. There is also a religious dimension to my pacifism. Of course it's very much part of the Christian pacifist's curriculum vitae that you have to know your Bible texts, what you'll do about the line, "I come to bring not peace but a sword." And "what did Christ say to the centurion?" I was coming to the conclusion that Christ was the number-one non-violent person. He made that point very clearly during his last days — he didn't bring in the legions of angels to defend himself, but knuckled down and turned the other cheek. But this was not the prevailing mood in 1939.

Tom Haley, printer's apprentice, Bethnal Green, London

Violence seemed to be the way of life around me, and fighting was the way in which you established the pecking order. The manly image was vital: you had to be a *man*, you had to punch and be able to fight . . . I remember vividly a march by Mosley's thugs through some nearby streets where the Jews were gathered to confront the blackshirts. They had marked the road, "They shall not pass." The bloodshed was dreadful: bricks, stones and all sorts of missiles were hurled from both sides. The fighting was beyond description; it was *horrible*. At this time I had this great feeling for the sanctity of human life and felt that I had to pursue this tremendous feeling within me of the wrongness of war. When I found the Friends' Hall it was a

90

tremendous relief to know there were others thinking like me, because I thought I was on my own, utterly miserable and an outcast . . . my mother told me that she had once met a conscientious objector. "What is a conscientious objector, Mummy?" "That's a man who is too frightened to go to war . . ." I promptly forgot this until my thoughts were forming when I was about 17.

Paul Townsend, undergraduate, Bristol University

I suppose I'm the typical sort of character who is likely to be a pacifist: a horror of violence, disapproving of blood sports, capital punishment, corporal punishment and the whole shooting match. I'd like to stress that because the whole temperament — the whole bundle of sympathies — seems to me to be important, quite apart from convictions about national or international issues.

Kenneth Wray, welfare worker, Sussex

The basis of my pacifism is the Albert Schweitzer movement. It's the sanctity of *life*. It's a reverence for life, and it applies not only to humans but to everything else too. I believe that everything in the universe is alive: the earth's stones, all her timber; everything in the world has *life* in it. This table I am sitting at today has life in it. I sometimes think the trees are an extraordinary example of living. They stand erect, immobile. They never harm man. They do nothing but benefit the world . . . There is an inconsistency, as I will chop down a tree as there has to be some kind of control in maintaining my garden, for instance. But my wife, who is of the same mind, almost *cringes* if a tree comes down or is lopped. But I take this only so far. I say that a cancer cell is a living thing and that we have no right to destroy it, but I *would* destroy it. There's my inconsistency. But I would never kill a human being under any circumstance.

Reginald Bottini, shipping clerk, London

I went to confession once and I was questioned closely by the priest as to what my politics were. I said, "I'm a member of the Labour Party." "Well, that's quite all right, my son," said the priest in the confidence of the confessional, "Holy Mother Church has no objection to that." "Well," I said, "I consider myself a socialist." "What do you mean by socialist, my son?" I said — coming out with the jargon of those days — "I believe in the public ownership of the means of production" etc. etc. "You are not a socialist, my son, you are a *Communist*, and I cannot give you absolution." Balham, south-west London, 1936. *Not* Spain. *Not* Ireland. I walked out and never went back . . .

Leslie Hardie, factory worker, East End, London

I suppose my objection [to war] was mainly humanitarian, but I was basically searching for a religious meaning. I'd gone away from the C of E, but I went to my local vicar and told him that the situation had me worried. He said, "The trouble with you is that you are yellow." That was the end of that! I had a try at various religions, tried the Salvation Army, but they were too jolly and enthusiastic for me — always ready with a hallelujah! Not for me. But they did fantastic work in the war when the bombs fell; I have great respect for them. I met the Friends quite by accident; they made me very welcome. I was in a meeting for worship when the sirens went on 3 September; several rushed out, but we just sat and an elderly Friend got up and said a few words. A calmness. I felt detached: they calmed me.

Rev. Donald Soper, Methodist probationary minister, Old Kent Road, London

After the First World War, there were a great many people who thought, "This is the end of war. We've learnt our lesson." And one took hope in the League of Nations and in the increased awareness of the terrible effects of war and that unless we put war behind us, it would overwhelm us. There was this hope that we'd never go to war again, and, of

93

course, gradually the situation developed in which that high hope almost became an idle dream. The days of the general strike and the increasing economic and political consequences of the First World War became vital problems. There was recognition in the Methodist Church, which held big conferences at the time, and the League of Nations was, for many thinking people, the way forward.

Reginald Bottini, shipping clerk, London

In my case, I never adopted the pacifist stand because I thought that in certain circumstances violence is inevitable. But in the sense that it's presented in neatly labelled nationalistic packets plus flags, it didn't go with me. So really you got a cacophony of views: the pacifists, the social-democratic conventionists, and the tiny minority of Trotskyist-influenced young people who didn't know where their urgings were coming from, but had a really healthy dislike of British imperialism and Nazi imperialism and American imperialism and were seeking to overthrow *everything*. That's very broadly where I was . . . I was known as an anti-war socialist within the Balham and Tooting Labour Party.

Lionel J. Redgrave, First World War absolutist CO, article in the Fellowship of Reconciliation magazine, Vol. 6 No. 5, May 1929

In the words of H. G. Wells: "War is no more to be ended merely by non-resistance, sarcasm, and gentle sentiments, than a tiger crouching to spring in a children's playground is to be disposed of by lofty disapproval." . . . Fundamentally, therefore, the problem of peace and war is not an ethical problem, as assumed by Tolstoy and most pacifists. It is essentially an economic problem . . . To prevent future big wars the world must frankly face prevailing economic conditions. This is the core of the problem . . . It is the conflict of national economic interests — this scramble by the big Powers for the world's markets — which is the main cause of modern war . . . It is futile for us pacifists to be content, as we too often are, to confine our activities merely to giving expression to peace platitudes; we must concern ourselves more directly, systematically, and intensely to the abolition of the causes of war, rather than with the partial and temporary abatement of the symptoms of war and deploring the horrors of war . . .

Peter Sharp, city clerk, Bermondsey, London

Mine was a very *personal* objection to war: I don't like taking orders from anybody if you object to them on principle. You hear so often the excuse, "I was only obeying orders . . ." I reject that. "War will cease when men refuse to fight." I have always believed that.

Vic Newcomb, office boy, Stoke Newington, London

None of the people I grew up with followed my particular path. In my experience, the anti-war people were very much the kind of people that make up CND today. If anything, most of them had a much larger religious background than those in CND today. Quakers in particular were very strong . . . I met so many people with special interests at that period that I became a kind of butterfly, drifting from one to another of the pacifist groups at that time; really I was experimenting where I stood . . . There wasn't a cohesive peace movement as such, rather a collection of organisations with their own objectives that came together on a very few occasions.

Gerald Gardiner, barrister (later Lord Chancellor, 1964–70), London

In 1918, I was just old enough to leave Harrow and join up in the Coldstream Guards Cadet Battalion. It never occurred to me at that age whether it was right or wrong to train for fighting in a war. If your country was at war, then you joined up. There it was. Fortunately for me, I was still training when the Armistice came . . . It was through meeting the Sheppards, after the war, that I began to become interested in pacifist ideas. Dick was a parson who had served as a chaplain in the war . . . He maintained that the modern form of warfare wasn't justifiable. He became an incumbent of St Martin-in-the-Fields after the war. The congregation were nearly all young men who had been to the war. I then joined a body called the Peace Pledge Union and became a pacifist, as most of his congregations were. My objection was that it was anti-Christian to kill and fight.

Leslie Hardie, factory worker, East End, London

When I joined the PPU before war started, I walked around the street with a banner and I was spat upon. I remember this bus-driver stopping his bus and shaking his fist and hurling insults at me, and one was pushed and molested as one walked along. In our street, people knew what I was and I was sent to Coventry, people whom I'd known for years turned their backs on me. It didn't worry me. I'd heard stories of what had happened to COs in the First World War and how some were carted off to France [to be shot]. I thought: could I stand this?

Sybil Morrison, London

I didn't become involved with the peace movement really until Dick Sheppard started his Peace Pledge Union. I was introduced to Dick Sheppard and I was fascinated with his whole attitude because he'd been a chaplain in the Army [during the First World War] and had decided that war is incompatible with the teachings of Jesus . . . I became a member right from the moment when women were admitted.

Denis Hayes, London

The thing about the PPU was that it did attempt to be a *union*. It was open to people of all persuasions who were prepared to be signatories of the peace pledge — it put people to an immediate choice, intimating to others that they took this view. You got all sorts of folk: people with political views, with religious views, humanitarian views, and people with no views at all apart from that they regarded it as wrong to take part in warfare in the future. It had many problems to face when it was forced to take action as a body because each of those people had marginally different views from others. But there were numerous rallies up and down the country led by well-known people whose views were respected . . . The type of persons who formed the PPU were intellectuals, not working people — these views aren't the easiest for working people to regard as important . . . The FOR was an exclusively Christian body formed in the First World War; it had less obvious effect than the PPU, but its personnel was of extremely high quality, and it worked together with the PPU and formed the basis of the pacifist movement.

Doris Nicholls (Steynor), member of the Fellowship of Reconciliation

I was working in the peace shops. Very much as Oxfam and War on Want have done recently, we would hire an empty shop and put up posters. The Quakers had some very good posters before the war and the PPU also had some. So we'd put these up and we'd have leaflets. And we would sit in the shop and just talk to people, sometimes stand outside and hand out leaflets. We had our own demonstrations. I don't remember ever getting involved in any fracas. But I do remember going with cardboard posters front and back and parading down the streets giving away leaflets.

Mervyn Taggart, city clerk, London

I think that in a general sort of way people signed the peace pledge because of a revulsion to war. I think it's always been a weakness of the peace movement that people unconsciously go into it for what they can get out of it because they enjoy a certain social atmosphere, and because they're interested in the problem in an intellectual, spiritual, philosophic or political way. I don't think they sufficiently realise that to bring about change and to change very deeply entrenched views on war requires immense personal sacrifice. I find that in the peace movement today, very few people indeed are willing to make that sacrifice — a sacrifice that is made by the ordinary soldier . . . I've always had great respect for the soldiers who take a very different view from me, but I have immense respect for their courage and their sacrifice.

Ronald Mallone, undergraduate, Goldsmiths College, London

Dick Sheppard was very sceptical of trying to keep peace by having an international police force. He said, "What difference does it make when you drop bombs on people whether you say, 'To hell with you' or 'With the blessing of the League of Nations'?" And he wouldn't have approved of the idea of having a United Nations armed police force. He did in fact try to get an unarmed force of pacifist people who would go out and stand between armies. This was feasible in the days of non-nuclear weapons . . .

The revulsion so many felt against war was fed by a proliferation of anti-war literature written by men who had actually served in the war. War poets such as Siegfried Sassoon and Edmund Blunden, with their message of the pity and futility of war, were very influential, with an appeal that extended beyond intellectual circles. In the late '20s, writings such as Robert Graves's *Goodbye to All That*, Erich Maria Remarque's *All Quiet on the Western Front*, and, later, Vera Brittain's *Testament of Youth* had great impact in the way they described the reality of war to those too young to have served in it. These, in turn, led to a later range of works by writers such as Beverley Nichols with his Cry Havoc!, a passionate cry against the "angels of death" — the armaments trade — one of the most influential books of the 1930s. Arthur Ponsonby, another fervent champion of disarmament, wrote that it was the "only absolute security". The eminent scientist Professor Albert Einstein supported Ponsonby; he had been influenced towards pacifism because of war's disruptive effect on science. He described himself as an "instinctive pacifist" on the grounds that "the murder of men is disgusting". A. A. Milne, who served in the First World War, now wrote that war was "silly", and that politicians were responsible for "lies, lies and still more lies". The impact of such outpourings was reinforced by the horrific images of human suffering and the devastated, fractured landscapes communicated so dramatically in the war art of painters such as John Singer Sargent, Christopher Nevinson and John Nash. The plaintive music of composers like Edward Elgar, George Butterworth and Vaughan Williams, in turn, added to an all-pervasive sense of sorrow and loss and a "never again" determination in large sectors of the British public.

Reginald Bottini, shipping clerk, London

Ethel Mannin stands out as the author that influenced me most in this interwar period. She was a prolific writer who wrote a lot on working-class life. I read her because she more closely equated to the position I had.

Ernest Goldring, bank clerk, London

Henry Williamson was one of the writers who had a considerable influence on my pacifist feelings. Although they were fictional, a lot of his earlier writings were based upon his own experiences during the First World War and his subsequent feelings of revulsion and rejection. In one of his books he made reference to the first Christmas in the trenches, when the British troops heard the Germans singing "Stille Nacht" and how they joined in. And on that Christmas Day how they played a football match together. I was also saddened when I discovered that two of the composers whose music I liked very much — George Butterworth and Ivor Gurney — were both victims of that war. That Butterworth had been killed and that Ivor Gurney had suffered from shellshock and subsequently finished his life in a mental hospital. Even when I was at school, I'd been introduced to Siegfried Sassoon's *Diaries of a Foxhunting Man* [sic]; and to Edward Thomas, a poet who was also killed. Vera Brittain's *Testament of Youth* also influenced me, the general impression being that the whole thing was a ghastly mistake — it confirmed my convictions that this war business is something which is utterly repugnant to me and I didn't want any more of it . . . I remember being slightly disappointed when I met her for the first time in the flesh. She seemed to be a rather quiet, mousy little woman who didn't have a lot to say. But because of *Testament of Youth* and all that meant to me, it was quite an experience to meet her and to talk to her.

Ronald Huzzard, draughtsman, engineering firm, Hull

Philip Noel-Baker wrote a book in 1936 called *The Private Manufacture of Armaments*, which influenced me a great deal. It convinced me that one of the main causes of war is the profit that people make out of war, out of armaments, and the way that behind the scenes disarmament talks are undermined by arms companies. Another book by Fenner Brockway, *Death Pays a Dividend*, is on the same theme. Those two books tied my anti-militarism, my pacifism, with a belief in the immorality of capitalism.

Tony Parker, sales assistant, bookshop, Manchester

The images of war I was getting from the books I read was, oh, the complete waste of life! The nonsensical trying to solve international problems in that way, and also the tremendously sad experiences that many of these writers went through in the war. And I remember one thing that most of them had in common: no one at home understood. Richard Aldington was a writer who was particularly good on that: *Death of a Hero, All Men are Enemies*. So it was a feeling of revulsion more than anything.

I was also very anti-authority and my feelings were increased by what I'd read about anarchism — Herbert Read and Prince Kropotkin, the great anarchist. As a young man, there was certainly that element in it. Many pacifists I've known have this and they're very aggressive.

Denis Hayes, London

I was drawn to pacifism by reading A. A. Milne's *Peace with Honour*, which dealt with questions chapter by chapter, and I cogitated on each as I went along and compared them with my own beliefs. Beverley Nichols's book *Cry Havoc!* was also important to me, but it was not of such quality as *Peace with Honour*, although compelling in many ways. It was terribly disappointing that within years of writing these books, each writer turned against what he had written . . . each with some very nasty things about the pacifist movement after the war had begun.

On 9 February 1933, ten days after Hitler came to power, the Oxford University Union, amid intense press interest, debated the motion that "This House will in no circumstances fight for King and Country." It was proposed by Cyril Joad, an ILP socialist and gifted speaker. In the first debate, 275 undergraduates voted never to fight for King and Country, with only 153 votes against. A few weeks later, in a second debate, the pacifist vote won again — 750 for to 138 against. This was after the first important challenge had been made to the League of Nations by the Japanese invasion of Manchuria in March 1931. This obvious act of aggression had rung the alarm bell for many in the anti-war movement. On top of this, hopes of disarmament were dashed by the failure of the Geneva Disarmament Conference of 1932. But it was the Italian invasion of Abyssinia in 1935 that was the real wake-up call, a blow to the League's core principle of collective security, that brought the issue of sanctions to the fore. On the vote for economic sanctions by the League in the Peace Ballot held in 1935, 10 million argued for sanctions, only 635 against. Even more significantly, 2,350,000 voted against military sanctions and 6,780,000 voted for the use of force to stop aggression, although the idea of collective security was still supported.

The hopes of peace were therefore fading when the debate regarding the use of military force intensified as the Spanish Civil War broke out in 1936. This caused acute dilemmas

105

especially to socialist pacifists, many of whom ended their pacifist commitment and opted to join the fray on the Republican side. Added to this, Hitler's increased belligerence in Europe and his persecution of German Jewry caused deep schisms within the anti-war movement, with a fundamental divergence of view coming to the fore — peace was no longer the clear-cut issue it had appeared in the 1920s. For religious pacifists, guided by doctrine, the situation was relatively straightforward. The Council of Christian Pacifist Groups in England started to promote a more united Christian opposition to war, the PPU, under the leadership of Dick Sheppard, playing a major part in this development. When Sheppard died, in 1937, Canon Stuart Morris took over his role.

Another peace organisation, the Federal Union (FU), was set up in 1938 to replace the discredited League of Nations with a federation of democracies. It gained great respectability and proved important as a home for those who had pinned their hopes on disarmament and collective security. William Beveridge (later Lord) was its leader and he was supported by Clement Attlee and Ernest Bevin. Intellectuals such as F. A. Hayek, Lionel Robins and Barbara Wootton served on its economic committee.

Vic Newcomb, office boy, Stoke Newington, London

It seemed to me that the picture I had of Spain was of an underprivileged and underdeveloped community, whose efforts to improve their situation through political means had fallen foul of the imperial interests of nations such as Italy and Germany, who intervened on a large scale. So it became a battlefield of ideologies, and at this point I began to understand what was motivating people on both sides of the fence and to understand that ideologies, politics, religion and all those convictions had a greater importance on life than I had given credence for . . . The Spanish Civil War was a turning point in my history.

Fenner Brockway, absolutist CO, First World War

The Spanish Civil War had two curious effects on me: it made me strongly anti-Stalinist, and at the same time it changed me from being an absolute pacifist. I went into anarchist Communist areas there — anarchist not in the sense of physical violence but philosophy. They were lovely places: villages on the coast where when they caught their fish and sold it, and what they sold it for went to the whole village according to the size of the family. And, oh, I so wanted them to win! I felt I couldn't want them to win without *doing* something to help them to win. That meant I could no longer be a complete pacifist, and I wasn't a complete pacifist of course in the Second World War . . . Strangely enough, I've never held a gun in my hand. I could never think of shooting a person; I'd much rather be shot. And so emotionally in that way I'm still a pacifist, but politically and realistically I can't entirely justify it.

Tony Benn, Westminster schoolboy, London

I remember things like the Japanese attack in Manchuria, I read about it and the horrors of it, and then the Spanish Civil War, I remember very clearly, we used to talk about it every night at home. I remember the rise of Fascism. My father and mother went to Marburg in 1933, just as Hitler came to power, and came back and reported on the anti-Semitism there. I met Oswald Mosley first in 1928 when he was a Labour MP, and the next time I saw him was seven years later in Parliament Square when he was leader of the British Union of Fascists. And I went to meetings with my dad that were broken up by the Fascists. This was all when I was about ten or eleven. I have a little article I wrote on disarmament when I was 11. "Keep armaments down . . ." So all this was deeply entrenched in me . . .

Colin Ward, schoolboy, Ilford, Essex

In the late '30s, the Left was in a strangely paradoxical position. There was this pacifist wing which claimed that warmongers like Churchill were pulling Britain into war and this anti-Fascist wing who were saying it's time to end appeasement and deal with Hitler and Mussolini. But they were much divided . . . Working through the list of movements, the one which I responded to with any actual interest was the ILP, precisely I think because you could recognise them as human beings, not as kind of mouthpieces like the Trotskyists, or theologians like the Socialist Party of Great Britain. The ILP's leadership tended to be of dear old chaps — a kind of parody of that kind of socialist: "sandal-wearing vegetarians" — who had been in the Labour movement for years and went for long walks as antiquated youth-hostellers. I think Lansbury, the ILP leader, was an out-and-out pacifist who was regarded by many as a kind of socialist saint. I remember his funeral in 1940 was a huge event at Bow Church in the middle of Bow Road . . . Relations between the ILP and PPU, the anarchists and Quakers, were friendly because they were united in being part of this minute opposition to the main current of thought. They would help each other out in a way which they wouldn't think conceivable with some of the other factions or, of course, with the Communist Party.

James Bramwell, undergraduate, Oxford University

I didn't really think about pacifism until the 1930s. There was the League of Nations failing to do anything about the Abyssinian War and that made a considerable impact on me — the failure to vote sanctions on the Italians. I was appalled by the rise of Fascism among the Axis powers, who were showing their true colours more and more, and then there was Mosley in the East End of London, baiting the Jews and Communists. There was a feeling of incredible gloom and depression among my friends that something ghastly was going to happen, a feeling of doom almost, and we all decided that we had to *do* something about it. And my good friend Charles Kimber started the Federal Union in the mid-'30s. Bertrand Russell was a founder member of this . . . The FU never really took off in a popular way and it was killed off by the outbreak of war. My link was through Charles. It was a good idea and I still think so.

(Sir) Charles Kimber, founder member of the Federal Union

It was pretty obvious that war was coming, and we began asking why the League of Nations had failed. The League was the thing that our generation regarded as *the* thing that those who were killed in the war had died for, and it had something that we were committed to. We were disgusted with the Kellogg-Briand Pact, where these top-hatted gentlemen were signing that they would never go to war with each other, and you knew perfectly well that they were piling up arms against each other . . . At the time of Munich, my friend Derek Raunsley rang me and said, "Look, we've got to do something!" By then our ideas were fairly clear, a league, but with powers of its own and independent of nation states ... The pamphlet we produced was just headed *Federal Union*, and the gist of the text was to say that the reason the League of Nations had failed was because you couldn't trust national governments to keep their word and what was needed was a federal government which had to be democratic. The difficulty was that obviously you couldn't federate with Hitler and Mussolini, so the question was whether you should say which ones to federate with, or just say that the British government was in favour of joining a democratic federation and see which countries responded. We adopted the second case.

James Bramwell, undergraduate, Oxford University

I certainly had nothing to do with the Oxford Union vote. I thought they had a perfect right to say what they wanted. The violent reaction from the press made it clear that the war psychosis was up and running, all mixed up with the gloom of unemployment and the situation in the mines — a very, *very* bad climate and the idea of war on top of it made it even worse ... Some of my friends joined up; I think that I was the only one who became a pacifist. I got the idea of joining the PPU as I was keen on Dick Sheppard, a charismatic man. I admired him, although I didn't count myself as a Christian. After I went down from Oxford, I sold *Peace News* for a while; I thought a lot of the articles were bad and felt quite ashamed of selling them. I was a member of the PPU until war broke out, when I abandoned it because some members even thought it rather treacherous of me to join the fire brigade. I felt uncomfortable with its dogmatism, and anyone who knows anything about pacifism realises its complexity, given so many *types* of pacifism. I became very impressed with the reasoning of Bertrand Russell and Aldous Huxley.

(Sir) Charles Kimber, founder member of the Federal Union

I was up at Oxford when that Oxford Union debate took place about refusing to fight for King and Country. I've always felt it was misrepresented; all the belligerent warriors at once identified it as a *pacifist* vote. It was nothing of the kind. Large numbers of people who voted that way fought subsequently in the Spanish Civil War. What people haven't realised is that it was very carefully worded: "in no circumstances will I fight for King and Country". This is what our generation was about and what the League of Nations was about: "my country right or wrong" was a thing that was not acceptable. And wording that resolution in that way enabled pacifists and League of Nations people to vote together. I've always believed that's how it should have been interpreted. It was not a vote against war, it was a vote against "my country right or wrong" — a nationalist war. That was the thing that finally allowed me to sign on [as a CO] when war came, that the war was a nationalist war. The pamphlet we [the FU] produced [in 1940], *How We Shall Win*, sought to make the Federation a programme of a European resistance movement. If that had been taken up, I think the outcome would have been very different in Europe. But Churchill really insisted on it being a nationalist war and a nationalist solution.

John Petts, artist, Wales

I felt proud that the youth of the nation could pass that resolution in the Oxford Union saying that under no circumstances would they go to war. This shocked the diehard militarists. How wonderful that the youth of the nation could make that affirmation — I really felt proud of that.

Tony Parker, sales assistant, bookshop, Manchester

I was frequently told that the Oxford Union debate vote had caused the war, because Hitler had apparently read in his morning paper that some students of Oxford passed this motion that under no circumstances would they fight for King and

113

Country. One had the image of Hitler reading this in his morning paper and saying, "Right, now is the time for me to strike at England!"

Ronald Mallone, undergraduate, Goldsmiths College, London

The Peace Ballot, done by the League of Nations, wasn't strictly pacifist, but it did bring out the differences between pacifists and non-pacifists. There were about 11 questions you had to answer. A lot of people did that, something like 13,000 people signed that. There was one questioning whether you believed in military sanctions and economic sanctions for the League of Nations. I was one of the minority who was opposed to military sanctions. I wanted economic sanctions.

Mervyn Taggart, city clerk, London

I had such a total revulsion to war that the possession of armies was so utterly, fundamentally wrong that I couldn't accept collective security.

Kenneth Wray, welfare worker, Sussex

Disarm, disarm! That's the only safe way of achieving a peace end, the happiness of men. We put it to the public that the Versailles Treaty was the basic cause of all the distress which was arising. And the thing was to get rectification of the

Versailles Treaty . . . In an infinitesimal small way we tried to do something *positive*. We ran an international peace camp in our garden in 1932 under the auspices of the International Friendship League. We were fortunate in having about two acres, and we erected about ten bell tents. We had something like well over a hundred one August, with France, Germany, Luxembourg and one or two other countries represented. We had Nazis and Jews. One of the Jews was a brilliant pianist and we asked him to play. We had to tell the Nazis, "You have to behave; you're here for friendship, not for political reasons; if you don't like it, you have the right to go back home." After that we had no more trouble.

Ronald Mallone, undergraduate, Goldsmiths College, London

I remember the very big Swanwick camp we had in 1936 in Derbyshire, and it says a lot for my pacifism because I don't like sleeping under canvas! There were about 500 people there. Dick Sheppard and Brigadier General Crozier were there, Stuart Morris, Max Plowman and various group leaders. We had lots of lectures every day. We also had social activities, music and sports. We had a marvellous sports meeting, divided — Dick Sheppard insisted on this — between the carnivores, who had to run with a big meat bone in their hands, and the vegetarians, who ran with a carrot in theirs. This was typical of the way Sheppard was not going to have anything become antagonistic in the movement, because there were those who thought you couldn't become a pacifist without being a vegetarian, and he didn't want any splits. Also, in one of the evening entertainments, he impersonated Brigadier General Crozier and the Brigadier impersonated Dick Sheppard. It was a sketch where one lot of people signed the peace pledge because Dick Sheppard made them weep with his sermon, so they signed in a sentimental manner; the others were terrified by the Brigadier standing over them, sword in hand, saying if they didn't sign he'd lop their heads off.

Vic Newcomb, office boy, Stoke Newington, London

It was the time when the public meeting was the basic means of communicating political ideas. People went to them, you could get audiences of many hundreds without too much effort — very different today [1986] . . .

Ronald Mallone, undergraduate, Goldsmiths College, London

Most of the public meetings were extremely well supported [but] very rarely reported in the press. The press was very antagonistic, very anti-pacifist. I remember a fine meeting in Battersea Town Hall, which was packed, at which Dr Salter, the Labour MP and a Quaker, and Dick Sheppard were speaking. It was a *marvellous* meeting. There was only one antagonistic question in the whole meeting, when an old lady at the back got up and shouted, "What about the Germans?" Dr Salter answered her. But the *South London Press* came out with the headline: "Salter Heckled Again!" That was the sort of reaction. Reporters knew their job: they were supposed to be anti. Dick Sheppard's address was reduced to one or two funny stories in the press, so you never knew what he'd said. The press still likes trivialities. It doesn't like people who make serious statements. I think this is the major reason why pacifism hasn't made much of an advance in the world.

Rev. Donald Soper, Methodist probationary minister, Old Kent Road, London

When I began to speak on Tower Hill in 1926, I was confronted with the practical difficulties of living out the Christian faith . . . Speaking in the open air was in the tradition of John Wesley. My motives for starting were mixed — not all of them holy. I wasn't doing well in the Old Kent Road and found it difficult to make contacts. I was answering the questions that nobody was asking, and I had to recognise that Christianity, if it is to be proclaimed, must have a rapport with events and not be distinct from them, and I very soon learned that lesson in the open air . . . One Wednesday I went along with a youngster from the church to Tower Hill. There were a number of meetings going on and I said, "I'd like to have a go." So I said to a fellow sitting on a wall, "How do you start a meeting?" He said, "Well, get up and they'll come." I got up and said, "What do I do now?" He said, "Well, clap your hands." And I clapped my hands and got him to clap his hands and I announced that I was prepared to speak on the Christian faith and would answer questions. And the first question was about Karl Marx, and I'd never heard of him! It was a baptism of fire! I said that I didn't want to give him a hasty answer, so I'd think about it and come back, and I've been coming back ever since . . .

Ernest Goldring, bank clerk, London

Donald Soper used to attract a crowd of anything from two to three hundred a day. I can certainly recall now seeing him standing on the parapet on Tower Hill. He had a very, very powerful voice and was a brilliant orator. He was particularly good at dealing with questions. He would be very provocative — deliberately so, I think — and he loved the arguments he used to have with people. From day to day there were the same old regulars tossing out the same sort of questions to him, but he had great charisma. He had people almost eating out of his hand. My recollection is that a great cheer would go up as he got up on the parapet.

Rev. Donald Soper, Methodist probationary minister, Old Kent Road, London

I tangled with the Fascists on Tower Hill; some were very difficult, quite violent. On one occasion I was knocked off a wall by a Fascist with a banner . . . But by that time I'd built up a sufficient number of supporters, people who found on Tower Hill a corrective to their experiences in their local churches, and I was grateful for it. So, although I did have some awkward and very dangerous situations with Fascists, on the whole they weren't a menace on Tower Hill . . . There was also a lot of humour. I remember an example of typical cockney humour, a little man, a rascal, who would sit on the wall beside me and whenever I was particularly obscure, he used to look down at the crowds and say "Now, is that clear?" and of course often it wasn't. That's what you have to face in the open air; in church you can get away with it.

Practical forms of peace work were ongoing from the mid-'30s, mainly to help refugees escape from Franco's and Hitler's oppression. The WRI, PPU and the Society of Friends were particularly active in facilitating the sponsorship and assistance of people, many of them Jews, desperate for refuge. During the last year of peace, attention was turning towards preparation for war. The annexation of Austria in March 1938 followed by the Munich settlement on 30 September caused great debate within the peace movement: on one side were those who were grateful for the way Chamberlain had preserved the peace, which they hoped would last. The other side, realising by now the evil nature of Nazism and the threat the Fascist powers presented reluctantly abandoned their anti-war stance, accepting that military force was necessary. The international situation they faced differed greatly from the old balance-of-power system that had existed in 1914, when Britain had fought to restore the balance that had been upset by Germany and her allies; the looming war seemed more difficult for them to reject. Therefore, as war approached, many in the peace movement perceived it as a war in which they must fight. But it was an agonising decision. Among their ranks were former pacifists like Cyril Joad, Bertrand Russell and A. A. Milne, who regarded his changed stance as a "practical pacifist", arguing that: "I believe that if it [Nazi rule] is un-resisted it will spread and corrupt the whole world."

The interwar peace movement, particularly the PPU, has often been accused of appeasing Hitler, citing, as it did, the onerous terms of the Treaty of Versailles on Germany as a reason for Hitler's rise, rearmament and expansion. Another accusation, with the disarmament campaigns they had so ardently supported, was that they had caused military unpreparedness. But as early as 1933 members were expressing their fears and hatred of Fascism, protesting against its advance, warning of the dangers it presented and the need to stand up to it short of force.

As the international situation deteriorated from the mid-'30s, governments made repeated assurances in Parliament that conscription would not be reintroduced in peacetime. In fact, a conscription bill had been in readiness since the end of the First World War. The government attempted to encourage men to volunteer by methods similar to the Derby Scheme of the earlier war. However, of the one and a half million men who responded to the Lord Privy Seal, Sir John Anderson's appeal, three-quarters opted to join the Civil Defence Service. Robust pressure for conscription was exerted by Britain's allies, and on 26 April 1939, the prime minister announced to the House of Commons that a limited form of conscription would be introduced for men aged 20 and 21. The announcement was received with only half-hearted opposition. It was made statutory in May 1939. The Act that introduced full-scale conscription — the National Service (Armed Forces) Act — was introduced on 1 September 1939, just after the German invasion of Poland. Conscription now covered men aged 18 to 41. Britain's participation was now inevitable.

Bertha Bracey, Quaker worker with European refugees, 1920s and '30s

Thousands of people wanted to get out; the difficulty was that there was barrier after barrier, after barrier, after barrier put up against them and it was all made more and more difficult. So if people were coming out of Germany, they were coming out empty-handed, they weren't allowed to bring valuables and money with them. The cream of the population was being skimmed off . . . In the main, I came to the help of refugees because it was at their request: help us to get out! They came to us because we had various centres: Frankfurt, Berlin, Nuremberg, Vienna and Prague. They came because they had known of the Quaker feeding programmes after the First World War.

Tessa Cadbury (Rowntree), Quaker refugee worker in Vienna and Prague, 1938–9

The Friends' Centre in Vienna was swamped with would-be refugees, and the people there were also very worried about a lot of people they'd been in touch with and from whom they hadn't heard. So they asked my friend Bridget and me to go and see if we could find them and see if they were all right. We did this for a week or two and got names and addresses, including Felix Salten, the man who wrote *Bambi*. We called on him and at first there was no answer; eventually this timid-looking man came to the door and there were these two English girls! He asked us in and told us that he was in hiding and that's why he was not in touch with the Centre. He gave us copies of his book, not *Bambi*, but the next one. It was the same day, I think, when we were out in the street, walking along, that there was a screeching of tyres and we were pushed into the middle of the road by a great crowd of people who suddenly appeared. It was Goebbels in a car, we were pushed practically near enough to touch him, and people were calling *"Vielen dank Doktor,"* *"Vielen dank . . ."* We were closer to him than we had been to Hitler when we had heard him speak earlier, but even then Goebbels was gruesome, really gruesome . . . Then an offer came in to go to Prague, and I was there for the best part of 1938 until March 1939, when I went out with a convoy of children to England.

Paul Eddington, schoolboy, Sibford Quaker School, Banbury, Oxfordshire

At school we experienced the first of several waves of refugees . . . I remember particularly a small Jewish boy called Gerhardt Dannenberg . . . He was in lederhosen, a little chap of nine, a little fat, round boy, not a word of English. He'd had to say goodbye to his uncles and aunts, brothers and sisters. The Quakers did quite a lot of work in getting children out . . . We heard the most horrific stories of children. Another friend of mine, Peter Gutkind, had gone to visit his grandmother in Buchenwald and she was thrown over the wall to them — I can't *bear* it! Meeting all these refugee children was a strong influence on us all of course. You might have thought that it would lead us to feelings of such extreme hostility towards Germany, and the Nazis in particular, that no thought of pacifism would have entered our heads. But of course our opposition towards Nazism, Fascism generally, even with that close contact with its

123

victims, was as keen as anyone's, but we felt that it ought to be expressed in a different way, and so did many of the victims themselves.

Mervyn Taggart, city clerk, London

I never felt at the time of Munich that the peace movement could stop the war. I think the peace movement at the outbreak of war is like a man who has cancer and the doctor says, "Look, there is no hope in dealing with this except for me to cut off your leg." At that point it is too late to stop the war. The time to do it is between the wars. It seems perfectly logical for me, for a person who believes that you can defend a country by armed force, to take up arms in a war to do that and I respect that. But at the same time, if you have a moral conviction that it's wrong to kill, then at that point you are entitled to say, "I've always believed it's wrong to kill, and the fact that there is a war going on doesn't alter that conviction."

William Douglas-Home, actor/playwright, London

My brother, Alec, was Neville Chamberlain's Parliamentary Private Secretary. I never knew Chamberlain, but I thought he was a good old thing and trying to do his best to stop the war . . . But having failed with his policy of appeasement, as they called it, I wanted everybody to switch to dislodge the German Army from Hitler. If Hitler had been thwarted in France, they would have got rid of him on the spot, and they tried to get rid of him four years later anyway, and nearly succeeded . . . David Astor and his younger brothers, Jakie and Michael, were friends of mine, and I stayed the weekend at Cliveden when Adam von Trott was there, who was later in the July plot of '44 and got executed. He was talking to people like Lord Halifax and you could tell that he thought it might be possible for negotiations to stop the war, but not necessarily with Hitler.

Jean Greaves (Catchpool), schoolgirl, Sidcot Quaker School, Winscombe, Somerset

At the time of Munich, I think there was more or less a universal sense of relief that there wasn't a war. I think people nowadays, especially those who weren't there, don't realise that we genuinely felt, "Thank God, another war has been averted." . . . The pacifists get blamed for that, don't they?

Paul Eddington, schoolboy, Sibford Quaker School, Banbury, Oxfordshire

Immediately before the war, the peace movement was very, *very* strong, and I think much bigger and more orthodox than it is now. I think it was perhaps rather shallower, because the moment the war happened the vast majority of people who had

125

professed themselves to be pacifists said, "Well, fundamentally I am a pacifist, but now this situation is with us we've got to do something about it." It's a position I can understand, but it did reveal their pacifism to be not very deep-rooted.

Vic Newcomb, office boy, Stoke Newington, London

I was aware of the way in which the COs of the First World War had been treated and were made subject to military discipline, put in prisons and had the "cat-and-mouse" treatment . . . We were in a different ball game. I think the anti-war movements and rights of COs had been widely respected in the years that led up to the war; even those who wanted to confront Nazism with military force still recognised that it was illogical and immoral for a lot of people.

Tom Haley, printer's apprentice, Bethnal Green, London

When the war started in 1939, I was 18. I knew my call-up was imminent: was I going to join the armed forces or sign on as a conscientious objector? Despite all my feelings against war, the decision was not an easy one to take. But this was make-up-your-mind time . . .

CHAPTER
THREE

1939–45: Second World War (I)

At the time of Dunkirk, when there was talk of "bloody conchies; what are they doing?" our shelterers said, "Don't you dare talk about them, about time you started to do something useful!" So it was a rewarding and happy time and we felt ourselves needed.

The news of the outbreak of war on 3 September 1939 was received sombrely. In contrast to the First World War, there was little enthusiasm and no rejoicing. The young men who intended to resist conscription were in a much better position to face the challenges ahead thanks to the legacy they inherited from COs of the earlier war. Also, the conscription process was well planned: compulsory military training was brought in three months prior to war, and full-scale conscription was introduced under the provisions of the National Services (Armed Forces) Act (NSA) of 1 September 1939, enacted on the outbreak of war, 3 September; a conscience clause was included. Those who drafted this Act were careful to avoid the ambiguity of the Military Service Act of 1916. The prime minister, Neville Chamberlain, had earlier spoken in Parliament on the need to respect the rights and status of conscientious objectors, and that experience of the previous war had shown that to act otherwise was "an exasperating waste of time and effort". The range of legal compulsion in this Act was much wider than in the MSA of 1916, covering civilians working in civil defence, defence regiments and fire-watching, as well as military service. Under the terms of the second NSA, passed on 18 December 1941, women were conscripted for the first time in British history.

For most people in Britain, the outbreak of war brought little change: although action had started at sea, there was no sign of the expected bombing raids and gas attacks, and there was stalemate on the land front. It was considered "the strangest of wars", as Neville Chamberlain put it, or the "Phoney War", as it came to be known. During this period, many pacifists felt there was a real chance that a negotiated peace could be achieved and the war stopped. The newly formed Stop the War campaign organised vigorous demonstrations throughout the country in which the majority of peace groups were involved. Pressures on the tribunals at the start of war were huge. During the period of the Phoney War, which lasted from September 1939 to the spring of 1940, more than 50,000 men had been processed at tribunals. At this time, the tribunals reflected the general public tolerance of COs, with 14 per cent of all objectors granted unconditional exemption in 1939. The proportion dropped to 5 per cent in 1940 and 2 per cent by 1941. This reflected the changes that had occurred with the *Wehrmacht*'s blitzkrieg through Denmark, Norway, then the Low Countries into France, leading to the retreat from Dunkirk. Following the fall of France in June 1940, the British people were urged by Winston Churchill, who had replaced Chamberlain as prime minister, to resist the Nazi threat and stand firm in the face of the Nazi onslaught. It was at this time, when invasion threatened, that many pacifists reconsidered their position and entered the forces. At the same time, public attitudes towards COs hardened.

As with the First World War, COs of the Second World War were a very mixed bunch: there was a huge range of religious objectors of all denominations and a diverse range of non-religious objectors, with a broad distinction between pacifist and non-pacifist objectors whose views ranged from socialists who would not fight in any international wars to those who had no objection to military service but had an objection to conscription for it. As with the tribunals of the earlier war, political objectors were the most unpopular. A number of objectors had been COs in the First World War; there were also men who had fought in that war whose experiences had led them to believe that, whatever the cause, war was wrong.

A major step forward was the establishment of the Central Board for Conscientious Objectors, under the chairmanship of Fenner Brockway. This was a welfare type of organisation, designed to advise and assist COs of all persuasions — non-pacifists as well as pacifists — and to keep a vigilant eye on legislation. It also served as a coordinating agent for the plethora of anti-war and pacifist organisations. It took its stand on the recognition that conscription was an abuse of human rights, and it did not engage in propaganda for the pacifist cause.

Harold Bing, CO, First World War

In 1914 there was a tremendous enthusiasm for war, war was a glorious thing, a crusade and so on. Those who went to the Second World War went there with a feeling, well, this is an unpleasant necessity. There was no glorification of war, no enthusiasm for it ... Generally, it was, "Well, Hitler's got to be disposed of somehow or other and we've got to see it through, but it's not a job we like." And one found that among the troops too.

James Bramwell, CO, London

I was in my aunt's drawing room, listening to Chamberlain's broadcast on 3 September, and I remember almost immediately after his voice had died away the sound of sirens, which seemed appropriate. And then a very dreadful silence when my aunt and I said nothing to each other, just sat. I thought there would be bombing right away. I don't think one could see what form the war was going to take ...

Ernie Trory, member and activist of the British Communist Party, Brighton

We were an anti-war organisation, but this is not to imply that we were against *all* wars. We were against *this* particular war. We followed the teachings of Lenin, who said that some wars are just and some are unjust. Wars of liberation, revolutionary wars and the like are just wars and so we fight them with everything we've got. We didn't register as COs. Far from being pacifists, we regarded ourselves as *revolutionaries*. As Comrade Lenin said in 1915, "Pay no heed to the sentimental whiners who are afraid of war . . ." We agreed with this and other teachings of Lenin, which said that in time of war one must go into the army because that is the key position in which to turn the war into a revolutionary war.

Colin Ward, sapper, Royal Engineers

One thing which impressed me very much was the change in the extreme Left — the Communist Party — whose attitude to the war was that it was a capitalist war until that magic day when Hitler invaded the Soviet Union in 1941. And curiously enough, I later came round to the view for quite different reasons. I think that it *was* a capitalist war.

Rose Kerrigan (Klasko), member of the British Communist Party, Glasgow

My attitude when the Second World War started was perhaps coloured by the underlying fact that I was Jewish-born. I was steadily convinced that it was a war against Fascism which was destroying

131

my people and lots of others in the process. Harry Pollitt claimed that we should be *for* the war because we shouldn't be supporting Fascism; he stood out in the executive committee against it. He was almost a pariah for a short period over this; I supported him. I felt that it was a just war to fight against them.

Letter from A. A. Milne to a pacifist addressee, 1 December 1939

I am afraid I am not with you: for I believe that war is a lesser evil than Hitlerism. I believe that Hitlerism must be killed before war can be killed. I think that it is more important to abolish war than to avoid or stop one war. I am a practical pacifist: In 1933 when I began *Peace with Honour* my only (infinitesimal) hope of ending war was to publish my views and hope that they would have time to spread before war broke out. They did not. One must try again. But since Hitler's victory will not abolish war; and since Peace now (which is the recognition of Hitlerism) will not abolish war; one must hope to be alive to try again after England's victory — and in the meantime to do all that one can to bring that about.

Ronald Huzzard, CO in a reserved occupation, Hull

I think a lot of people who had been PPU members up to the time war started and up to the time they received their call-up papers had a change of heart. The last war was not an easy war to oppose. I'm an anti-Fascist, I read as much about Nazism and Fascism and what was going on as I did about war. It was a real dilemma. But I felt at the time that each war was getting worse, the destructive power of armaments that were being developed was making war an even greater evil, and there was obviously going to come a time when war was a greater evil than the evil it was opposing. I think we've reached that stage. We reached it at Hiroshima and Nagasaki, if not before.

Mervyn Taggart, absolutist CO

People's minds changed from Dunkirk onwards. There were a great many who were pacifists up to the time of Dunkirk, but when they saw a real possibility of England being invaded, at that point they changed. And this would go for people who were lifelong pacifists.

Tony Benn, Westminster schoolboy, evacuee, Herefordshire

Dad's Army had a junior brigade, and when I was 16 I joined the Home Guard. I was taught to use the bayonet, to use a rifle and to fire a revolver. I was taught to fire a very elementary missile — a Blacker Bombard — it was a piece of piping and you dropped a bomb into the bottom and it went out again, completely aimless. I also had to throw a grenade, a Mills bomb with a pin — you pulled it out and counted four and it went off . . . But the thing about that was that it made me think about violence because, although I'm a deep follower of Gandhi, who believed in non-violence, I think the right to defend yourself is one you *have* to recognise, and if the Germans had arrived, I would have thrown a bomb. Would that have made me a terrorist or a freedom fighter? That made a deep impression on me and something else did too. To make bayonet practice more realistic, instead of having balloons to put your bayonets in, they put pigs' blood in the balloons so that you'd be splattered with blood. The Archbishop of Canterbury objected and I thought to myself at the time: "Why is he objecting to pigs' blood when he doesn't seem to object to sticking it into real people?"

(Lord) Hugh Jenkins, officer in (Royal) Observer Corps, Maidstone, Kent

I was very worried at the time. On the one hand, I loathed the idea of war and was, I think, a pacifist at heart. On the other hand, I came to the conclusion that Nazism had to be stopped, and I was uncertain about what I ought to do. My friends and I knew that eventually we'd be called up — would we be COs or wouldn't we? . . . When I entered the Observer Corps I had no doubts, no problems once I was in it. I was as keen as anybody and *proud* of the RAF and what they were doing, and it was only later, when I was in the air force, that my doubts began. But even then, in the air force, acting as an air controller, I was still *wholly* engaged. I'm inclined to think that it was the last war in which any gallantry, any nobility, was involved. Because at that stage it was a struggle for *existence*, and it was clear who the aggressor was . . . I still retain the sensation of being involved in the defence of my country . . . In the early days of the war, we still had scruples. If one of our aircraft went over and couldn't find their exact target, they would come back and drop their bombs in the sea. I know one case where a volatile pilot blew everyone up because he tried to land with his bombs still aboard. So a real scrupulousness. A very different world in those days. We really *did* believe that we weren't supposed to kill civilians.

Now [1992] the object of the exercise is to kill civilians.

John Marshall, CO, volunteered for the army, NCO in Royal Corps of Signals

I joined the army in January 1942 . . . I was told to report to the Royal Signals Training Centre, at Prestatyn in north Wales . . . I got into the first barrack hut and found myself among people I can only describe as unconscientious objectors . . . All of them, to every young man present, *loathed* the idea of being called up, was lamenting bitterly and saying so in no uncertain terms as well. I think I was the only one who didn't say this, and I was also the only volunteer in the entire barrack hut as well.

Dr J. E. A. Bartlet, RAMC, Argyll and Sutherland Highlanders, Malaya, 1941, later POW, from his memoir

In the early days there was no conscription for doctors. I volunteered for the army. My surgical chief had a "good 1914–1918 war" . . . One of his favourite expressions was "the only good German is a dead German". I had a very high regard for him but never felt quite the same towards him after, when on telling him of my volunteering he said, "I thought you would soon be wanting to join the fun." In retrospect perhaps it was just a semantic misunderstanding related to the generation gap. However, it was not how I or, I think, many of my generation looked at war. War was something unpleasant that one's government had become involved in and had to be got on with.

William Douglas — Home, actor/playwright, London

I went on acting until July 1940, when my call-up papers arrived . . . I wrote and said, "I'm not a conscientious objector, I don't think I'll go before a board because I don't think I'll get off because I'm a political objector, therefore I'll accept my call-up papers. But a situation might arise in the future when you wouldn't find me all that reliable." They never answered that. Then I was called up and went down to Maidenhead, where the 7th Buffs, which formed part of the Royal Tank Regiment, was . . . It was a difficult decision for me because I was against the whole idea of the war and wanted peace aims — there weren't any. But I don't think I would have liked being a conscientious objector and digging a hole in a field . . . I preferred protesting against the thing rather than actually packing it in right away. I am not a pacifist.

Denis Allen, absolutist CO, Feltham Borstal, Wandsworth Prison and Wormwood Scrubs

I did not register as a CO. I took the view that if I registered and took exemption in the normal way, I was subscribing to the pattern of war. The government was liberal, enlightened in providing that opportunity for people like me. I recognised that and compared it to what would have happened had I been in Germany. But that didn't alter the fundamental principle, so I wrote and said that I wasn't going to register . . . The stigma of prison for COs was much less than it had been for COs in the first war. My friends were all supportive, although my mother and stepfather excommunicated me.

Reginald Bottini, shipping clerk, London

I went to the company secretary, who was a nice man by the name of Mr Brown with whom I'd had excellent relations for five years. I said, "Mr Brown, I have to register tomorrow." "That's right," he said. And I said, "I think it's only fair to tell you that I propose to register as a conscientious objector." And it reminded me of the advertisement of the man in the chemist's shop who wondered whether Howell's aspirin was the best. He went *white*, poor man. He'd never had such a shock because I was such a good clerk and generally reliable. So he said, "I think Mr Stewart will want to see you" — Mr Stewart being the deputy chairman — and Mr Stewart did. And Mr Stewart used some insulting expressions and said, "Get rid of him!" No one dared to speak to me during that week. Being thoroughly awkward, I enjoyed making everyone feel embarrassed being there and I marched out very proudly and thought: "I've struck my blow." It didn't really do any good at all, I should have kept my trap shut until I'd been to the tribunal. But that's how it was. One thumbed one's nose at the world.

Denis Hayes, CO, CBCO member, London

When the inaugural meeting of the CBCO was held, we looked around for a suitable chairman and thought we couldn't do better, in order to unite all the different factions, than to have Fenner Brockway, who had been court-martialled four or five times between 1916 and 1918. In 1939 he was almost an elder statesman. Even the Society of Friends were prepared to accept that in the forefront there was a person who, although he had a great peace background over many years, would not regard himself as a complete pacifist . . . The CBCO took the view that there was a conscientious movement which was broader than the pacifist movement.

Fenner Brockway, absolutist CO, First World War, chairman of the CBCO during the Second World War

In the Second World War, though I was not a pacifist and though I was tremendously anti-Hitler and couldn't oppose the Second World War as I did the First, I remained chairman of the CBCO because I believed in the liberty of conscience so much. But it was very different in the Second World War, it was easier for the COs . . . It was the resistance during the First World War that made them [the politicians] so tolerant in the Second.

Kathleen Wigham (Derbyshire), absolutist CO, Blackburn, Lancashire

When I went to register, this gentleman came and spoke to me. I said, "I've come to register as a conscientious objector because I object to doing any work which will relieve anyone else to do military service." He said, "Oh, you're one of *those*, are you, we didn't expect *women* coming along." I said, "Well, I may be the first but there will be more to follow." So he took various particulars and dropped some casual remarks about being a coward and not being able to see straight and told me, "Well, you'll be hearing from us."

(Bishop) Freddie Temple, Balliol College, Oxford

The Master, A. D. Lindsay, used to say to those of us who were thinking of pacifism, "Be sure you are not just wanting others to wash your dirty linen and get their hands soiled on your behalf."

Harold Bing, CO, First World War

The National Service Acts were more generously drafted, the tribunals were more carefully appointed and there was no military representative on them. And the hearings were all, I think, much fairer. I went as visitor to support various applicants and they got much fairer treatment . . . There were not many absolute exemptions granted.

Significant changes were made regarding the membership and procedures of tribunals. In the earlier war, they had been under the aegis of the War Office until 1917 and there had been very little liaison between tribunals and central control. Now they were administered by the Ministry of Labour and National Service, which strictly controlled their membership. They were called Conscientious Objector Tribunals and were to deal with applications from those wishing to be exempted for all or part of the war effort. Local tribunals consisted of a chairman, who had to be a county court judge (or his Scottish counterpart), and four other "impartial" members, one of whom had to be appointed with the agreement of a trade union representative. Unlike tribunals of the earlier war, army

141

representatives were not mandatory, although there were cases of military men serving on panels. However, it is generally accepted that the war ethic, which had so strongly pervaded the tribunals of the First World War, was largely absent. The hearings were to be held in public unless the chairman decided otherwise, and the applicants were allowed the support of a relative, friend or legal representative.

Although still an ordeal for the young people facing them, the British tribunals of the Second World War are generally regarded as having been relatively fair, with panel members more open-minded, tolerant and striving to understand the young men and women standing before them. But there continued to be great differences between tribunals, and the attitudes of judges varied, ranging from tolerant and sympathetic to hostile and insulting — Fulham, in London, being considered one of the harshest compared with the South-Eastern, seen as fair and more understanding. Between the first sitting of a tribunal in July 1939 and the end of the war in May 1945, sixty thousand British men had successfully claimed conscientious objection: 1.2 per cent of those liable to be called up and almost four times as many as in the First World War.

The categories of COs followed the same pattern as in the First World War: Category A, unconditional exemption, the absolutist position, continued to be difficult for tribunal panels to accept, although government and Parliament had adopted a more conciliatory tone and gave tribunals the power to grant it. Category B, conditional exemption, was the most common, whereby COs were directed into work of national importance, under civilian control. In April 1940, the Non-Combatant Corps had been formed expressly for receiving Category C objectors into the army. If applicants failed to convince tribunals of their sincerity, they could be directed into military service, the Category D decision. From 1941, women who registered as COs were directed into civilian work as no NCC had been formed for any of the women's services.

Angela Sinclair-Loutit (de Renzy Martin), undergraduate, Somerville College, Oxford

I was pleased to have a tribunal. It was rather like passing a driving test, being like all the others, to have some status with the men . . . Tribunals were a subject of gossip; we all compared them. It was stressed that what they were after was sincerity of belief, not in fact what the beliefs were. How difficult it is to judge sincerity! . . . I do remember being embarrassed at times: my father had quite a number of diplomatic acquaintances and most of their sons and daughters were serving in the forces. I was never accused of being a coward, but I do remember feeling embarrassed occasionally on his behalf.

Donald Swann, undergraduate, Oxford University

I found that I was judging them, the panel. But that shows how arrogant I was. I didn't believe they had any status at all and that they had been themselves brainwashed into an impossible situation . . . that there was another world that I was trying to create and they didn't know too much about it . . . After me, they got a man who said he was a butcher. He immediately said, "You're all murderers. I won't do anything for you." That was his one and only statement. "No good," they said, and dismissed his objection. He was totally inarticulate, he had no way of expressing himself . . . Fortunately he was swept up by the CBCO people who said, "You must have an appeal. We will tell you how to write it all out."

Doris Nicholls (Steynor), pacifist, general secretary FOR, advisor to COs, social worker

Many of those coming before tribunals were only 18, and some of these poor little devils weren't articulate. But the remarkable thing was that eight times out of ten, the tribunal members not only saw through those who were being smooth and trying to get away with something, as many of them undoubtedly were, but they also got through to the inarticulate. One I shall never forget, a young man who could in fact have got exemption on medical grounds, but who was a convinced pacifist and felt that this was not fair and that he ought to go to the tribunal. When he got there, it was literally the case that he was struck dumb. One question after another came. And there were these great silences. Then, whoever had put the question would rephrase it: "Well now, try that." They were kind, they realised that the lad could not find enough moisture in his mouth to utter and that his mind had gone . . . Very occasionally there'd be a halting sentence, but that was all they could get out of him. I was there to speak on his behalf and the chairman turned to me and said, "Can you help us?" I said, "Well, I've had a number of conversations with him, and it was easier for him in my nice little room to talk, and as I understand it it's this and this, you see." And from time to time they'd just turn to him and say, "Do you agree?" or "Is this true?" and things of that kind. And they gave him unconditional exemption.

Ronald Mallone, absolutist CO, English master, Eastleigh, Hampshire

I was in Eastleigh at the time so I went to Southampton for my tribunal . . . Of that tribunal, the most unpleasant was Dover-Wilson. He always used to ask educational questions. Whoever was before him, he would say, "To what standard were you educated? Did you go to grammar school? Did you pass matric?" When he'd done that, he subsided. If they mentioned anything about history, he'd say, "How can you tell us anything about history when you didn't even have your matriculation?" I happened to have a first-class degree in history. As soon as he discovered that, he didn't ask me any questions at all. I felt this very unfair: he was picking on the uneducated . . . Really their attitude was to prefer whatever the government wanted: if it wanted ambulance people then they were sending people into the Ambulance Corps, and later, when they filled that, they sent them on the land. They also varied as to the attitude of the CO and how many raids we'd had the night before. If there had been a raid the night before, the judge was always in a bad temper and antagonistic; if there had been a peaceful night, he was more like a judge.

Kathleen Wigham (Derbyshire), absolutist CO, Blackburn, Lancashire

On the 2nd of July 1942, I was summoned to appear in the Sessions House on the grounds of why I had objected and refused to pay the five-pound fine at the industrial tribunal I'd been sent to after I had registered. Again I stated my reasons. And, scratching his head, the chairman says, "Well, there's nothing more we can do only to send you to prison, and we're giving you the shortest period of sentence that we can possibly give anyone. We hope this will help you change your mind. Fourteen days in Strangeways. If at any time you change your mind, all you have to do is let the governor know that you'll pay your fine and you'll be released immediately." They were almost *begging* me to pay my fine . . . A wardress and prison warder came and took me down to the cells.

Nora Page (Watson), absolutist CO, Holloway Prison, London

The sentencing was very arbitrary; the chairman would say, "By the law I will sentence you to three months, six months, twelve months . . ." It could be anything according to the mood of the magistrate on the panel. For my sentence I got fourteen days, but a week afterwards a Tottenham girl got a month, others got three months, and it was exactly the same offence — refusal of direction of labour. In my case, they had directed me to serve in a greengrocers which would release girls that could then be taken into the services.

Ian Serraillier, CO, Birmingham, extracts from his notebook

From a previous Tribunal

J. "You say you will not take life. Are you a vegetarian?"

C. "Yes."

J. "Do you refuse to take life of any sort?"

C. "Yes."

J. "Cabbages are living things. Do you eat cabbages?"

C. "Oh, no! I don't eat cabbages."

J. "Apples grow on trees. Do you eat apples?"

C. "Oh no, I don't eat apples."

J. "What do you eat?"

C. "I live on bread and water."

J. "What is your work?"

C. "Draper's assistant."

J. [announcing decision] "You'd better go on being a draper's assistant."

Nora Page (Watson), absolutist CO, Second World War, London

They used to say, "What are you pleading?", and the solicitor would say, "Conscientious objection to the Military Service Act so and so . . .", and this chap says, "I'm a conscientious objector too." And the magistrate says, "It's not on his papers. What's your objection then?" So he says, "I ain't going to live with my wife any longer, I've got a conscientious objection to living with her." He was actually there on a maintenance order that he hadn't fulfilled. This was the lighter side of it . . .

James Bramwell, CO, London

Lytton Strachey, I remember, had a rather amusing answer to the question, "What would you do if a German raped your sister?" "I should try to interpose myself."

Mervyn Taggart, absolutist CO, agricultural worker

My position was very much easier than most because people understood the Quaker position, it was an historical one, and this made it relatively easy at the tribunal . . . I was one of a very, very small number of people who were given unconditional exemption. That means that they left it to me to do what I thought was right during the war.

Reginald Bottini, Fulham tribunal, London

I will never forget my tribunal because I was trembling, trembling more with indignation than anything else. It was Fulham, which was credited as being very harsh on COs. Seven lads who were obviously religious fanatics of various kinds went before me one by one; they all based their objections on the Bible. It struck me that the members of the tribunal seemed to have a list of counter-quotations from the holy book so that when one of these unfortunates quoted the saying, "That if thine enemy strike thee on the right cheek turn unto him the left," they only had to turn up counter-statement number 26, "And he took whips and beat the money-lenders out of the temple." They were all refused registration as COs and ordered to be transcribed on the military register. So I became convinced that when my number was called that I would be dealt with in a similar fashion. And in a rather confused and inarticulate way, I adopted the most aggressive posture possible to their very hard questioning. In fact, they gave me conditional registration, the only one out of eight. I reached the conclusion, cynical youngster that I was, that it wasn't on the basis of conscience at all, but that here they saw a red-haired trouble-maker of Irish/Italian descent that might be difficult for army discipline . . . I said to Groves, who was supporting me there, "I'm going to object, I'm not going to do anything for them." And I was told with the aid of an expletive to shut up, that I had been extremely lucky.

Rev. Donald Soper, Methodist minister, Kingsway Hall, London

The great difficulty of course is the Bible — a very dangerous document which caused me no end of trouble. You can make up your mind what you believe and find a text which supports it and you can find a text for any darned thing that you want to . . . War is over and over again justified in the Old Testament . . . The concept of the Just War is a contradiction in terms — there may be just *motives*, but they are corrupted immediately in the prosecution of war, and justice flies out of the window as soon as you embark on mass destruction and the bombing of innocent civilians . . .

Peter Sharp, CO, Bermondsey, London

There's no other word for it: the tribunal members were pigs; they were most unpleasant to these Christian pacifists. They were quite weakish sorts

150

of people and they started bullying them, telling them they were lying, that sort of thing. When it came to my turn, I showed my truculence, stuck my hands in my pockets and just stood there . . . They dismissed me right away. I was quite prepared and thought I was going to prison, but I didn't really want that so I appealed. Well, the difference! There were about a dozen chaps at the appeal, they would go up to the panel, who would ask questions, and before they were halfway through, the chairman would say, "We understand." I mean, what a difference! They could sense the nervousness of the objectors and were understanding. I was given a chance to go on the land, and I got a job with a very mixed bunch of pacifists at Ripley, near Guildford . . . My three brothers were all in the forces and they continued to be very supportive of me. Not once did they say to me, "Pete, why aren't you going?" It was conscription, you see; if anyone refused they were "cowards". My brothers went like many others, but they were not exuberant about going . . . I can remember the talks I had with my family and friends, all agreeing that war was ridiculous, but they didn't think *politically*; like most they went along because, well, there's no trouble, you don't annoy people.

Douglas Beavor, Jehovah's Witness, absolutist CO, London

I am not a pacifist, the war of Armaggedon I would support, although not by bearing arms or taking part, but I would be in complete agreement with it . . . I knew that I would have to stand up and bear my witness if called up. At the beginning, Jehovah's Witnesses were recognised as conscientious objectors and were given exemption, but this changed after about a year and after that we were not recognised as COs. The pressure was on after Dunkirk and our stand, being absolute, brought down the wrath of the authorities on us. Towards the end, it was the maximum sentence every time.

Fewer COs were involved in breaking the laws relating to compulsory military service in the Second World War than in the First. This is attributed to tribunals offering a much larger number of applicants alternative work that they could conscientiously perform. Absolutists, as in the earlier war, wanted nothing to do with the military machine and few received unconditional exemption at their tribunals. By refusing to accept the tribunal's decision, they faced court martial. The process would be similar to that of the First World War: absolutists would initially refuse to report for duty when summoned; they were then arrested and taken to an appropriate guardroom. A court martial would then take place, which would be followed by a detention sentence. Forcible dressing in military uniform and, in the Second World War, a compulsory medical examination were then attempted.

Refusal to accept the rules led to repeated court martials and prison sentences. A sentence could start out as a fine, then progress to indefinite detentions (for a maximum of two years) or what would have been a huge fine of £100. Also, fewer objectors were imprisoned for more than a year, compared with at least 800 COs incarcerated for 20 months or more in the First World War. By 1943, much publicity had been given to the cases of two Jehovah's Witnesses who had been repeatedly imprisoned; this led to an administrative concession that on completion of a third sentence, a man would be discharged. At last the hated "cat-and-mouse" was ended. It meant that no CO, whether judged genuine or not, would have to spend more than three terms in prison if he claimed that the offence was committed on conscientious grounds.

Of the 62,301 COs who faced tribunals in the Second World War, of whom 1,074 were women, 2,937 were awarded total exemption and the rest were undertaking various forms of civilian work, serving in the NCC or just trying to keep their heads down. Of the latter group, 6,500, including over 400 women, served prison sentences, with very few imprisoned for more than a year. It is generally accepted that the treatment of COs in prison was far more lenient than it had been in the earlier war and they were no longer forced to work. Yet the stigma remained and many stories of brutality have been recorded. Pockets of intentional cruelty also existed — in Dingle Vale, for instance, where gaolers were later prosecuted for their inhumane treatment of COs.

John Radford, absolutist CO, Dingle Vale School detention centre, extract from letter to Dr Donald Soper, 27 September 1940

I expect that you will be disappointed to hear that I have given up the fight after fourteen days . . . I will outline the last few days of our resistance. I can liken it only to a Nazi Concentration Camp, and what is more it was here in free and democratic England . . . On Monday morning after breakfast (one slice of bread) about six R.P.s came to take three of us to work. We refused and were beaten up on the spot then dragged to the butcher's shop and ordered to clear up the blood and mess on the floor. We still refused and were then given another beating up then we were cuffed all the way back to the Guard-room. Later in the morning we were taken before the R.S.M., another bully, who gave us the option of scrubbing a floor or doing an hour's exercise. We chose the latter and were placed here and there amongst a squad of soldiers with rifles. We were marched up and down for an hour or so, I should imagine that they had been given some instructions because at every turn we were tripped and kicked about the legs, rifles were jabbed in our backs and knees used on every possible occasion. At the end of the exercise I had several bruises and was pretty well in a state of collapse. After a dinner of one slice of bread we were given an hour's hard exercise by ourselves, orders and abuse were hurled at us the whole time

. . . this treatment continued until Wednesday when my whole head was cropped, this was the last straw, it broke me up finally. I was then told that a political C.O. called Foster, the backbone of our company had given in, so in this moment of weakness, I gave in too, it was the fourteenth day . . . I feel pretty badly about my failure to stick it out. I am now in the NCC . . . I have applied for a transfer to the RAMC which I suppose is a little more humane in its work.

William Heard, Jehovah's Witness, absolutist CO, Feltham Borstal, Wormwood Scrubs, London and Oxford prisons 1940–4

What amazed me was the meanness of the individuals in Feltham Borstal. In the tailor's shop, part of the job was preparing the suit for a man due to leave, and these people would say the day before, "If you don't give me your meal today I shall leave the iron on your suit." And they would, and they did. They were horrible, and this was to their own kind. I was there quite a few weeks and all the time having these beatings up. Eventually I had my teeth knocked out in the front — somebody tapped me on the shoulder and just hit me. My teeth were gone. No dentist, just loss of teeth. They had started bullying me immediately, the first night, that's when I had the slop pail poured over me in bed. I had to sleep in it. They knew why I was there and that's why they bullied me. Another nasty habit they had was putting my boots in this bucket all night and the warder would make me wear them the next day. And when the rations came, one particular officer cut mine down. The officers would turn a blind eye when anything happened. Weekends were terrible. From Saturday afternoon until Sunday, I was with the rest of them in a big dining hall. We were supposed to read, but the books and everything were thrown around. Then the meal would come up and I'd sit at this long table in a quiet way and all of a sudden you'd get a cup of boiling-hot cocoa poured down your neck. Nobody saw it, of course. So I hated weekends.

Kathleen Wigham (Derbyshire), absolutist CO, Strangeways Prison, Manchester

A gruelling factor of my prison sentence was that this was the time when Liverpool and Manchester were being badly bombed each evening. And at night at eight o'clock it was lights out, so there was nothing to do, only to lie down, and you virtually just stared up at the window with everything in darkness because of the blackout. And then you'd hear the sirens going, and hear gunfire and bombs dropping, and this would aggravate the girls; there would be terrible tension. And you'd hear a girl shouting, "Let me out! Let me out! Take us to the air-raid shelters!" And nothing, *nothing* happened. You heard no comforting voices, no one even saying, "Shut up!" It just gave the impression that all the officers and wardresses had gone to their safety shelters and we were just left. Sometimes I would shout and say, "We'll be all right, you know we're being watched over." But they would swear back at you, it stopped me from even saying a prayer for them because they would tell you to "b— off" and so on; the language was pretty foul. Really it was mental torture, there's no other description for it.

Nora Page (Watson), absolutist CO, Holloway Prison, London

Then you started to see who was next door to you. The conversation is always, "What you done?" "I haven't done anything at all; I won't take part in this war." "Oh! They put you in here for *that*?" Well, they'd all done something: knocked off a whisky bottle, fiddled the rent book, done the Underground — all things that were worth doing, but here were people who hadn't done *anything*, it was a big talking point. I was in the workroom one morning, all of us sitting in a row doing needlework, and our officer says, "The visiting magistrate is here, this is the time you can make your complaints, and there hadn't better be any." In comes this old man who could hardly walk, tottering along: "Any complaints?" And old Vera got up — she was a very tall woman, used to come in every Monday, got out every Friday, get drunk, come back again — and she said, "Yes, sir, I have a complaint. This place is coming to something when they've got people in here who ain't done anything." By then there was Kathleen Lonsdale [physicist and Quaker] and this Jehovah's Witness and me. He looked at her: "That's not a complaint." And turned to the officer and said, "I recommend that the prisoner be mentally examined."

Kathleen Wigham (Derbyshire), absolutist CO, Strangeways Prison, Manchester

The cell door was open and there stands the doctor: "What's all this about refusing your meat?" "I'm a vegetarian, I haven't eaten meat for a number of years, and if I eat meat I know I'll be ill, the authorities know because I've written to them about it." ... He just pulled the cheek down to look at my eyes with a flashlight, turned to the wardress and said, "You can find her a bed in the hospital, she's barmy." ... He went out and the wardress started on me and didn't half give me a dressing down. "Our men are fighting for sluts like you. Fold your blankets and you carry them down to the laundry . . . if I had my way you'd be hanging from the end of a rope." Prodding me all the time, a nudge almost knocking me over when I was wrapping the blankets up. I found it difficult to talk, a lump was in my throat and I was very close to tears . . . I'd visions that she was going to trip me up going down the steps because she was

constantly pushing me, couldn't leave me alone
. . . When I got to the ward, I thought, "Good
heavens above, this is almost like being in a mental
ward!" There were patients shaking, one woman's
tongue was lolling backwards and forwards,
another girl was screaming and making noises and
pulling her hair out, and some were just sitting
quietly . . .

Sybil Morrison, CO, PPU activist, Holloway Prison, London

It was through my activities with the PPU that I
got arrested . . . I got into trouble right at the
beginning when the doctor who was examining
me asked me — which she had no right to do
— what I was in for. When I told her, she was
simply furious and said, "If you were in
Germany you'd have been shot." I said, "Yes,
very likely." And she said, "That's what I'd do
to you." So I, forgetting that I wasn't speaking
in Hyde Park, and that I shouldn't answer back,
said, "You mean you agree with Hitler?" She
was really furious and unpleasant to me all the
time I was in there. She was a bit of a Hitler;
they were all very frightened of her. You soon
learn that it's a great mistake to answer back.

Kathleen Wigham (Derbyshire), absolutist CO, Strangeways Prison, Manchester

Prison has left a lifetime's impression on me because when I came out of prison I couldn't speak without stammering, and for a long, long time I found it difficult to find the right words for what I wanted to say. And this has remained . . . I think in some ways this has stopped me in going further in my [teaching] career . . . Mentally, if it had been any harder it would have broken me in health, in mind and body. I'm fully aware of course that Quakers and COs in the First World War went through a lot more . . . When I came out, I did write my experiences down and sent them to the Prison Reform authorities. I just felt that something had to be done to improve conditions in prisons.

Harold Bing, CO, First World War

There wasn't that sort of cat-and-mouse business — come out of prison, into prison again, and so on for the duration of the war . . . That meant, of course, that there never developed the same kind of strong fellowship among the COs of the Second World War as it did among the First, when we were in the same, or many, different prisons together and there for two or three years; whereas even those who went to prison were only at a local prison perhaps for three months and then they were off, scattered on farms, and never really got to know one another as we did. That explains the comparatively small number of the Second World War COs found active in the pacifist movement today compared with the absolutists of the First World War active in the interwar period.

Denis Allen, absolutist CO, Feltham Borstal, Wandsworth Prison and Wormwood Scrubs, London

In the prisons I always had a cell to myself, but there was a fair bit of contact during the day in the workshops, where we were free to talk; we also exercised together, so there was much more social contact then than now, when, due to staff shortages, the lack of supervision requires prisoners to be locked in their cells for most of the day. In these kinds of ways, the situation's gone downhill quite a lot . . . What I learnt in prison is that prisoners are not a different breed, so to adopt a them-and-us attitude is irrelevant. The experience reorientated me entirely and it certainly affected my social work when I had the opportunity to employ an ex-prisoner.

The Second World War was proving a very different conflict from the earlier war. Major technical developments in the machinery of war — aeroplanes, tanks, artillery and bombs — and the involvement of the whole globe in the waging of war, the mass mobilisation of populations, and the blurred

161

boundaries between the home front and the battlefield, meant that it was a Total War of epic proportions. Civilian deaths on the home front outnumbered those of the services up to September 1941, and by the end of the war they totalled 66 per cent worldwide. The huge humanitarian need was soon apparent, which meant that Category B was the ideal decision for tribunals as well as many COs who felt the need to bear witness through practical action. The work on offer was varied and much of it highly satisfying. It included agriculture, forestry, community projects, hospital and ambulance services, coal mining, and serving as guinea pigs for medical experimentation. From March 1941, COs could also be drafted into civil defence; many willingly undertook such work, although the element of compulsion was objected to by many, particularly Jehovah's Witnesses, with their fundamentalist stance. One Witness, George Elphick, was prosecuted nine times for refusing fire-watching duties in Lewes, Sussex. The sort of men who sought CO status were, on the whole, individualistic and disposed to be socially useful and so welcomed the opportunity for worthwhile work. Therefore many COs found their work in the humanitarian field hugely rewarding, even life-forming. The "alternativist" label used in the earlier war was rejected by them: it was considered misleading, disguising the compulsory nature of military service, indicating that conscripts were free to choose between military or alternative service. Instead, they preferred "humanitarian service" or "work under civilian control".

The RAMC had a very good record so far as COs in the earlier war were concerned. The problem did, however, arise that since the RAMC was not officially an NCC service, objectors might have to take up arms. This was resolved in

March 1940, when the War Office made it clear that drilling with, or handling, lethal weapons would not be required for those performing non-combatant duties.

Tony Gibson, CO, Pacifist Service Unit, London

When raids started in September 1940, I did a bit of shelter work in Stepney and Poplar. I then heard of the Pacifist Service Unit to be told that I was *it*! Over the next few months we got three sections of ten going, which we dispersed around Chadwell. The main thing was going around the shelters in the mornings, taking the buckets of shit and throwing them down manholes and covering the lot with bug powder. Then in the afternoons we went to houses that had been bombed, rescuing people's possessions. We weren't much use at rescue work or fire fighting, but we were regarded as "good people". At the time of Dunkirk, when there was talk of "bloody conchies; what are *they* doing?" our shelterers said, "Don't you *dare* talk about them, about time *you* started to do something useful!" So it was a rewarding and happy time and we felt ourselves needed.

Ernest Goldring, CO, agricultural worker

Well, after working in a bank, farm work was pretty tough. I never had been particularly robust in health, so at the physical level it was certainly very

163

exhausting and demanding. In addition to which we had to look after ourselves: cook, wash our clothes, empty the loo bucket, things like that. But looking back on it, I think I enjoyed it very much. I'd always had a great feeling for nature and it was pleasant living in rural surroundings. I learnt some skills such as milking cows and to plough and dig properly . . . Also, for the three of us this was our first experience of community living, and there were times when we got a bit irritated in the evenings when we came back tired — about the rota system of cooking, washing and the like. It didn't reach any serious levels and the experience was probably good for all of us.

John Petts, CO, agricultural worker, Derbyshire

This farm manager said, "Today we're carting quicklime and don't forget it's bloody *quick!*" He meant corrosive, the sort of lime they dissolved bodies in during the Great Plague. My body started to dissolve too. There was always this rain and wind. You marked the field out and placed these pyramids of pure white in patterns across the field. The wind was blowing this corrosive dust about and the rain was wetting my face. I had two livid lines from my eyes straight down my face, raw-meat canals. I felt I would be scarred for the rest of my life as I was sent out on it day after day — nothing was said about my burns. It was impossible to complain. The answer would have been, "You shut your mouth; men are dying out there."

Ian Serraillier, CO, labourer, Birmingham area, extracts from his notebook, 22 November 1940

Instead of £5.10 [£5.50] a week I now get 25/- [£1.25]. Instead of working a 6½-hour day, I do a 12-hour day, 7 days a week. I mend boards, plaster up walls, lay pipes. 4 men work with me, 2 sacked schoolmasters, a schoolboy, and a sacked civil servant. We work all day and sleep on the floor upstairs at night heavily and peacefully, for we are far from sirens. Soon this ratty barn will lose its 30 years old cobwebs, and it will be a palace for the families from the industrial centres where homes have been shattered.

Peter Sharp, CO, agricultural worker, Surrey

This farm near Guildford was my first contact with so many different "isms". It was a surprise to me how many reasons there were for being war-refusers. To start with there were the spiritualists, whom we referred to as the "crazy gang"; they were most odd and didn't seem to have any idea of pacifism or anything else. Then there were the Christadelphians — they were all right. There were straight anarchists, some who had been Communists but now had more mixed feelings, and one Jew. We came from very mixed backgrounds, professionals and artisans all working together digging ditches. We all got on well; people would listen to others when they were having their say. Some who were used to hard work, worked hard; others didn't; those who hadn't worked with a pick and shovel before found it difficult. We got on well with our supervisor, although he didn't agree with our views.

Nigel Walters, CO, agricultural worker, extracts from letters to fiancée Sheila Donaldson

Feb 1942: manual work is a great hindrance to intellectual development . . . It is difficult to retain a pleasurable conception of life and I do hope I shall not develop strong mucles [sic] or acquire in any way the faintest expression, or attitude of a yokel . . .

11 March 1942: work is most depressing for me, having been levitated for a while to a higher plane of appreciation, farm-work appears contrastingly vulgar, being a purely material and physical thing . . .

19 April 1942: Barry is a very amusing pacifist and a remarkably insincere one, but I wish him success. We at college are egotists inwardly, and consider our lives too valuable to be taken, game

fashion, one for one with the enemy. War is strong-headedness, I am not strong-headed, it is cruel and I endeavour to be kind, it is base and I consider myself to be enlightened. Others fight, I neither hinder or assist them. Political opinions or religious beliefs, which are only colours and aspects of life, should never be valued above life itself. War is not civilised and we dear Sheila are.

Mervyn Taggart, absolutist CO, agricultural worker

I saw these communities as a brave new world, a microcosm of what the world might become: cooperative and thoroughly unselfish, very giving, giving being the very basis of life and progress. I got tremendously caught up in them and, in fact, at one of them I just worked to the point of exhaustion. I felt they had *tremendous* potential. They failed for three reasons: they were mostly land communities and members didn't always have the necessary technical skills, the abilities needed in farming. Secondly, they failed because the people running them were very strong individualists and there tended to be a conflict of personalities. And they failed because they didn't provide a totally different economic system, a sound financial basis for a reasonable standard of living. People who lived there often lived under the most appalling conditions.

167

John Marshall, CO, agricultural worker on a commune in Hampshire, volunteered for the army 1942, NCO in Royal Corps of Signals

We had some Austrian refugees working with us. When France fell, Hannah, the fiancée of Gustaf, was in utter and total panic and horror. I have never seen anyone in such a state of abject *terror*. I could understand why because they had mentioned the nature of the Gestapo to me in passing . . . I didn't know what to say to her and this was when the question of "to be a pacifist or not a total pacifist" came out in all its stark reality. And one of the most intelligent and hard-working members of our commune, a chap called McCann, said to me in private, "The country that gives you the liberty that we've got makes you want to fight for it, doesn't it?" . . . And so we were facing another hideous dilemma . . . Another blow was when the arch intellectuals who provided and stoked up the rational, intellectual side of the pacifist movement, Bertrand Russell and C. E. M. Joad, both virtually recanted following Dunkirk. So now, as a youth on the receiving end, one felt totally betrayed. First of all we felt betrayed by the fact of the war itself. Then betrayed intellectually . . . So one felt completely abandoned and betrayed.

Denis Hayes, CO, CBCO member, London

It was the COs to some extent who added their little bit of upgrading to the status of agricultural workers. They were town folk, had the education, known other standards, it soon got around — why should farm labourers live in feudal conditions? The COs gave a push in the right direction.

John Petts, CO, agricultural worker, Derbyshire

The terrible thing is that you never considered that you had any rights at all. So you were overworked and endured conditions that no one else would have endured. But I used to say: "Well, there are people dying, being smashed to bits by explosives."

Tony Parker, CO, coal miner

I was the only CO in the pit, so I was looked upon as a rather strange being from another world, and I had definitely a grammar-school accent . . . I was terrified when I worked below the surface. Most of the tunnels — or roads, as they called them — radiating from the pit bottom were not high enough to stand in, and very often you had to crouch, and then the further in you got towards the seam, the lower and lower they got until you were on your hands and knees . . . Your only lighting was the lamp on your helmet and it was all shadowy and changing and strange. And there'd be rumblings of the transport of the tubs along the lines, and explosions of course because in those days they used to dynamite and blast the coalface and then dig it out. But I think the thing that impressed me most was the feeling of solidarity among the workers . . . The colliers were the men who got out the coal, and they were the crème de la crème. They hacked the coal out with their picks, and if you were a collier's lad, that was something very special, and two or three times I was a collier's lad and had this very privileged position — to be behind this man and, as he hacked the coal out, to shovel it back . . . They were not highly emotional, but every now and again you'd sit down for a break and I remember having some quite extraordinary discussions with colliers . . .

The FAU, which had provided ambulance and emergency services with the French and British armies on the Western Front during the First World War, had been disbanded in 1919. In 1939, it was quickly reactivated with the aim of giving young COs — not only Quakers — the same opportunities for humanitarian service as had existed in the earlier war. It offered an outlet for those who believed that pacifism should show in action just what it is capable of doing in relieving the effects of war. One thousand three hundred men joined, women were admitted in October 1940, and by the time war ended, ninety-seven women had served in the unit. Whereas in the First World War, not all members had been COs, in the Second World War, almost all had to attend a tribunal to establish their CO credentials. Also, the FAU in the Second World War had a far greater international flavour, with 91 members coming from overseas, the majority from the United States and Canada.

Michael Cadbury, CO, FAU, medical orderly, City Hospital Gloucester

We were up against quite a lot of hostility to start with, both from the City Council and from within the hospital itself. One or two of the doctors refused to have us on their wards. One or two of the sisters made life hell for us "shirkers". But we expected that, and once they got the colour of our eyes, they were more understanding and realised that we really wanted to help and were making a good contribution there. That was the thing that helped all the way through: we weren't running away from anything, we were trying to get *into* things . . . We came in as conscientious objectors who had been through first-aid, ambulance and hospital training, and it was that training which enabled us to do work all over the world during the Second War.

Donald Swann, CO, FAU, medical orderly, Orpington Hospital, Kent

My most important hospital time was in Orpington, a branch of Guy's Hospital. I was a mortuary trolley operator and then, the most interesting of all, I worked in an operating theatre for about four months. I was the one who pushed the patient in, then helped, watched the whole thing, then cleaned it all out, then pushed them back to the ward . . . I remember vividly bathing chronics — the very sick, old men. We each had to bath nine a week in our own time . . . They couldn't move and you had to lift them out of their nightshirts and put them naked into a trolley and take them to the bath and put them in. Some could hardly speak and some of them were incontinent . . . What a hard finishing to life that is, lying in beds very close to each other. They didn't worry that we were COs. You see, this is the thing: a medical passport is probably one of the most wonderful things, because they were glad that there were men around who could produce a bed pan or whatever it was and they'd got us to talk to. So we struck up a few friendships.

Deryck Moore, CO, FAU, medical orderly, Hammersmith Hospital, London

You occasionally met a theorist who said, "This is a wrong move, we should all be on our knees praying." But I tended to write those off as somewhat on the cranky side of Quakerism, not really my line of country at all . . . I think the thing that affected me more than anything in Hammersmith was the kids who were injured in the war, that was the one point that I really began to say, "Shouldn't you be going away with a gun and sorting out this evil?" I think we were human enough to challenge our stand. Trench warfare is one thing, but when it starts affecting kids, and they're getting arms blown off, legs blown off and their lives totally altered because of it, this is the time you began to say, "Is my pacifism right?"

(Dr) Alan Taylor, FAU, medical orderly, Lewisham Hospital, London

Most seriously, the fire from the flying bomb which fell on the hospital had spread to the dispensary, in which we had a whole stock of oxygen, carbon dioxide and nitrous oxide cylinders. These were now dangerously exposed and liable to go off like shells if overheated. Three of us [COs] cleared them from the fire. We got recognition for this with a British Empire Medal . . . I could see there were arguments for both sides in accepting this: one shouldn't accept awards from a government one didn't agree with; on the other hand, I did feel a bit of natural pride. And it was a little demonstration that COs and cowards are not synonymous.

Tessa Cadbury (Rowntree), CO, FAU, Yorkshire

Then I was asked to form a women's section of the FAU. It was always put like that — as a "women's

173

section" . . . It seemed quite obvious that women were ideally suited for shelter work — helping with children, making sleeping conditions better, that kind of thing . . . Our set-up was very different to the men's . . . We weren't bothered with bureaucracy and theory, we were definitely more pragmatic. Give us the jobs — shelter work, rest centres, hostels and, later, foreign work — all those places that called out for a woman's touch. Do the job, then move on to where the need is.

Mervyn Taggart, absolutist CO, agricultural worker

On balance I think I took the wrong attitude, that I would have nothing to do with the war effort. I remember a woman doctor saying, "Why don't you go into the hospital service during the war?" I didn't because it seemed to be in support of the war effort and the war effort was wrong. With the wisdom of hindsight, I can see that *this* was wrong. One should do a thing because it is right or wrong in itself and not so much for the implications. The idea of saving life is right in itself and an overriding consideration. I think many pacifists went too far in this uncooperative attitude.

Leslie Hardie, CO, medical orderly, Winford Hospital, Bethnal Green Hospital

For three weeks, we had a lot of hostility from these military patients: "I don't want bloody conchies touching me!" There was deliberate harassment: bottles would be poured onto the floor, trays tripped over — deliberate mess for us to clear up. We were told not to react to it, just get on with the job, no argument . . . The staff sergeant was *the* man. He would come and say, "Got a particularly nasty job here" — a case of gas gangrene say — "my chaps flake out with this sort of thing . . ." He'd come to me for that sort of unpleasant job . . .

Molly Sugden, Air Raid Precaution (ARP) volunteer, Hampstead, London

Being in Hampstead, there were a lot of artists, actresses and writers, a lot of whom were conscientious objectors. Probably a lot of them saw more action than those who joined the services. You imagine: if a house is bombed and collapsed, the rescue squads would have to go and shore up houses to get to people who were trapped, and it was a *very* dangerous job. Then the first-aid people would be there to administer first aid to the victims. The COs were doing all this.

175

(Dr) Alan Taylor, CO, FAU, medical orderly, Lewisham Hospital

At one time during the war, the Medical Research Council appealed for volunteers for the guinea pig scheme. Six of us went to the National Hospital for Nervous Diseases in Queen Square . . . Various experiments were done: there was one on our blood volume — we were injected with a dye and they assessed the volume of our blood. We had to lie on an operating table for long periods until we were totally relaxed, and then we were tipped up, and the pooling of the blood made all except one of us faint. We wore a big metal boot which measured the increased flow of fluid to the leg. We were also at times given extra plasma to try and vary our blood volume during experiments. Another was carrying heavy weights up and down stairs with big bags attached so that gas analysis could be done and our oxygen consumption measured. There was an experiment in which we were immersed in sea water to check the effects of the salt and the cold — this was the first time that wet suits were starting . . . On the nutrition front: we lived for weeks on a controlled diet of saltfree dried food, to which vitamin B was added . . . I also remember that whilst working in the Hammersmith Hospital, I was rather shanghaied into having one of the early cardiac catheters inserted into my heart. I remember a great furore about this because the doctor who was responsible for the FAU people found out about it and was very incensed.

Bernard Nicholls, CO, shelter work, Hungerford, London

With the crowding in the shelters and the amount of body, pubic and hair lice that were around, there was fear that there could be an outbreak of typhus. So a crash programme of research was put on under the leadership of Professor Mellanby and his assistant, Dr Busfine. We undertook to supply them with clothing that we took off verminous people and also to supply vermin if we could collect it in any other way. We made history so far as the School of Hygiene and Tropical Medicine was concerned by producing the clothing of the most lousy person that had ever been known to exist. He came in very ill so we took him to St Stephen's Hospital and carried him in a sort of hammock to the casualty department. The orderly there just deposited the poor man on the floor and with this can of disinfectant, ran a ring around this man. I said, "Look, if we undertake to undress him and if you'll give us a bag, we'll undertake to stand within this circle of disinfectant and take off all his clothing; will you take him on from there?" So we very carefully put all his clothing in this bag and closed it up. When we got down to his skin, I was in fact absolutely horrified: all the outside skin, on this man's back particularly, had gone. And the whole of his back from his neck to his buttocks was just a wet mass of puss. The hospital in fact saved his life. The researchers were terribly pleased. They stoved the garments and killed off all the lice, then they meticulously went over every square inch of all that man's clothing and one by one picked off the dead lice and registered each one on a counter. My recollection is that their count was over 15,000 lice.

Donald Swann, CO, FAU relief work, Palestine

I was sent to a refugee camp called Nurseirat, just south of Gaza, to work with a whole host of Greek refugees from the islands. These were people who had left their German-occupied Dodecanese islands — Kos, Rhodes, Kárpathos, Sími, Kásos — because there was no food, and they had tracked through Turkey and Syria and eventually into Palestine, where the British Mandate was looking after them until they could be returned home. They'd had a pretty poor war and we were learning about it all the time. I see it all so vividly that I am reliving it: we're now on the Mediterranean coast in very desert-like country with this big Arab town, Gaza, to the north. The camp is enormous — mostly canvas with some huts, in about three fairly large sections — one by the sea, the others more inland. The two or three thousand refugees are mostly living in family units, but with several single men and women. The army is responsible for the general administration and security, and the voluntary workers, including the FAU, are responsible for the welfare and getting on with what needs doing — cooking, registration. Certainly those of us who had learnt to dig latrines at last get their chance! We have been trained for this and it is marvellous really being able to meet the circumstances.

Wilfred Littleboy, absolutist CO, First World War

I did a certain amount of fire-watching duty in my office building. Some people felt a hesitation about doing fire-watching because it was required of them under a sort of civil-defence regulation. I've no recollection that it was required of us in that way, but it seemed reasonable to take your share in the fire-watching in the offices which you were using. I was there one night when Birmingham was badly blitzed.

Harold Bing, CO, First World War

As far as public opinion was concerned, it was much more tolerant in the Second World War . . . The fact that conscientious objection was now fully recognised meant that the COs of the Second World War were not looked upon as traitors or skunks or cowards: they were recognised as people who have a legitimate religious, moral or

179

other acceptable objection. A much more tolerant attitude. Many still regarded COs as a bit queer, but it was a queerness they could tolerate . . .

Although few COs suffered the persecution or organised brutality the pioneer conchies of the First World War had endured, the majority suffered discrimination, ostracism and disapproval in the workplace, in public places, even in churches, and many lost their jobs. This is when organisations such as the PPU and the CBCO came into their own, providing much-needed fellowship and support. Many COs who had contact with the military explained how they found service personnel more sympathetic towards them than civilians, especially civilian women. War events seem to have been an important influence on public opinion, although those in contact with the work COs were doing in shelters, rest homes and hospitals during the Blitz appreciated and admired them and would stoutly defend them against their critics.

Eric Turner, CO, milkman, Kidderminster

The most difficult part, which still upsets me, was the pain and embarrassment I caused my parents in doing what I did. They could not understand, nor could I make them understand, why I wanted to be a conscientious objector. This meant that my relationships with my own family, friends and neighbours were much more difficult than going through the tribunal, which was a clean and clinical experience compared with the torment I experienced at home. In working-class communities like ours, having this odd character who wasn't going along with the rest of the chaps to fight this evil man Hitler was very hard. I think my mother suffered more as I was her youngest child and she was very fond of me . . . So this was the most painful part for me.

Donald Swann, CO, FAU, London

I think I began to learn to fear certain types of family meetings when the remote person would turn up who didn't understand. That actually was the worst that I ever encountered. I did not encounter people spitting or pushing me around.

Kathleen Wigham (Derbyshire), absolutist CO, Strangeways Prison, Manchester

There was some hostility. I got a white feather, the sign of cowardice, sent anonymously through the post. It was in a piece of paper in an envelope; it fell out and Mother just picked it up and put it on the fire and said, "We don't want any of *them* here."

Frank Norman, absolutist CO, Lewes Prison and Wormwood Scrubs

About 60 per cent of the neighbours were antagonistic . . . One man in particular sticks in my memory. He was ex-Indian Army, had a high position in it. He was then about seventy and lived three doors away from us. He would be walking down the street and if nobody was in the street apart from our two selves, he would sing very loudly patriotic songs such as "Land of Hope and Glory", "Hearts of Oak". If anybody was in the street — stranger or not — he'd go across and tell them about me, and point at me. I took no notice of this; I felt sorry for him in a way.

Reginald Bottini, CO, agricultural worker, Peterborough

There was nobody coming up, as I understood they did in the First World War, with insults and white feathers or leaflets through the door, or screams from agitated women. Nothing like that, just a bleak incomprehension as to how one could take this view. But with some men, not many, thinking that anyone who can get out of this bloody lot is wise. But that's a masculine point of view. The feminine viewpoint seemed to me was "my husband's had to go" or "my son's had to go, why shouldn't you?" But never to the point of hysteria.

John Petts, CO, agricultural worker, Derbyshire

The Miss Bassetts, the owners of the farm, never said a word to me. I was an embarrassment to them, they didn't acknowledge my existence at all: better to keep away from someone so untouchable as a pacifist. One grew to wear this really — daily, monthly, yearly. There was never any malevolence or insult, but implicit in the manner that people withdrew because your stance had put you beyond the pale, you no longer deserved to be treated like a human being in the community — a judgement you had to wear. It became a habit: you hunched your shoulders and had this weight to bear like Pilgrim in *Pilgrim's Progress* . . . One had to forgive that attitude because their sons and husbands were dying; they had to believe they were right. We were second grade, despised.

Kenneth Wray, absolutist CO, welfare worker, Sussex

It wasn't easy, very difficult in fact. The main thing was the sense of isolation, and I think my wife felt that also. It was Rabindranath Tagore who said, "The greatest enemy of the state is the one man who says 'No.'" The one man. That's true. I was going to stand absolutely solid, four-square. And nothing would shake me. Nothing would shake me now. But it wasn't easy . . . *No* . . .

James Bramwell, CO, NCC, Pioneer Corps

It wasn't a poster of Kitchener pointing at you, "Your country needs you!" But much more sober, quiet and sad . . . I felt an outsider.

Sydney Carter, CO, FAU, Palestine

When I listened to Vera Lynn singing "bluebirds over the white cliffs of Dover", and all the war speeches, I felt: "A whole lot of *me* is in there, but I'm cut off from it." I wanted to *belong* so much and be able to sing those songs along with everybody else and feel the warmth, but I felt pulled in two directions. That was the hardest part. People didn't give me white feathers or persecute me very much; it was this internal split which I found the hardest thing . . .

Tony Parker, CO, coal miner

I think you did feel very alone, or at least I did. I think most conchies did because it was never a clear-cut issue. All the time one was saying, "Am I doing right or am I doing wrong?" and "Ought I to rethink this?" This was especially so if you had a friend who was killed or injured in the war. That was the time you felt rather bad about it, rather guilty.

Rev. Donald Soper, Methodist minister, Kinsley Hall, London

I was very well treated as a pacifist, apart from the occasional violence from an Irishman who'd had a liquid lunch. There was a chap appointed from the Home Office to stand in the crowd and listen to what I was saying, and instead of standing surreptitiously he rang me up and told me he was coming. I used to stop in mid-sentence and say, "Am I going too fast for you?" He'd say, "No, all right." That is the anachronism of war: a mix of ferocity and humour. You had to be careful; I learnt the lesson that behind the most violent disagreement there may be a personal tragedy. I took one chap to task and he asked me afterwards how I would feel if I'd just heard my son was missing?

Mervyn Taggart, absolutist CO, agricultural worker

I think my general feeling about the treatment of COs by the government is one of great respect. I think it's quite remarkable that when a nation is threatened by invasion from one of the most barbaric and horrific regimes in human history that young men are given a chance to convince a tribunal of their sincerity and have the opportunity, having done so, of not taking part in any way in the war. I think it's quite *remarkable* and a tribute to British justice and British fair-mindedness. That's one of the finest things of the war.

185

Tony Parker, CO, coal miner

I don't think the system of dealing with COs in the Second World War was well organised. No. It was typical bureaucratic *shambles*, because I've met other COs who just went along and asked to be put on the register for COs and they never heard any more from anybody. And in my case, when I came out of the mines, the Ministry of Labour was supposed to send me somewhere else and make me do other work. The man there responsible for COs became very friendly with me . . . he used to come round our house and listen to gramophone records with me in the evenings. And yet it was his job to make sure that I was toeing the line.

Ernest Goldring, CO, agricultural and social work, Kingsley Hall, London

I was very impressed with the stand that Bishop Bell of Chichester took in his condemnation of massed bombing. I met a number of priests who were members of the APF [Anglican Pacifist Fellowship], PPU or FOR, who gave me consolation. But there was this feeling of considerable disillusionment with the established churches. I remember reading about John Middleton Murry's book called [The] Betrayal of Christ by the Churches, which reinforced my feelings that there was a betrayal taking place.

Mervyn Taggart, absolutist CO, agricultural worker

The hardest thing I had to bear during the war was a lack of understanding from my Quaker church. Many of them, from their sheltered and respectable position, didn't appreciate how much of an outlaw and an outcast one was with regard to employment and with regard to society as a whole. Many of us were forced to wander about the country picking up jobs where we could, sleeping rough, and life was very hard. I don't think they appreciated that under those conditions it's rather difficult to live a conventional life, stay in a steady job and live in a conventional way.

Defections from the ranks of COs occurred throughout the war when dilemmas, doubts and guilt got the upper hand. Such feelings continued after war ended. Within the armed forces, many servicemen, like their counterparts in the earlier war, became disillusioned, deploring the Allied war policy and the way the war was being waged. Many continued with their service, protesting when possible; others felt they could no longer continue serving and were brought before court martials. COs shared the enormous relief felt by their fellow citizens when war ended, although many eschewed the victory celebrations, instead engaging in heart-searching as to whether they had done the right thing. This was particularly acute when the full horror of the Nazi death camps became apparent. As with the conchies of the First World War, few found their old jobs open to them or found it easy to gain new employment, and many continued to suffer social disapprobation.

Mervyn Taggart, absolutist CO, agricultural worker

It was hard to get work after the war. Quite rightly, jobs went to the ex-servicemen and one was, I suppose you could call it, being underprivileged; it was more difficult for people who had been COs. I think this was really the first time that one really felt one's situation financially. At the start of war I lost my job because of it, and after the war it was difficult because naturally the servicemen got the jobs and the training grants.

Denis Hayes, CO, CBCO member, London

People found doors were closed to them that had previously been open. No explanation was given, but they knew what it was . . . I was pretty popular when I was a youngster and I found it quite a serious problem to find that there was always a black mark against me for a long time, and I think it affected my confidence for many years.

188

Denis Allen, absolutist CO, Feltham Borstal, Wandsworth Prison and Wormwood Scrubs

Yes, my prison experience has proved a handicap: in the early 1960s I was invited to be Quaker minister at Winchester Prison, but the Home Office said "No." Later I applied for a job in the prison service; the interview went well and I heard on the grapevine that I had been accepted, but I heard nothing. Fenner Brockway wrote on my behalf and was told the decision was not to employ me on the grounds that I was an ex-prisoner. This seemed extraordinarily blind. The Home Office also intervened when I applied for a post in an approved school. This seems to epitomise the totally inappropriate attitude that underpins the Prison Service: once a prisoner, always a prisoner . . .

Colin Ward, sapper, Royal Engineers, budding anarchist

The Second World War was different, it was said, because of the attempt to exterminate the Jews. Now here we're into a very tricky point: the persecution of the Jews and extermination camps was revealed to the great British public in these terrifying films shown in the mid-1940s. But I think the intelligent reader of the serious newspapers and other printed literature would know perfectly well that this was happening much earlier . . . But it's also evident that the British government's war aims were not in any sense to remove the threat of extermination of the Jews of occupied Europe . . . I would never dream of whitewashing Nazism or to minimise the atrocities of the Second World War, but would claim that the British war aims were not in fact to liberate European Jewry and that the facts now shown to us show this to be so. I don't know whether this was the issue which divided the pacifist movement, but if it wasn't, it should have been.

Kenneth Wray, absolutist CO, welfare worker, Sussex

Just before the war, Bart de Ligt, a Dutchman, wrote a book following up the theme of non-violence. He said, "This is the non-violent way if you are in an enemy-occupied country. You can defeat your enemy by non-violence." He put it all out in absolute detail exactly what everyone should do. It would have worked against Hitler in those countries. He'd shoot a thousand, two thousand, three thousand. But what is that compared with the Jews and others who were killed? Those Jews would not have been killed had it not been for the war. It was the war which allowed Hitler to shoot or gas all those Jews. He couldn't have done it in a peaceful world, but because of war he could just exterminate them. War has caused all that. Hitler was there, yes, but *you* are responsible, *I* am responsible for those Jews because we made Hitler.

(Sir) Charles Kimber, CO, founder of the Federal Union

If one had known then what one knows now about the final solution and the concentration camps, would I have still registered as a conchie? That's a very difficult question. But the answer is, yes, I would.

Leslie Hardie, CO, agricultural worker, hospital orderly, East End, London

I did what I wanted to do during the war, but there was always a slightly guilty feeling that I was a survivor, that others were being killed. I always felt very privileged and very lucky to have survived, but guilty; I felt I had to repay. I stayed on in voluntary work after the war and did two and a half years in India, working in a voluntary capacity far longer than most pressed servicemen because of it. I remained a pacifist due to so much militarism, so much unwillingness to face up to situations. But I have to think about my doubts. But I now know that I can say: I know where I stand.

Mervyn Taggart, absolutist CO, agricultural worker

There were two dilemmas that faced pacifists during the war, both very central and inescapable: how to stop Hitler without going to war in that particular moment in history. But a much more difficult question was when people said, "All right, you are prepared to suffer the consequences of refusing to fight — be prepared to go to prison, to be shot, you would be prepared to have Hitler's hordes taking over the country. That is reasonable because it's within your right to make that sacrifice. But are you justified in placing your family in danger? Of the Nazis coming and raping your wife? To allow your children to live under Nazi rule for the whole of their lives and perhaps their children's lives? Have you a right to commit them to these same sacrifices?" That is a very difficult question to answer indeed.

Ronald Huzzard, CO in a reserved occupation, Hull

It's very difficult to give an answer as to how Hitler could have been coped with short of force. In fact, some countries which were overrun by the Germans — the Danes, for example — did in fact attempt to resist by non-violent means and had quite successful outcomes in their struggles . . . I have faith in believing that in the long run evil can be overcome with good. It may take longer. Nazism may not have collapsed by non-violent means as quickly as it did under six years of war. But I think the things that were done during the Second World War are going to be with us for a long, long time.

Tony Benn, RAF pilot, Southern Rhodesia (Zimbabwe)

I was in Rhodesia [Zimbabwe] at the time, training as a pilot, and got the telegram saying that my brother [Michael] had been killed and I was deeply distressed by it. Many of my school friends were killed, and although I never killed anybody, thank God, and I never saw a dead soldier or civilian myself, hatred of war became very, very deeply entrenched.

Professor Joseph Rotblat, nuclear physicist, Manhattan Project, Los Alamos, USA

Niels Bohr used to come to my room at eight every morning to listen to the BBC. Afterwards we'd talk about matters. He explained what was likely to happen, the consequences of making nuclear weapons. He said if we go on making these weapons, then eventually the Russians would also have them, and then we'd have a nuclear-arms race. This was 1944! And he told me of the terrible consequences of such an arms race to the whole world and the danger of complete annihilation. This made me even more worried about continuing to take part in such a project. I resigned from the project — the first time a person had resigned from Los Alamos. I had to promise not to tell the reason why I was leaving. They were afraid of the effect this would have on the other scientists . . . Most scientists were against the use of the bomb against civilian populations, but of course the military didn't take any notice of this.

(Lord) Hugh Jenkins, RAF Fighter Command, 12 Group HQ, Bombay

Having arrived in Bombay harbour, we heard the news about this great new weapon and its effect, and everybody was very happy about that because we knew we were going down to Burma and had survived as a result of this. We were stuck there in the harbour for about a week and the mood changed. It was realised this wasn't just a bigger bomb; it was something new. There was a certain uneasiness, not generally felt, but with some, and I think I shared this uneasiness. But something happened which has been a motivation of mine ever since. Going down the gangway preparing to disembark, an airman came down after me and he said, "Do you know what I think, Sir?" I said, "No, what do you think?" He said, "I think they may have saved our lives at the expense of our children's." Oh God! It was as if he'd *hit* me! I've had that thought in my mind ever since — what an extraordinary piece of prescience!

CHAPTER
FOUR

1939–45: Second World War (II): Conchies in Action

In China, I had become a conflicted and confused conscientious objector, then had changed to become a conflicted and confused soldier. I could never decide whether I had been a failed conchie and a failed soldier, or whether to be both at the same time is the only real human condition.

Although many COs were content to remain on the home front providing relief and humanitarian services, they were determined to keep aloof from the military. Others were keen to serve overseas, insisting on a civilian setting whilst accepting that this could only happen under broad military control. But there were many others who had a strong urge to be in the thick of the fighting, to perform their humanitarian service nearer the action zones, alongside the troops, but without renouncing their CO status or bearing arms. Reasons were complex: mixed with the straightforward urge to share the suffering of battle was the need to face danger and risks in order to end the feeling of segregation from society; there was also the anxiety not to be labelled a coward — some felt they had to justify themselves not only in their own eyes, but also in the eyes of family, friends and society.

As well as the valuable humanitarian service performed by the FAU in civilian settings, there were others in the unit who felt the urge to offer relief and medical service in conflict zones. They had joined the FAU hoping for "the arduous and dangerous" to "Go Anywhere, Do Anything", as their motto "GADA" indicated. And many readily accepted attachment to military units and work under military discipline. Because of its need to move in military circles, drills, route marches and kit inspections were included alongside the basic training of keeping fit, first aid and nursing skills. This ostensibly military aspect proved difficult for some COs, although all those who entered conflict areas vouched for its importance. The FAU served in most war zones from as early as December 1939; these included Finland during the Winter War, Norway in early 1940, the North African campaigns, Syria, the Lebanon, Greece, Burma, China, Ethiopia and India. After D-Day, 6 June 1944, the FAU followed closely behind the invasion forces doing whatever humanitarian work was at hand, flexibility being its keynote and strength. Unit members often found themselves behind German lines and many were taken prisoner.

The Hospital of the Hadfield-Spears Unit (HSU) had been set up by Mrs (later Lady) Spears (alias the novelist Mary Borden), the wife of General Spears, in cooperation with Lady Hadfield, in the autumn of 1940. The hospital was attached to the 1st Free French Division, which consisted of those who had rallied to de Gaulle in 1940. The medical team included eight English nursing sisters and six women drivers of the Motor Transport Company, who drove the staff cars. The FAU had been asked to provide a section of 15 men to drive and maintain the hospital's trucks. The unit also supplied medical orderlies. Eventually FAU numbers went up to 38, taking on a far greater variety of tasks. The HSU served in Syria during the internecine fighting between the Free French and the Vichy French, in the Western Desert, North Africa, Italy, and with the invasion force landing on the coast of the French Riviera on 15 August 1944. Another group of 33 FAU men served in the Medical Battalion of the 2nd Division of the Free French, under General Leclerc, working in North Africa and in France with the invading forces.

Many COs served with the Pioneer Corps, to which the NCC was attached. Some soon became dissatisfied with the boring, menial nature of the work, a far cry from the active service they were seeking, and volunteered for bomb-disposal work with the Royal Engineers. There was a huge demand for this during the Blitz and further raids on London and other cities in 1940 to '42. But with the raids lessening the work eased off, which once again led to frustration and a further urge for action. In early 1944, the opportunity arose when the War Office asked for volunteers for the Parachute Medical Services. As the invasion of France drew near, the Field Ambulance of the Parachute Regiment had been transformed into a parachute unit, the Parachute Field Ambulance (PFA), which was attached to the 6th Airborne Division — the "Red Devils". The War Office found it was unable to find enough volunteers for this dangerous work and decided to admit conscientious objectors, guaranteeing their CO status.

As the spring of 1944 approached, the "Red Cross Devils", as they called themselves, were training hard alongside the troops. The first task of the 6th Airborne Division's drop over

Normandy on D-Day was to secure the eastern flank of the main seaborne invasion army while its forces landed along the French coast from Cherbourg to the River Orne. Three PFAs dropped with the troops. The function of 224 PFA, to which the conscientious objectors were attached, was primarily to treat and clear casualties sustained by the 3rd Parachute Brigade, to deal with any other wounded troops in the area, and to deal with civilians and enemy wounded who were taken prisoner. Ninety per cent of the PFAs who were dropped in Normandy on D-Day had never been in action before. Later, survivors of the 224 PFA served in the Ardennes Campaign in the bitter winter of 1944–5. As the advance continued in early 1945, the 224 PFA was part of operation "Varsity Plunder", the drop over the Rhine. It then advanced with the 6th Airborne Division across the Reich to the Baltic. As the war in Europe ended, it was destined for another parachute operation in the Burmese jungle. An advance party of the PFA was en route to India when the atom bomb was dropped on Hiroshima; plans were then changed for a move to Palestine to deal with troubles there.

Another group of active pacifists were those who had, after much heart-searching, renounced the CO status they had been awarded and found an acceptable niche in the newly created Special Operations Executive (SOE). They were attracted by the amateurishness of the organisation, and the scope for flexibility and independence it offered, as well as the chance it gave of thwarting the enemy and working with resistance groups in occupied countries, thus advancing liberation and the end of the war. All COs in conflict areas faced the prospect of injury, capture and death. Those serving

199

with the SOE were not treated as POWs if captured and faced torture and execution.

After years theorising about war and peace, many of the young COs working in front-line areas found deep satisfaction that they had finally found themselves where they wanted to be. They were no longer detached from the war but right in the heart of the action. But they had to face bitter criticism for their motivation and service by more purist COs who felt they were making a dangerous compromise with the military machine.

FINLAND

It was the Winter War between Russia and Finland, which started on 30 November 1939, that provided two different groups of COs with their first experience of working alongside fighting troops overseas. One was a small group of eight Auxiliary Fire Service (AFS) fire fighters accompanied by a staff officer from the London Fire Brigade headquarters, sponsored by the Finland Fund and equipped by the Home Office. The other was a larger group of 60 FAU men under the aegis of the British Red Cross Society.

Michael Harris, CO, FAU, Finland

When the Finnish war broke out, the fighting was very intense, and the British were dithering about wondering whether to go in and help the Finns against Russia. So the government was quite keen for us to go; in fact, the country was very pro-Finnish because the "great Russian bear" was playing up and trying to occupy a small country. We went into further training, which involved a lot of driving with heavy trucks. Our ambulances were painted white as camouflage for the snow. We were fitted out with sheepskin coats and fur hats — it was all very primitive and rather, I imagine, like going to the Russian Front in the First War.

Denis Allen, absolutist CO, Feltham Borstal, Wandsworth Prison and Wormwood Scrubs

One basic objection to the FAU from my viewpoint was that it recognised the *legitimacy* of war-making. I was in those days an absolutist. I felt that I wasn't prepared to join in the war-making, even to the extent of being told that I could be exempt from military service providing I was willing to join an ambulance service.

James Bramwell, CO, AFS, Finland

The [London] Blitz was going to come sooner or later, and I imagined that we were going to Finland to gather information about fire-fighting and to help the Finns. The Russians were bombing the Finnish towns and, being wooden buildings, they burnt like matchwood — one or two on fire would have gutted a whole town. Our AFS would be very useful. I was very keen to go; the bombings had made a stir in our newspapers and aroused everybody: "Poor little Finland." We all felt they were taking the brunt of the war.

There were nine in our team, not all pacifists — just my cousin and I. We had one big engine and two smaller ones; they were still bright red — later in the war they were painted grey, very drab, and they had a big LFV painted on them, London Fire Volunteers. We had a send-off in Berkeley Square by the Finnish minister, the head of the London Fire Brigade and one or two Home Office worthies. We were all lined up and photographed, and Madame Gripenberg, the minister's wife, broke a bottle of champagne over our fire engine to baptise it.

Michael Rowntree, CO, FAU, Finland

Our work was transporting Finnish casualties back to the base in Savonlinna. Driving back on one occasion, we had our first experience of being bombed by a Russian plane. There weren't many casualties on the front where I was stationed — I probably didn't see more than 30 during my time there. The winter of '39–'40 was intensely cold: our dugout was freezing; we had a wood-burning stove in it, which was a bit of a hazard, but at least it kept the dugout warm. This only lasted for about two or three weeks because peace was declared after that.

James Bramwell, CO, AFS, Finland

By the time we and our engines arrived it was too late; the war was over and the south-west part of Finland was ceded to Russia. We were very disappointed, but we helped evacuate the Hangö area. It was a big job; we drove our big lorries across the frozen ice. We did everything; picking up people from their homes in the forest, humping furniture, and on one occasion we pulled a coffin across the ice for a funeral. It was a stimulating and rushed job as the evacuation had to be done within ten days.

Michael Harris, CO, FAU, Norway

We crossed into Norway, 1 May 1940. We did a certain amount of evacuation of the wounded, but not really very much because the retreat was so very rapid back to Namsos, which was the evacuation port. We got there one day and it was entirely in flames, very badly bombed. We had to drive all our ambulances onto one big heap and disable them . . . We sailed out in convoy and were very badly bombed. The British troops were very bolshie — they felt the whole thing had been grossly mishandled. The air cover had been non-existent; they hadn't really fought but been pushed around, and the British Tommy doesn't like being pushed around.

GREECE

Ronald Joynes, CO, FAU, Greece, 1941

With the Germans coming into the fray, the Greeks were retreating and we were retreating with them . . . Our journey back to Athens was under air attack most of the way and the ambulance I was in was hit by a small bomb. I was with Freddie Woods and we had secreted a bottle of gin — good Quakerly beverage — in our ambulance and our first thought was for that! The vehicle was towed into Athens in the dark of the mountain road. A small group of us stayed in Athens for a week, transporting the wounded around the Athens area, which was being badly attacked by then; the remainder transferred to the Australian Army in the north . . .

When the time for evacuation came — by then we had got to Navplion to the south — the entire column closed ranks and marched out into the sea, but only one craft came in and pulled away when it was full and we waited in the sea for another. This time I just made it because I was at the back, and I am indebted to one of my colleagues who, as I was disappearing beneath the water, hauled me up into the landing craft . . . We were then taken down the coast and unloaded and told to hide until the next night. We carried on in that fashion for three days. Happily we ended up on the beach where the rearguard was being evacuated . . . This was *it*. We were eventually rowed out to the destroyer *Isis*, where we were given hot cocoa, which tasted just like nectar.

NORTH AFRICA

David Rowlands, CO, HSU, Western Desert, 1942

We then moved on to another site — a piece of sand called El Azragh on the map. We dug in there and had an operating theatre dug into the sand. One day we were eating our meal when we saw a single plane. There was just time to scatter into the slit trenches we had dug. Nik Alderson, our leader, was in the neighbouring trench. We heard a tremendous crunching as this stick of bombs landed and there were flames and smoke. This gradually dissolved away, and when we looked around we found that Nik was no longer in his trench and the parts of his body, some of which were recognisable, were strewn around. We collected the pieces into a rubber sheet and carried it into one of the tents. What is one more death when we had seen so many killed! But when it was someone as near to us as Nik had been, then we were all very deeply affected.

Hugo Powell, CO, HSU, Western Desert, 1942

We were then in El Alamein. Imagine being in a small surgical tent, with the surgeon getting on with an operation and I would be preparing people. Then, suddenly, you realised that the infantry were coming up from behind us, spreading out around our tents with fixed bayonets, and you realised how close to things you were ... I have to say that at El Alamein, the system didn't work particularly well because the battle was so fast-moving. We seemed to spend ages scurrying in and out of minefields, digging holes to put the tents in, then building up with sandbags, then getting the tent up and ready for patients. Then the order would come, "Move!", and because we had to carry as little as possible each time, we had to empty the sandbags — it was a very energetic time. I was conscious that I had chosen to do this. I was a pacifist and had found the best way of expressing my belief that one ought to relieve suffering.

Michael Rowntree, CO, HSU, Western Desert, 1943

I recall the good games of football we played. One was against the Foreign Legion — this side, of course, being made up of a range of nationalities. There was a great bearded Spaniard called Jesus de

Mendoza. I remember one of the semi-blasphemous shouts from the touchline: "Bung it in, Jesus!"

Jack Daniel, British radar operator, gun layer, Royal Artillery, Siege of Tobruk, 1940

What accelerated my conviction that I was basically a latent pacifist was, after we broke out of Tobruk, I got involved with the New Zealand division, with [General] Freyberg . . . We had 88-mm guns captured from the Germans, *marvellous* guns. Between Mareth and Enfidaville we brought out the artillery and blasted the Germans. Suddenly, we were caught in air bursts and had no time to get into slit trenches, and I caught a very slight packet . . . I was shipped back to this advanced field dressing station. I must have passed out. When I opened my eyes, I was astonished to see the palm leaf and scroll of the Afrika Korps on the chap lying on the stretcher alongside me. I really wasn't badly hurt at all. I raised myself up and saw that three other chaps on the far side were also German. This was confirmed when the orderly came round and said: "Char up! Char for the old Jerries!" Really the crunch came for me because they could speak English, and after a time we started talking. The "old Jerries" were about 20 years old, just like me.

They were talking about what had happened to them. "Oh yes, we got caught by the bang whops." I said, "What do you mean, the bang whops?" "Well, the gun that can fire so fast that the explosion sounds before the firing of it." There was only one gun that did it, the 88. Then I knew that those men lying on the stretcher were the men we'd been firing at that morning and this was the result. One died; he never came round. One kept asking for a *Spiegel* [mirror]: "Anyone got a *Spiegel*?" "Where's the fucking *Spiegel*?" Eventually somebody said, "For Christ's sake, give the bloody Jerry a looking-glass." What he wanted was to see that the scar he'd got on his head hadn't marred his face. And he had something wrong with his feet, and the other guy had something wrong with *his* feet. For the first time I was made aware that I personally was responsible. Now that rarely happens. If you fire your machine gun, you get up and move onto the next thing; there are a lot of bodies lying around, but *you* are not personally responsible: there's so much going on and you don't have time to think about it. But I did. I had a *lot* of time to think about it. I didn't like what I thought: "You're in the wrong place, mate; this is not where you should be; you should not be doing this." So the erosion was taking place . . .

BURMA/CHINA

Tom Haley, CO, FAU, Burma/China Convoy, Burma, 1942

We quickly realised that we were working with a retreating, not a fighting, army. There were so many casualties; we operated for nine hours continuously until the Japanese were within minutes of our position. It was *hectic*. Those who hadn't survived had to be buried. We had to wash down, clear up, repack and reload, and then move on as quickly as we could before the Japanese caught up with us. Then we'd start all over again . . . There were men who were badly injured and who were going to die. What could we do for them? We had to use our own discretion since there was no way we could leave them for the Japanese to bayonet. This was a terrible dilemma, a dreadful compromise position that everybody finds themselves in in wartime: wanting desperately to do the right thing, but being forced to do something which is abhorrent to them. I backed up the doctor and the surgeon . . . As a pacifist, this was the most horrible and distressing thing for me in the whole of the war and it has lived with me ever since . . .

Charles Besly, officer, Royal Berkshire Regiment, Burma

We had a slight scuffle with some Japanese . . . there we all were, about a score of us, feeling pretty low, we'd lost blood. Suddenly, along the very rough, crude jungle track came a jeep with a couple of stretchers on it, and a fellow dressed in a yellow open-neck shirt and grey flannels — no steel helmet, no rifle, no nothing, driving along as happy as could be. I was absolutely *stunned*, so I got out of this hole we were in. He looked at me and said, "What are you fellows doing?" He was a kind of freelance Quaker ambulance unit. He said, "I've got stretchers here, I'll fix you up." And three at a time he took us back to Company HQ, where an amazing little aeroplane, called a Lysander, landed on a postage stamp of a paddy field and took the wounded off.

David Morris, CO, FAU, China Convoy, 1942

Before the China Convoy started, the International Red Cross had been responsible for distributing drugs, but once we set up, from then on the only medical supplies being moved around in China were being moved by us. At this time inflation was increasing and drugs were extremely valuable. The FAU was trusted. What difference did we make? We were in China trying to do something to help and I think we did do a little ... But when you consider that this small band of people, with a bunch of battered, old, cheap production-line three-ton trucks, were trying to move these drugs over mountains to mission hospitals and front-line medical teams and central distribution depots, with worn-out engines, inadequate spare parts, and fuels which covered fourteen different kinds, you can see that the nature of the roads were such, the age of the vehicles were such, the wear and tear of the fuels being used was such, that an extraordinarily large proportion of time was spent on repairing and cannibalising trucks and getting them to move ... You can see that it was totally pitiful and inadequate in comparison with the vast need for drugs by this enormous population. But I don't know who would be doing it if we weren't there ... We were ordinary human beings trying to live extraordinary lives in China.

Evelyn White, CO, FAU, China Convoy, 1942

This rail accident on the Yunnan-Szechwan railway was bad. People were lying around dead, some badly injured ... There was a farm nearby in which we began the work of dressing wounds and splinting fractures ... Towards the end of the day, we took the badly injured back to a Chinese Army hospital in Kutsing by train. The conditions were like those in Crimea during that war: beds would

211

be planks on a trestle of bricks, straw palliasses for a mattress and they would be lucky to have a cotton blanket for covering. There was no running water, the floors were mud with bamboo walls and the place was infested with lice, which brought them relapsing fever, typhus and all types of malaria . . . We found later that those whose wounds we had splinted and plastered had torn the plaster off because they thought that if they died and entered their heaven, their leg would not be there because it was bound in plaster. This was the sort of frustration we'd meet from time to time in China.

INDIA

Alec Horsfield, CO, FAU, Calcutta, India, 1943–6

We heard rumours of a disaster down towards the sea. It was confirmed that a cyclone had brought a tidal wave up, a large area had been flooded and 30,000 people had perished . . . It was a difficult journey; we could only move when the tide was going downstream. After we had arrived at our destination — a local rajah's palace in Mahishadal — we set off for the villages, long walks in the sun through stinking mud and water. As we approached, people melted away. We stood alone in deserted villages. Gradually they came to trust us. From dwelling to dwelling we walked and waded, inoculated, walked, waded, and inoculated again. Dogs and jackals howled and fought over putrid flesh and bone; packs of monkeys bounded angrily through the bamboos. We went where Europeans hadn't been before. Jean [Cottle], one of our members, tended the purdah women, banished from the eyes of men. Her fame spread; men and women alike demanded her painless needle. She became a symbol. In their tragedy, we felt the warmth of friendship. Cholera broke out. The people fought back in the only way they knew: to our weapons of syringe and flask, they added eerie processions in the dark with discords of conch-shell, cymbal and drum and the call of prayer.

ETHIOPIA

Tom Barnsley, CO, FAU, Addis Ababa, 1941–5

When we arrived at the Hammanuel Hospital in Addis, it was only a shell with inadequate beds, mattresses, no drugs, sanitation appalling and people just congregating there to die . . . I worked as the medical orderly in charge in the Tekla Haimanot Clinic, the satellite clinic of the hospital . . . I did this clinic in the mornings from eight until midday. Then in the afternoons I went to the leprosy camp some 15 miles outside the city . . . The lepers were treated very much as outcasts by the local community because there was still a hangover from the old biblical times: leper, unclean. That is why, when a man or woman suspected they had the disease, they hid it. I suspect it had got the same stigma as Aids has now.

Ted Dunn, alternativist CO, FAU, Ethiopia, 1941–5

I was thrown in at the deep end, but it was wonderful. There was no other public health service. I was *it*. I worked myself to death over the excitement of it. Patients would appear not just from the village, but from the countryside around. I dealt with all the common diseases: rheumatism, tropical sores, syphilis, eye diseases, tapeworms. Once a man came in who had been mutilated by an animal which had got under his house and mauled him . . . I once did a Caesarean operation. I had never seen this done, but I looked up "Caesarean operations" in my book and thought: "Well, either I have a go, or she'll die." So I had a go. I was surprised how straightforward the operation was. The uterus was very, very thick and I was trying to hack my way through it very carefully in case I ruptured some blood vessels. Getting into the uterus and getting the baby out was quite straightforward, really. I had been concerned all the while for the mother, so I took the baby out and put it down, and carried on caring for the woman; the assistant said, "Look, the baby's moving!" But it died.

Harry Burbridge, RAMC doctor, Diredaua

The Ethiopians had their suspicions of us, as we were military. This is why the FAU was so important and very useful. On one occasion, for instance, one of our Ethiopian assistants, when cleaning up, emptied a small amount of white powder into a clean jar thinking it was barium meal. Actually, it was arsenic — you see, he couldn't read. Well, a bit later, one of the local chiefs, who was suffering from stomach pains, was given this, seeming, barium meal for an X-ray, and he died. This caused a furore because we had "murdered" the local chief. This was where the FAU came in: because they had the confidence of the local chiefs, they were able to calm the local ill-feeling.

ITALY

Roy Ridgway, CO, HSU, Italy, 1944

We were right by the battle at this point. We could see the monastery on Monte Cassino being bombed by the Allies. This was the dominant position that had to be taken. This was the "Battle of Cassino". We weren't aware of it at the time; we only knew there was a lot of slaughter and that we were breaking through the German lines . . . This is where I *wanted* to be. I'm very glad I was there to see what the *reality* of war was. I had talked about the horror of war and here I was in the midst of it, seeing human beings doing the most horrible things to each other, yet fundamentally having the same needs and feelings. And because of some politicians, or a madman like Hitler, they were drawn into this terrible conflict. I felt: "I have been there, and seen the hell of war and the bravery and courage and the way 'enemies' can get together. There is no enemy really. I am a pacifist."

THE SOE IN FRANCE

Harry Rée, former CO, British officer SOE, F Section, Montbéliard, France, 1942–5

We all knew that the Peugeot car works had been turned over to making tracks and engines for tanks for the Germans. So it was obviously important that the factory should be, if possible, put out of action. The bomb damage to Montbéliard was pretty nasty and there wasn't any anti-British feeling for the [RAF] raid. But I was seeing Rudolf Peugeot the next day . . . I said to him, "Wouldn't it make more sense if we organised sabotage inside your factory rather than have the RAF come again?" And he said, "Of course," and put me in touch with some foremen inside the factory . . . I was able to provide them with suitable explosives, which we'd got stored away from parachute drops . . . I sent through to London a long report about the Peugeot business and said, "Can you arrange with the RAF not to come and bomb the factory again while we continue to sabotage it inside, from the ground?" Evidently [Colonel Maurice] Buckmaster and the SOE people had awful difficulty with the RAF in getting them to agree to this. But in the end they said, "If you can send us monthly reports of the sabotage undertaken and we're satisfied that it's doing a useful job, we will lay off." Well, this was a wonderful job for an ex-conscientious objector — to stop bombing by blowing up machinery!

Frances Cammaerts, former CO, Lt Colonel, F Section SOE, France 1942–5

We walked through the town [Digne] without any difficulty, and when we found the car on the other side we got in and went off and there was a roadblock further along. We were checked through and just moving off when a couple of Gestapo officers arrived to disperse the roadblock, and they rechecked the papers and they found that the two of us had some bank notes of the same series. We had said that we were simply hitching lifts and that we weren't associated with each other at all. Well, the sequence of numbers of the notes obviously contradicted that to a certain extent. We pretended afterwards that we'd been engaged in a black market deal, but they didn't believe us, and the road we were going on was known to be the road that led up to the headquaters we were using at that time. The Gestapo must obviously have thought we were resistance people. There was no way in which they could check on us because their communications had been non-existent for a couple of months. So they simply decided, having questioned but not tortured us at all, that it was better to execute us and get rid of us, so that was determined . . . Our escape involved a tremendous bluff by a very very courageous lady [Christina Skarbek] that got us out.

BOMB DISPOSAL

James Bramwell, CO, NCC, Bomb Disposal

We were a section of the Royal Engineers stationed in Bedford made up entirely of conchies of various types . . . I thought it a combatant service, can't think how we got in. It could be dangerous; many officers were blown up in bomb disposal. I helped dig out an ordinary 50-kilo bomb. I was in the hole when someone hit the bomb with a pick. We all rushed out. I was so impressed with the officer, the way he went down to defuse it with me peering down from above; he was very calm, treated it as an engineering problem. I was frightened of it, a devilish, mysterious device . . .

Vic Newcomb, CO, NCC, Bomb Disposal

There were many bombs; they were on isolated farms, in the Fens area — it was very pleasant work digging in open country . . . It was physically demanding, which I never shirked. In fact, all through the war there was a conflict between my physical urge to be aggressive and do something and the restraint of this urge by the straitjacket of my pacifism . . .

We were proud of what we were doing and identified with the army very clearly, and I don't think many of us disguised this. We were photographed in uniform with our officers in traditional form — the "group photograph". I don't think we behaved in any way dissimilar to the soldiers. The basic distinction was what we were likely at any stage to do — we never carried arms or paraded with them and were never put in a position to kill anybody.

PARACHUTE FIELD AMBULANCE

John Petts, CO, Pioneer Corps

We were paraded one sunny morning, detached into sections of fifteen, and told to don our gas masks. We were then marched into a gas chamber. We stayed for x minutes with the gas spraying out of a pipe and were reassured to find we could breathe quite comfortably. We were then taken outside and took our masks off. Then the NCO said, "Now, something a bit tougher to make sure you can stand the presence of gas and still survive." So again we were marched around the edifice with masks on, then the command came over the tannoy: "Masks off!" We stood there choking and spluttering, breathing in this poison gas for two whole minutes. It seemed much longer. We were then told to put our gas masks on and run at the double on the parade ground outside until we were unable to continue. We ended rolling about in agony on this rough asphalt coughing up saliva which was bright red. "Good God!" I felt. The NCO realised he had gone too far and told us to make our own way back. This really angers me, our lack of rights as "bloody pacifists", a most despised unit. Who were we to complain or even to report sick! One just endured. I coughed blood for two days and I'm still having trouble with my lungs . . . The only way to get out of this and into the

RAMC was to volunteer for parachute duties as a medic. They took me up on that immediately.

Vic Newcomb, CO, 224 PFA, 6th Airborne Division

We were getting nearer to the real thing with all this training for the PFA. I was feeling more satisfied at this stage than at any other stage during the war, working in those kinds of parameters, and I certainly enjoyed the company of the COs and others around me. But I never lost sight of how the whole activity was one that was severely questionable. But this was a prospect of bringing the war to an end and with the prospect of not having to rebuild Europe — this was the important thing uppermost in most of our minds.

James Bramwell, CO, 224 PFA, 6th Airborne Division

Once we knew our destination, northern France, I think we all felt a sense of history. We knew from the messages of Churchill and Eisenhower that we had an important task. The taking of Varaville was crucial: we were supposed to hold the flank of the invasion coming behind us, and the ships. It was postponed for 24 hours because of the weather; we were all very keyed up.

Vic Newcomb, CO, 224 PFA, 6th Airborne Division

It was sometime after midnight when we emplaned, the actual drop in Normandy was to be about 2a.m., 6 June . . . The atmosphere was particularly quiet and intense. I was indeed conscious of taking part in an historical event . . . We were used to the jumping routine, but we knew that we were being met with hostility and that some of us weren't going to come back. Yes, I was frightened. I was facing something new, and my first experience of going abroad was going into a battle of some kind. I could see the contradiction within it and could reflect on the transition from somebody who had persuaded himself that he wasn't going to take part in any single act that was directly connected with the war into somebody who was involved in what was a spearhead operation.

FRANCE

James Bramwell, CO, 224 PFA, 6th Airborne Division, Normandy

In "Bomb Alley", the Bois de Mont, it was very tough. There was a tremendous flow of wounded and the battalion had lost most of its medics, so both the padre and I were very busy . . . I remember once that Corporal Cranna and I were detailed to take possession of a small house near the battery to be used as an emergency dressing station. He was armed and there to do the fighting, whereas I, who spoke some German, was to do the linguistic part of the exercise. I remember him saying, "Just my luck to be in a tight corner with one of you conchies!"

Vic Newcomb, CO, 224 PFA, 6th Airborne Division, Normandy

As reports came in that there were wounded, we were sent out to give them attention and bring them in. One in particular I was sent out to with three others was a parachutist with a broken leg. On the way back, because of the confused situation, we were overtaken by a German patrol. This was in a kind of no-man's-land, which was happening in lots of areas around our zone. It was led by a lieutenant who fired a couple of shots over our heads, but recognised us as medics and didn't fire upon us. But when they caught up with us, they insisted on taking us prisoner and took us with them until they found that carrying a stretcher with a wounded man on it was hampering them. So at one stage, we found ourselves standing in the middle of the road with the officer deciding what to do . . . He couldn't release us for fear we'd betray his presence and yet he didn't want to be lumbered with a wounded man. He told us all this because he wanted to be fair. So in the end, he was persuaded to leave me alone with the wounded man and take the other three with him . . .

On a later occasion, I was sent off to find a wounded man in a nearby village. I was given a jeep and driver. On the way we passed a couple of British sentries who peered out from the side of the road, and they warned of a mine they'd placed in the middle of the road further down, which we carefully avoided. But they didn't warn us that on the other side there were Germans. So when we approached the village, we were met with a burst of fire over our heads and told to stop. We were POWs, my second time . . . I was handed over to a unit where British and American wounded were and, with another medical orderly from the glider units, given responsibility for nursing these wounded men.

James Bramwell, CO, 224 PFA, 6th Airborne Division, Normandy

In Normandy, a chap was brought in with the top of his head blown off and his brain spilling on the stretcher. I took one look at him and asked the surgeon, "Is there anything we can do about this?" He shrugged his shoulders and I myself gave him a lethal shot of morphia. That was the only one [act of euthanasia] I saw and took part in myself.

224

Some of the Germans didn't expect to be treated well. One case I remember was a tall panzer grenadier who came into our tool-shed dressing station carrying his arm, which was literally hanging on by a ligament. I gave him morphia and put him on a stretcher and we carried him into this room in the villa which we were now using as a hospital. We put the stretcher on the floor; he was grey in the face by this time. He signalled that he wanted a urine bottle, I got it and put it down, but he couldn't make it work. I thought it might help to loosen up things if I put a hot-water bottle on his stomach. When I tried to put it on him, he started tossing about so much that the drip came out and the dressing torn off his arm pouring blood. I said, "What the hell's the matter?" One of his mates in perfect English said, "Oh, he's a victim of our own propaganda, he thinks you're going to castrate him!" That was German propaganda. But ours didn't suggest that Germans could be trusted if you were in trouble. There was a man, for instance, who used to shoot German prisoners coming in. Quite a lot were shot.

William Douglas-Home, British officer, 7th Battalion East Kent Regiment, Normandy, June 1944

Then off we went to Arromanche. I was still in command of the reserve squadron. They kept saying that the young Germans wouldn't surrender even if you stuffed a rifle in them because they'd been told they'd be shot, after the unconditional surrender policy . . . Then I started writing letters to the *Maidenhead Advertiser*, the paper in my constituency, saying that I thought the war had gone on long enough and that unconditional surrender was the greatest mistake and wasn't helping anybody to reach a compromise with the Germans . . . and saying that I really wanted to resign my commission, and I wrote to the colonel asking him about this.

James Bramwell, CO, 224 PFA, 6th Airborne Division, Normandy

As a CO I was just as interested in how the battle was going, in fact totally absorbed in it, and hoping to hear the "griff", the news, of anyone coming up from the melée to eat or drink. It wasn't possible to be impartial about the progress of the battle — no. I was definitely onside; one depended on it. It would have been superhuman not to be. Even the padre was onside. I particularly admired the troops who were remarkably skilful, so deft with their weapons and so efficient. They were nice chaps, except for a few, and it was incredible how human most of them were considering this intensive course in death-dealing . . . They were well aware of our pacifism and we had no trouble. We had more trouble with the RAMC people, and when we were in battle, they thought they'd have trouble with us, that we would let them down. Quite the reverse took place; we didn't let the side down.

Vic Newcomb, CO, 224 PFA, 6th Airborne Division, Normandy

There were a number of casualties in my section [of COs], and three or four who died. These were talented, sensitive people, and this is one of the things that impressed upon me what war does to people and communities if it robs them of people of that quality.

Private James Baty, 9th Battalion, Parachute Regiment, Normandy, 1944

Brigadier Hill, when he opened a commemorative plaque on the wall of this farmhouse where we worked, said, "Some of the bravest men of the war were the 224 Ambulance men." He said they were all conscientious objectors who would not bear arms but they would fight for their country and they all became stretcher-bearers and medics. They went out right into the battle and brought in bodies and wounded, British and German, and you couldn't ask for anything more than that . . .

William Douglas-Home, British officer, 7th Battalion East Kent Regiment, Normandy, June 1944

Then we approached Le Havre. At this time I was fed up with the whole thing, thinking it was going on for ever . . . We were about three miles from Le Havre and the colonel said, "You must go as a liaison officer with the infantry tomorrow." I said, "All right, sir." We went right up to the edge of Le Havre and the intelligence officer, Captain Bailey, said, "Something's just happened right up your street, the German commander in Le Havre has just asked if he can evacuate all the civilians." I said, "That's a good idea." Then he said, "But we've refused him." This wasn't our colonel but the High Command, a Canadian division. I said, "Why have we refused them?" and he said, "Because our division commander said there's no time, they'll get knocked about with a battle going on." We then proceeded to sit for three days outside Le Havre with nothing happening whatever and the civilians could easily have walked out. Then they did the air raid in daylight, killing three or four thousand people. I went to the colonel after this air raid and said, "I'm not going to take part in the battle because the civilians ought to have been let out."

I don't think the colonel was going to court-martial me at all because he knew I'd written several letters saying could I resign my commission, which he hadn't replied to, nor forwarded either. So he was just making me hang around. Then about a fortnight later, when we were outside Calais, this letter of mine appeared in the *Maidenhead Advertiser* and was all over the press. The day after it had been in the London press and on the BBC news service. I was told that the German commander in Calais had asked the Allied commander to evacuate the civilians in Calais, although, unlike Le Havre, where it had been quiet outside, the battle had begun and this request was granted. After that letter came out, I was sent to be court-martialled and then returned to Wormwood Scrubs via Scotland Yard . . . I was sentenced to a year's hard labour . . . Being cashiered was the bit I didn't like . . . they take your lapels off and your captain's badges and throw them in a corner and all that, and you're dismissed from the service. You're *out*. You're not worthy of being in the army. Cashiering was abolished in the 1970s . . .

Bill Spray, CO, Medical Battalion, Free French 2nd Armoured Division, France

We were excited beyond words being COs in total war, doing at last what we had wanted to do . . . In the battle areas, we worked through finding our wounded; there were always obstacles to get around and snipers in the forests on either side of the roads. We were several times in front of front lines. On one occasion, Derek and I drove out of a village to see a German column just ahead of us. The French never worried about the fact that our lorries were not as well protected as their tanks. I remember the tank commanders were astonished that we had been allowed up there . . .

David Rowlands, CO, HSU, Surgical Commando, invasion of the Riviera, France

Although the advance had been tremendously swift, there had been great resistance at Toulon, which meant that the hospital had been overloaded. The less severely wounded were sent back to us and it was at this time that we were working day and night, almost falling asleep on our feet — the colonel operating and Jiberet giving anaesthetics. We were then attached to the Medical Battalion for the advance up the Rhone Valley. There were still pockets of resistance, but it was an incredible experience to be on the move at last. We passed through Toulon with the shattered dock area and, once more, the sickly smell of death, then on to a desolate and empty Marseilles. Next we went to Aix-en-Provence, and here the contrast was staggering: the pavement cafes were in full swing, with waiters wearing little waistcoats handing out drinks. We went into a nice little bistro where we were served — sunshine and wine flowing well. We were among the first to cross the Rhone. All the bridges had been blown and our vehicles — jeeps by then — went over on the pontoons . . .

Bill Spray, CO, Medical Battalion, Free French 2nd Armoured Division, France

I can't ever see or use the word "liberation" without thinking of that day, 25 August, rolling into Paris. We were the first lot in, the only ones to make a public entry because the Americans had given the division the honour of liberating Paris. So it was the 2nd Division and these 30 conscientious objectors who rolled in on that splendid day. We were bang behind the tanks. People came out onto the streets, great crowds of them, cheering, throwing flowers, hugging every soldier they could see and, suddenly, discovering that we were English, transferring their affections to us quite as much as the French. It was a brilliantly sunny morning and the French ladies looked magnificent — the widows in black looking motherly, the young ladies so beautiful — where had they got their lovely dresses from? We lifted them up into the tanks and ambulances. It was enormous fun, a great *outpouring* of joy and relief, and everything else fell into what seemed the right perspective on that wonderful, *wonderful* day. It was a great revelation of the human spirit and astonishing that, in a sense, it required a war to produce it.

OVER THE RHINE, 224 PFA

John Petts, CO, 224 PFA, 6th Airborne Division, Rhine crossing

I felt survival was hardly likely because, believe it or not, the headlines in the paper the day before the drop said, "German ground forces prepare for airborne drop. Every field on the eastern side of the Rhine is armed, is bristling with machine-gun posts in every possible open dropping zone." So the thought of landing in the open with machine guns in the woods was a nightmare. I don't know anyone who slept that night . . . Suddenly, in the middle of the night, there was this sound — one of the most *primitive* things I had come across — the sound of the sharpening of knives and daggers on stones. It seemed that one was going back hundreds of years to hear soldiers sharpening their knives in the night before going into battle. The "naked blade" . . . Speaking for myself, I was quite *craven* with fear.

James Bramwell, CO, 224 PFA, 6th Airborne Division, Rhine crossing

25 March 1945, "Varsity" operation: we were driven to the airfield at dawn. We were the last plane of this enormous formation of planes, with the propeller already turning. One of the unique things about this Rhine crossing was that the

whole of the 6th Airborne were going in one go . . . As we took off, there was a great deal of singing — I remember "Macnamara's Band". We were silent at our end of the plane, we'd been to Normandy, and I remember exchanging a sickly grin with the colonel — let them sing! I remember looking out at the white cliffs still to be seen and immediately the French coast. I fell asleep and awoke when someone tapped me on the shoulder and pointed through the window. I could scarcely believe my eyes! There was this simply *enormous* fleet of gliders which had formed up astern of us — these almost motionless, huge craft with their wings slightly dipping, all suspended above their tugs, as far as the eye could see. That was really a reassuring thing, this enormous back-up force. We stood up, hooked up, checked each other's parachutes. From my position as number three, I could see out of the door a landscape of shell-cratered fields . . . Someone shouted: "Over the Rhine!" The red light, then the green and I was outside. We were quite high and all seemed remote for a moment. I found myself drifting down and began to hear the sound of bullets past my ears, *schwoo, schwoooo*, rather alarming in its quiet way. My morale was done great good when I remembered the brigadier saying, "It is a form of egotism, gentlemen, to imagine that they are shooting at *you*!"

John Petts, CO, 224 PFA, 6th Airborne Division, Rhine crossing

Then, *wooof*, one came down and was immediately covered up, protected by all these young trees . . . When we were crouching, above my head was the colonel commanding the 1st Canadian Parachute Battalion, hanging upside down, killed before he hit the ground, his parachute caught up in a tree. It was a fantastic sight with all these big pine trees festooned with dead men swinging gently in their harnesses. The Canadians were *livid* with anger. All the Germans dug in on the strip were either killed or taken prisoner, and that's the first time I saw the dreadful murder of prisoners with their hands up. That is what I saw . . .

Vic Newcomb, CO, 224 PFA, 6th Airborne Division, Rhine crossing

A number of the paras were wounded on the way down. In running for cover, we had to stop and put on a dressing on somebody and shepherd them along with us. This situation on the DZ [Drop Zone] meant once we got under cover and assembled in the trees there was a frequent necessity for medics to go out and pick people up. I think this is the occasion on which the only recorded military medal was awarded to a CO for what he did, bravery under fire and bringing the wounded in on a DZ. His name was Lenton: a unique case, I think; he was just an ordinary CO medical orderly.

John Petts, CO, 224 PFA, 6th Airborne Division, Germany

There was so much work for us to do after we landed. I can only remember a whole chain of casualties, many of them very young men. From my shelter I rushed across to a man who was writhing on the ground. A lad of 18, I think. He must have had a grenade burst right close to him because I opened up his tunic and all his gut was completely smashed, the whole gut just fell away. He looked at this and said to me, "I've had it, haven't I?" All you can say at such a time is, "No, no, that's OK, don't worry, you'll be all right." Most of his trousers had been smashed away. And a visual thing that stays in my mind — this was like a verse from *A Shropshire Lad*, the tragedy of the soldier of the king — the tendons of his thigh were holding a coin with the king's head on it; it was an effigy of the sovereign and a lad of 18 who had died for his country. All I could do was to hold him like a mother for a moment and give him a big shot of morphine . . . It was always one's decision: you knew how many grains would be an overdose and send a man quickly on his way. I can't say that I have killed men by giving an overdose; I've only made their inevitable death a little more bearable. And if you say who am I to make the decision that a man was going to die or not, one only did this in the very extreme cases where the man clearly was not going to survive in any way.

James Bramwell, CO, 224 PFA, 6th Airborne Division, Germany

Once, we were standing on the edge of this wood where we had been searching for casualties, with one of our dead and one seriously wounded, waiting for a jeep to take us to the dressing station. Suddenly Petts said, "Germans!" I looked round and saw a couple of badly frightened German parachutists pointing a gun at us running down the path. "*Hände hoch* [hands up]," they said, and then took us into a farm where there were a number of their group. A big corporal was standing by the fireplace. He asked who we were, and we pointed to our red crosses. "Oh, you're medics, are you? Perhaps you could answer something: why have you been shooting prisoners on the DZ?" I remembered the behaviour of some of our chaps in Normandy and said that whatever the battalion had been doing, it was nothing to do with us: "We are medical orderlies, stretcher-bearers." He said, "Let's see, turn out your pockets. If you've got any revolvers or fighting knives, I'll shoot you." I translated this to Petts and it had a chilling effect. This was a vindication of our refusal to carry arms . . . I think the fact that we were unarmed gave a sense of immunity. You didn't feel any hostility, you didn't want to shoot anybody and you didn't expect them to want to shoot you. We were trying to rescue them, Germans or anybody else.

Clifford Barnard, CO, FAU, Sandbostel concentration camp, Germany, from his memoir

As we entered, a fearful smell, impossible to describe, drifted everywhere. A huge pit had been dug in the centre of the compound by the Germans before they left into which row upon row of half-clothed or naked bodies had been thrown and lime scattered over them. There were some 8,000 male political prisoners dying at the rate of twenty or thirty a day . . . Once outside areas had been cleared the huts were entered. Most of the men were lying in tiered wooden bunks, without blankets, but many just lay on the wooden boards of the floor. The huts were deep in filth and excreta. It was dark, the smell unbearable and the RAMC doctors had to face the terrible job of deciding between the living and the dead . . . The FAU were asked to be responsible for organising the feed arrangements.

Vic Newcomb, CO, 224 PFA, 6th Airborne Division, Germany

We were part of the front-line troops which were advancing across Germany . . . We met up with the Russians; they laid on concerts to which British troops were invited and tributes paid to those involved, all very spirited. The Russian Army carries with it a concert party in every unit and someone who is able to sing "Old Man River" in English! And the dancing was great . . . We recognised the fear the Germans had of the Russians. In the hospital we took over in Wismar, when a rumour went round that the Russians were taking it over, it emptied within two hours of patients on foot whether they were fit to walk or not — they'd risk anything rather than face the Russian hordes.

John Petts, CO, 224 PFA, 6th Airborne Division, Germany

I remember a middle-aged man coming up to me and in broken English and German he said, "*Komm!* [Come!]" And he took me to his house, and his daughter was weeping and being held by her mother. He said, "She has been raped by one of your men. What do I do?" And I had to say, "Look, I can do nothing, I'm sorry." I put my hand on his shoulder and said, "This is part of war. I agree that what has happened is terrible . . . Don't forget that Hitler started the war and this is part of it." That is all I could say.

Vic Newcomb, CO, 224 PFA, 6th Airborne Division, Germany

The only misbehaviour I witnessed was by British troops; this was because I was *with* British troops. The only incident that sticks was with a British officer who had been a POW of the Germans for a short period and had suffered some ill-treatment in order to get information out of him. He took it upon himself to sort out members of a particular German regiment and publicly execute them. I'm not saying this was typical, but it comes back to me as the sort of typical effect on ordinary people that the war situation has. It confirmed my original idea of war as a dehumanising activity, and the British Army, like any other, will have its catalogue of looting, raping and so forth. The scale may be different, but the instincts are there in a lot of people if put into a perilous situation like war.

John Petts, CO, 224 PFA, 6th Airborne Division, Germany

It was a tremendous moment as a pacifist in the British army to be handed a loaded weapon from a German soldier who had been ordered to hand it over. And there were several of us who stood in the middle of the road while a queue of German soldiers came handing in their weapons, and after checking the bullets, we held them by the barrels and smashed the butts and put them into a great heap of smashed weapons, good to see. And that was the only bit of destruction that I joined in during the European holocaust.

One of the major challenges for all the conchies in action zones concerned the need to work closely with the army without violating integrity of conscience. Many have spoken of the sympathy, respect and friendship they came to feel for the fighting troops with whom they shared dangers, wounds and, sometimes, death. As pacifists, they realised how blurred the boundaries were, how their detestation of war was shared by many of the front-line soldiers. They were constantly aware of their privileged position as volunteers, with a degree of choice denied those acting under military discipline and having to obey orders, however distasteful or terrifying. Though most experienced conflicts of conscience at some stage of their experience, many coped and remained confident that theirs was the right way, the only way for them. But there were others who questioned their own pacifist stance. Such doubts arose for a variety of reasons. One had to do with the test of being in a war situation, of seeing evil at first hand and realising that something had to be done to stop it even if it meant bearing arms and joining in the fray.

(Bishop) Stephen Verney, medic with HSU, Syria

My mind began to change when I was in the Syrian Desert and began to get toughened up to the reality of things. Then, as the rumours began to get through of Hitler's extermination of the Jews, one began to think: "What am I doing just keeping my hands clean?" And thinking that love and service was going to heal the world while others suffer and die. It was then that I decided that I would have to join the fray.

George Parsons, CO, FAU, China Convoy

It was just a feeling which had grown on me; perhaps something had been there underground from the very beginning, but it had begun to take shape during the Burma Campaign of 1942 [engaged in humanitarian work]. I began to realise that I was cheering our side on to myself, but then feeling this was completely wrong: wasn't I supposed to be a pacifist and neutral? Then it arose: "I can't be a pacifist if I feel like that." Somehow it bubbled up of its own accord, it wasn't a conscious decision I came to, it broke out finally until I thought: "I can't stay with this, I've got to do something about it." Once it was out, I could think my way through things freely. I decided on the army, not the RAMC. I felt the RAMC would still be a compromise. If I were to be absolutely honest then I had got to be prepared to do anything the army wanted me to do. I thought about bearing arms and having to kill. I wasn't the only one . . . I entered the army with a direct commission as a captain.

(Bishop) Stephen Verney, medic with HSU, Syria

I joined the army and ended up in the Political Warfare Branch of the Intelligence Corps and was trained in sabotage, explosives, firearms and knives in preparation for being ferried into occupied Crete in 1944. My mission was to undermine the morale of the German forces there. I was called Stephanos Stephakis and became a *zornpotod* — a buyer and seller of cattle. I built up a little network of anti-Hitler Germans and had many adventures and several narrow escapes. Once we heard of someone giving information about us to the Germans. We thought we knew who he was, so my gang went and captured him and brought him in front of me. He was very frightened. The boys said, "Let's beat him up." I had absolute power over this man and I felt the desire rising up inside of me to smash him, to break him. It was really a *terrifying* feeling because it went against all my instincts, a violence erupting out of the very depths of myself. And I came to realise that this was the Hitler in me. That was a fundamental, mind-changing thing. I suddenly knew that the violence I was fighting against — the concentration camps, the sadism, the torture — was boiling up inside my guts. That has been a profoundly important insight for my life — that one should recognise the darkness. I sometimes feel that if you become a total pacifist, the danger is that you begin to think that you haven't got these things in you. You become very gentle and smiling, but underneath you're boiling away.

Bill Brough, CO, FAU, China Convoy (awarded two Bronze Stars, the Silver Star and Medal of Merit whilst attached to the United States Army)

For some time, I had become increasingly uneasy inside myself about my position as a conscientious objector. From the beginning, it had never been black and white. It was enough that I should refuse to kill. Then gradually it did not seem so right . . . Someone had told Colonel, Dr Seagrave, that I was leaving the FAU to join the army. I received a letter from him telling me that there was a place for me in the US Army as a medic . . . I joined Dr Seagrave's unit in November 1943 and moved into the OSS (Office of Strategic Services) guerrilla force, 101, during the last chapter of war there [as a combatant], the point where General Slim and the 14th [British] Army were pushing the Japanese out, and the Chinese had taken Michainar. We jumped in by parachute and organised guerrilla units behind Japanese lines . . . I had no wish to avoid the danger and the hardship of war. I was not afraid and I lost the phobia of killing once I entered the army . . . In China, I had become a conflicted and confused conscientious objector, then had changed to become a conflicted and confused soldier. I could never decide whether I had been a failed conchie and a failed soldier, or whether to be both at the same time is the only real human condition.

James Bramwell, alternativist CO, NCC, 224 PFA, northern France; 6th Airborne Division, Germany

When VE night came, I was in a ward with mostly German Luftwaffe wounded. Sitting out on the balcony, I was watching these great fires of rejoicing from our lines and all the different coloured flares; it looked gay and strange, and then further away were the Russian lines with their smoke fires, real, home-made fires, little cones of light, the vast area all illuminated. It was a great deal to reflect on really, the almost ghostliness of the end of this war. And one wondered about the celebrations at the end of the Napoleonic wars, the troops all bivouacked and possible rejoicing. And then the next war would come along . . . So it wasn't for me, anyway, and certainly not for the Germans behind me, a moment of rejoicing.

Bill Spray, CO, Medical Battalion, Free French 2nd Armoured Division, France

The French were very keen on giving us medals and it was desperately difficult to know what Quakers ought to do about it. I know those operating with the First Division had the same dilemma. We came to the conclusion that we wouldn't mind if a citation and some recognition to us in general was made. In the end, it was left in the good old Quaker fashion to everybody's individual conscience. I don't think anyone in our group refused a medal. I got the *croix de guerre*, which I must say, as a conscientious objector, gives me perverse satisfaction. I accepted it for two reasons: I knew my mother would be pleased; then I thought it would be a good thing to have up one's sleeve if ever one was accused of being a CO for cowardly reasons. It was such a nice name, too!

Vic Newcomb, CO, 224 PFA, 6th Airborne Division, Normandy and Germany

When I reflect on it, the compromise we made was bigger than we felt at the time. The ranks of the PFA without the COs would have been very, very thin indeed and might have jeopardised the existence of the 6th Airborne Division. It couldn't operate efficiently without a strong field-ambulance section. The PFA was much more a psychological boost to the division than the quality of work provided. It was their presence on the battlefield that was important to the fighting soldiers. This back-up the COs provided boosted the war effort much greater than was appreciated at the time. In retrospect, this was a great renunciation of the total pacifist position. This activity, however, went some way in removing from the public image that pacifists were pacifists because they were afraid for their own skins . . . There were one or two articles in the popular newspapers that appeared in the immediate aftermath of D-Day which did highlight an incident or two relating to COs on the battlefield, but there was certainly no effort to create in anybody's mind a picture of the glorious CO!

James Bramwell, CO, 224 PFA, 6th Airborne Division, Germany

After the European war ended, we were asked to go into weapon training . . . I had been told by my brother, who was serving in Burma, that the Japanese did not observe the Geneva Convention and the red cross was meaningless. So, not only would I be shot if unarmed, but my wounded would be as well. I agreed to have a Sten gun. I think I was the only armed conchie in the war. I would have killed to protect a patient.

Vic Newcomb, CO, 224 PFA, 6th Airborne Division, UK

We were to see action in South East Asia . . . We were expected to drop into the Malayan territory for the assault on Singapore. It didn't take place because of the use of the atom bomb and subsequent surrender of Japan. I had an immediate repulsion about it. I recognised an inevitable succession to previous weaponry. It may have saved me from a vastly more terrifying experience than the one I'd been through in Europe, but I never accepted the morality of dropping it.

When atomic bombs were dropped on Hiroshima and Nagasaki on 6 and 9 August 1945, killing 150,000 Japanese civilians and maiming thousands, initially the exact nature of these weapons was not apparent. But, in effect, it marked the end of conventional warfare and the opening of the nuclear age. It presaged a new, terrible dimension to warfare and was to have a great effect on the next stage of the anti-war movement.

Kazunori Yamane, soldier in Japanese Imperial Army, Hiroshima, Japan

I was about 2.5 km from the epicentre of an atomic bomb when it was dropped on Hiroshima on 6 August 1945. I was in hospital in Mitaki, Hiroshima, which was in the north of Yokogawa Station. The hospital belonged to the army. I was getting well at the end of July and was in charge of taking care of the rabbits that were kept at the hospital. I was mowing grass for the rabbits with two other soldiers when I heard the roar of a bomber. I thought that the sound was strange because there was no siren warning. When I looked up at the sky, I saw something flashing high up. When I said, "There it is!", pointing at it, I was blown by the blast into a rice field, crying without knowing what had happened to me. I asked the two comrades how they were and stood up and found the hospital completely destroyed. I saw fire starting in Hiroshima City. I heard an explosion and guessed that some kind of bomb had been dropped and decided to escape to a mountain nearby. Soon it started raining heavily . . .

We went back to the hospital, where I saw bloody nurses and comrades who were helping injured people. I started to help them and carried heavily injured people on a stretcher to a mountain. Shortly bloodstained people in rags and tatters started to escape from Hiroshima City to the countryside. Some people fell down and said, "Soldiers, please give me some water," and "Help!" Others died without drinking the water that I brought. I was busy rescuing injured comrades and people until sunset.

Donald Swann, CO, FAU, relief work, Rhodes

I was still on Rhodes when the war ended, and was in a camp called Efialtis, which is Greek for "nightmare", when I heard about the atom bomb. I was as far away from Nagasaki and Hiroshima mentally as I've ever been in my life . . . Our war had ended. I remember feeling that somewhere a long way off, statesmen were trying to work out the peace . . .

CHAPTER
FIVE

1945–90: Cold War (I)

What you could say at the moment of CND is that our impact is to keep the nuclear issue alive and to make people aware of the dangers of the world in which we live. Whether we shall get into power governments who will act in the light of those facts remains to be seen. We haven't been successful so far.

Chie Yuasa, worker at Mitsubishi Electrical Machine Factory, Nagasaki

An atomic bomb was dropped at 11.02 a.m. on 9 August when I was at the factory. I was blown off by a blast and it became dark with a cloud of dust. It was just like night although it was a sunny day. When I managed to enter a shelter, it was full of injured people . . . I went back to the dormitory on 10 August. On the way back I used a boat from Mizunoura to Ohhato which was full of dead bodies of men and women as well as horses and cows. We stayed at the dormitory, which was four kilometres away from the epicentre. We went to the factory on the 12th and it was like hell. The shelter

249

was full of people who were burnt and it was hard to recognise who they were. I began to help them as a tentative nurse . . . It was said that people were supposed to say "Long live the emperor!" before they died, but it was not true. Many said "Mother!" before they passed away. Many people became full of maggots and died. The shelter was full of a bad smell, which made me sick. I also had to carry dead people from the shelter to a place where many bodies were burnt. I became sick and had a high fever on 15 August when the war ended . . .

Kazunori Yamane, soldier in Japanese Imperial Army, Hiroshima, Japan

On 15 August, when Japan was defeated, I was carried to a truck on a stretcher and was taken to Hiroshima Station, where I was put on a train. I could see Hiroshima City destroyed by the bomb and the fire as far as I could see from the window of the train. I was taken to an elementary school in Ibarashi which was used as a temporary hospital. I had to sleep on a mat all the time because I could not walk. Citizens were also in the classroom and I heard injured people groaning. My comrades looked fine, but some of them began to lose their hair and have their gums bleed. My burnt arms and legs began to get better, and I began to walk little by little. I felt very good when I had my body washed for the first time in a stream near the school.

John Hersey's slim volume Hiroshima, published in 1946, gave a full and graphic account of what the atom bomb had done to a city and its population, including a new sickness that was later diagnosed as radiation poisoning. Although the full implications of atomic fallout were unknown at first, there had been much public debate about the ethics of this new weapon since it had been dropped in August 1945 with just two bombs killing 150,000 people and maiming thousands more. With the publication of Hersey's research, the debate became far more intense, with those like the physicist Dr Kathleen Lonsdale protesting that nuclear weapons were "a new crime against humanity".

Eileen Daffern (Clough), Brighton

And then came the dropping of the atomic bomb, and that happened a matter of weeks after the UN had been formed — the timing couldn't have been worse . . . As Einstein said, it changed everything but our way of thinking, but it changed *my* way of thinking . . .

Professor Joseph Rotblat, Director of Research into Nuclear Physics, Liverpool University

Once the news [of the dropping of the atomic bomb] was confirmed, it brought to me terrible worries because I remembered what [Niels] Bohr had told me would happen. Moreover, I already knew what others didn't: that the fission bomb, the atomic bomb, was only the *first* step. Because a bomb 1,000 times more powerful would be prepared, because in the office next door to mine in Los Alamos was Edward Teller, who was working on the so-called "super project" [the hydrogen bomb]. I was in despair because I felt that if we went on like this and began an arms race with the Soviet Union, it was bound to end in confrontation . . . I decided to change the line of my research. Nuclear physics had become so much involved with military research that I didn't want to do it any more. So I decided on a line of research to help people directly; this is why I decided to work on the medical application of nuclear physics — the use of isotopes, of radiation.

Tony Benn, undergraduate, New College, Oxford

I realised the enormity of what had happened. When the war ended and I went back to Oxford, Group Captain Cheshire, who had been the British War Cabinet's observer on the plane that crossed the bombed area at Nagasaki, said, "Whatever you do, it'll be a complete waste of time unless we get this right." He made a deep impression.

Ronald Huzzard, CO, Second World War, Hull

August 6 1945. I bought a paper and read on the front page that one bomb had destroyed a whole Japanese city — Hiroshima. Atomic energy had been developed for military purposes. And the very fact that the Allies had gone and actually *used* it made me feel sick. War had now developed to the point where the human race could wipe itself out. Then three days later a second bomb was dropped, on Nagasaki. I remember that two clergymen in Hull called a meeting on VJ Day in Hull as a protest against the use of nuclear weapons. There were very few in the audience, 20 or 30 people. And that was the first meeting that I went to protesting against nuclear weapons. It might be the first meeting *ever* held in Britain to protest against the use of nuclear weapons . . . With the publicity given to the Nazi concentration camps, I regarded what had happened at Hiroshima and Nagasaki as as big a crime as what the Nazis did in the gas chambers.

Bruce Kent, schoolboy, London

A headline announced: "Wonder bomb destroys Jap city." I remember saying to myself, "Bloody good show, that's great, they had it coming to them. The war's over." It took me a very long time to think of the moral and legal significance of what had happened and to see how the arms race spun on from there . . . Later, I began to realise that what had happened in Hiroshima and Nagasaki, like Dresden in the Second World War, had stepped outside any traditional Christian Just War thinking, and very rapidly I found that if you begin to think that sort of thing in a church [as a Catholic priest] then you rub up against a very, very deep nationalism.

Tony Parker, CO, Second World War

My first reaction to the news of the dropping of the atomic bomb on Japan was to feel that I didn't want to have any children because I was quite sure that the world would not survive for very long, that the human race would destroy itself. I still think that it probably will.

Very soon a nuclear-arms race became the most significant feature of the new international system known as the Cold War. When the Second World War ended in August 1945, it was soon apparent that the post-war system of power was a bipolar one dominated by the United States and the Soviet Union that was to divide the world into two competing spheres of influence. This lasted until November 1990, when the Cold War's official conclusion was affirmed in the Treaty of Paris. The Cold War was characterised by a state of tension and hostility between the two superpowers and their allies that did not deteriorate to the point of "hot war" between them. Their rivalry was expressed in ideological competition,

254

espionage, numerous proxy wars and a massive conventional and nuclear-arms race. Relations between the two blocs froze and warmed during the years between 1945 and 1990, thawing dramatically during a period called "Détente" in the early 1960s, when successful negotiations on the reduction of both arms and nuclear testing in the atmosphere occurred. It was the Soviet invasion of Afghanistan in 1979 and the subsequent cancellation of arms-limitation talks that led to a new stage of intensive nuclear weaponry competition along with the freezing of relations once more.

During the early years of the Cold War, conscription was still in force. It was retained after 1945 to meet Britain's worldwide defence commitments as well as fears connected to the onset of the Cold War. The 1948 National Service Act, effective from 1 January 1949, made every male citizen between the ages of eighteen and twenty liable for eighteen months' compulsory military service, with four years in reserve. Military service was extended to two years in 1950 after the Korean War had started. Northern Ireland was excluded from the Act. Deferment was granted for those about to enter university and those who were engaged on work of national importance. Provisions were also included for conscientious objectors. National Service intakes ended on 31 December 1960; the last conscripts left the army in May 1963, since when all full-time members of the armed forces have been volunteers. Peacetime conscription differed from that of the wartime situation, where the purpose had been fighting a clearly identifiable enemy. Duties ranged from clerical duties in the UK and serving in the occupation forces in Germany and Austria to armed conflict in places such as Malaya, Palestine or Korea.

A total of 3,631,500 men registered for National Service in the period 1945–60. Just over 9,000 registered provisionally as COs — a much smaller proportion than in the Second World War. The tribunal system continued to function and, as with both world wars, a large number based their objections on the grounds of Christian religious faith. Moral and political bases were also in evidence, with some objectors taking exception to particular wars — the illegal invasion of Suez by Britain, France and Israel in 1956, after President Nasser nationalised the Suez Canal, for example. Also, with increasing knowledge of the devastating nature of thermonuclear weapons, many took issue with the new mass extermination methods of contemporary warfare. As with the two world wars, perhaps the true numbers of those who objected to peacetime conscription will never be known, as many young conscripts found themselves in distasteful situations, defending the principle of Empire perhaps when they no longer had any faith in the concept, or placed in dangerous situations of which they wanted no part; they would serve out their time just trying to keep their heads down. Between 1949 and 1963, 395 peacetime conscripts were killed in action.

Michael Randle, CO, National Service 1951–2, Operation Gandhi, DAC activist and Committee of 100 (C100)

Nineteen fifty-six — that was a watershed year! I think the 1960s started in 1956! Because two things happened: one was the invasion of Suez by the French, British and Israeli forces, and the other was the Soviet invasion of Hungary. I was absolutely *outraged* by what happened at Suez, and it led to quarrels within my own family and within lots of other families too. There were violent disagreements about it. I remember coming up to London on several occasions and Donald Soper had made a statement calling on people to undertake direct action and civil disobedience against what was happening . . . The seeds of the anti-nuclear movement of the late 1950s and of the new Left really came from that period . . . It was also a time of great cultural resurgence, a new generation of playwrights like John Osborne, John Arden, Christopher Logue, and film directors like Lindsay Anderson, and the plays at the Royal Court. So the feeling was that something was on the move. All these things came from Suez . . .

David Morrish, National Service CO 1955–6, FAU International Service

Suez was for many a critical point. It didn't always connect with pacifism, but had a seminal effect for many people's politics — a watershed. It brought up for public debate the ethics of war, and this thing which had been lying dormant now came up again for public discussion — the use of armed force for the use of peacekeeping . . . At that time there was a great growth of nuclear weapons and the H-bomb was beginning to cast a shadow . . . Many of us had fears in the possibility of a nuclear conflict triggered off by accident and we felt this a far greater threat to world peace than the rather clumsy behaviour of the British in Suez and the Russians in Budapest.

Bill Hetherington, former National Service, coder, Royal Navy, 1952–4

In a 1957 White Paper, Duncan Sandys, as Minister of Defence, said that we were committed to the bomb and because of that we can afford to dispense with — he didn't use the word "cannon fodder" — National Service.

The Soviet Union had exploded its own atomic bomb in 1949; Britain followed up with testing its own nuclear weapon in 1952. A small group of pacifists from the PPU had reacted to this by setting up a Non-Violence Commission, which soon developed into another organisation called "Operation Gandhi" (which later became the Direct Action Committee [DAC]). Its members had decided to use Gandhian tactics of satyagraha, non-violence, as a challenge to nuclear weapons. It demanded an end to the nuclear programme, that Britain should leave NATO and that American forces should leave the country. The first testing of an even more destructive weapon, the hydrogen "H-bomb", by the US in 1952, followed by the Soviet Union exploding its own hydrogen bomb in 1953, and rumours that Britain was developing this weapon, fuelled their protest.

It was the US tests of a much bigger hydrogen bomb in 1954 that swelled the ranks of protesters who felt that something had to be done to stop the slide into nuclear war.

This was a seventeen-megaton blast in the Bikini Atoll, where huge quantities of radioactive dust fell onto four inhabited islands, causing long-term radiation effects on land and inhabitants. But the trigger for the mass mobilisation that was to result in the formation of the Campaign for Nuclear Disarmament, on 17 February 1958, was the outrage felt at the testing of the British H-bomb on Christmas Island in 1957. On top of this, the British government, as part of NATO, had agreed to house US Thor missiles, capable of attacking Soviet targets, in 15 American bases in different parts of the UK, making the country, it was argued, a prime target for Soviet attack. This was the context in which the first Aldermaston march took place in April 1958. This first march, organised by the DAC, was far more modest than the later five CND marches that followed. On arrival in Aldermaston, a resolution was passed that called on Britain, the United States and the Soviet Union "to stop testing, manufacturing and storing nuclear weapons immediately".

The Rt Hon. Tony Benn, MP, Bristol

The day I was elected to Parliament for the first time was November 30 1950. President Truman said he might use an atomic bomb in the Korean War, and Attlee, the prime minister, flew straight to Washington to stop it. That was the first hint after Hiroshima that this thing was an ongoing threat, and I got involved with the peace movement of one kind or another ever since. I was a member of the Peace in China Movement, which my dad was president of, because at that time there was a serious threat of an attack on China.

Ronald Huzzard, CO, Second World War, peace activist

I was at a peace conference in the Black Forest, Germany, in 1954 as a trade union representative. At that conference there was a Japanese scientist who had been present when the Japanese fishing vessel — the *Lucky Dragon* — had been caught when the Americans exploded the first hydrogen bomb in the Pacific Ocean. He brought along fish that had been examined and they were all radioactive . . . It was out of the groups that were formed to protest against the nuclear-weapons test, like the one I belonged to in north London, that led to CND being formed in 1958.

(Lord) Hugh Jenkins, founder member CND and chair 1979–81, Labour MP and minister 1964–79, House of Lords 1981–2004

It was the result of a decision by a Labour government to enlarge the lethal capacity of atomic weapons by transferring from the atomic bomb to the hydrogen bomb that really energised me . . . I was in the [anti-nuclear] campaign from the beginning and took part in the first Aldermaston march — an inspiring occasion because of the newness of it and the great *hope* we had then, which we've lost nowadays. Things in those days were simple and straightforward, we were not engaging in all the technicalities that we do nowadays, we simply said: "Ban the Bomb!" We thought if we got enough public support we'd make it clear to the government that the world did not want weapons of such mass destruction that might have the effect, if not of abolishing human life, at least setting civilisation back, as the Americans once put it, to the Stone Age.

Michael Randle, CO, National Service 1951–2, Operation Gandhi, DAC activist and C100

When we announced this three-day Aldermaston march in November 1957, I originally thought it was going to be on the scale we'd done before with previous marches. But it soon became clear it was going to be something quite different. The planning was done on a shoestring . . . One evening a man rang us up called Gerald Holtum; he was an artist and he had some ideas for the march, and so we met. He had an idea for a symbol for this march — the semaphore signals for *N* and *D*. He had drawn all these sketches and said we should have these symbols all along the route with no slogan at all to begin with, and then the slogan should be added . . . And of course this was the famous nuclear-disarmament symbol . . . He had imagined it so vividly and we were really fired

261

up and said, "Yes, we'll adopt it as our symbol," and the first leaflets that came out about the march had this strange symbol on them. Because it came at the right time, its strength was that people could attach their own meaning to it, and the meaning that they attached to it was: "Aldermaston and anti-nuclear." You can hardly go to any radical protest in the world without seeing this symbol, so I feel a certain pleasure at being one of those who said, "Yes, we'll adopt it."

That march, which took place over Easter, 1958, was a big success. At the maximum 8,000 people came and that was the worst Easter for 40 years! We had sleet and snow, but the weather actually enhanced it, as headlines went: "They're still there!" The first was from London to Aldermaston, and the emphasis was on persuading those at Aldermaston not to carry out this work. Michael Foot was one of the speakers in Trafalgar Square. I remember that as he raised his voice, all the pigeons flew up around Nelson's Column. One of the other speakers was the American Bayard Rustin, who gave a very powerful speech. He was terribly impressed with that march and afterwards said it was one of the inspirations for him to organise the march on Washington which he coordinated in 1963 when Martin Luther King made his famous "I have a dream" speech . . . In the following and susequent years, CND took over the Aldermaston march and turned it into a major annual event.

Pat Arrowsmith, DAC, CND and C100 activist

The march was very impressive going in silence by the [Aldermaston] base, and we had a final rally in the Falcon Field. I think this is where I would date my having become a kind of news figure . . . The McWhirter brothers who had formed a group called Common Cause, which was totally against the nuclear-disarmament movement and quite right-wing, drove into the field to break the event up. Marchers and demonstrators started to close in and it looked as if it could get violent. Hugh Brock insisted, and it was very clear to me, that this was a non-violent march, it was for peace and was to be peaceful. So I belted out into the field with a loudspeaker and shouted out repeatedly that there was to be no violence, and it *worked*. They departed. It got picked up by the press and this stocky little young woman shouting out for non-violence evolved into a mini profile in the Diary of the *Guardian*, and it made me known to the press seriously for the first time and seems to have remained ever since — partly because my surname translates as an arms manufacturer, which is rather funny . . .

Rev. Donald Soper, Methodist minister and peace activist, Kingsway Hall, London

I marched to Aldermaston on the wettest day of the year, a marvellous occasion. That was the high point, a possible breakthrough, and if the Labour Party had taken that plunge, I believe they would have had a very different history.

Denis Hayes, CO, Second World War

By the 1950s, the Second World War CO movement had come to an end. The people who went on Aldermaston marches were young and very likeable. As a CO from the First World War said, "They are more like the people we had in the First World War, more political and more extrovert about it." He felt that all these immense marches occurred without a blow due to what the earlier COs brought to them.

(Monsignor) Bruce Kent, London, CND chair 1977–9, vice president 1987–90

My first connection with CND must have been the Easter of 1959 — the march that went from Aldermaston to London. I remember standing on the steps of my church and complaining bitterly about the bride being late because the cars couldn't get through the mob of people marching up the high street . . . My next memory is when I was driving Cardinal Heenan on Easter Monday in '63 or '64 to his country house in Hertfordshire. Our route took us through Trafalgar Square and I'd forgotten about the CND demonstration. All these people were milling about the square and I remember Heenan saying, "Looking at this lot, as far as I'm concerned, there's only one answer: that it's better to be dead than Red." That the Roman Catholic Primate — a very worthy Christian — would actually say something like that, in deep contempt for what was going on in the square, really *shook* me. I realised that these thousands of decent people were by no means Red, but didn't want nuclear testing and nuclear bombs and were moved by a deeply moral point of view. I was wise enough just to suck wind, but it struck me. I've never forgotten it. *Never* forgotten it. I thought: "What does he mean by being dead?" Not just being dead but murdering millions by the same process. I couldn't swallow it. By that time, I was getting influenced by arguments in the *Catholic Herald* and by listening to Archbishop Roberts. But I still wasn't active in CND until the mid-'60s . . .

Eileen Daffern (Clough), CND executive, Brighton Branch

Brighton had a very strong CND movement and I was on the executive . . . We went on a big Aldermaston march in '61 or '62 and it was so *inspiring*, we walked eight abreast up Whitehall and you really felt that you were part of a line of radicals who'd been protesting from the Peasants' Revolt or much earlier, and it was a *marvellous* feeling, you get such *empowerment* when you're involved in campaigning, you feel you can change the world, and we had that feeling so rarely.

By 1959, CND had tens of thousands of supporters and had declared its unilateralist position (the argument that if one country gave up its nuclear weapons, others would follow). The second Aldermaston march, organised by CND, reversed the order: the march started at Aldermaston, where over 4,000 set out in wet and cold weather. By the time they reached Trafalgar Square, their ranks had swelled to 15,000. A further 5,000 greeted them in the square, including many former COs from both wars. Conspicuous by their absence were those pacifists who believed that "nuclear pacifism" was over-simplistic. Sybil Morrison, speaking for the pure pacifist view as she toured the country, announced: "Weapons are not the cause of war. It is because of war that weapons are made."

Myrtle Solomon, PPU activist, PPU chair in the 1980s

I'm not so involved with the nuclear aspect of war as many peace people are. Obviously I realise that it's infinitely more catastrophic than anything we've ever met, but I think that it's war we've got to get rid of, the method of war, because if you're prepared to use a gun, you'll be prepared to use a nuclear bomb at some point — or somebody will. So I don't get involved with this selective resistance, though I'm glad that others are doing it. It isn't quite for me.

Tony Parker, CO, Second World War

I can see how you can be a CND-er without being a pacifist, but I don't see how you could be a pacifist and not be, at least, sympathetic to CND.

Jack Daniel, Royal Artillery, Second World War, post-war pacifist

I joined CND right at the beginning, but it was rather like domestic Christianity. At the meetings there were a small group of us who said, "Well, disarmament must be *total* disarmament. Cut out the N. It's not just that we're objecting to nuclear arms, we're also objecting to guns and bayonets and grenades." CND said, "How are you going to do that?" "We will refuse to pay part of our taxes that relate to the public commitment to defence. Find out the amount and refuse to pay that bit." They wouldn't have it. They said, "You can't antagonise society like that." So we're back onto the original Christianity thing. You've got a watered down version of disarmament and anti-war. It's an accommodating thing.

As well as the schism between pacifist organisations like the PPU and WRI and CND, there was friction within the anti-nuclear movement between those who favoured direct action and techniques of civil disobedience and those who felt that their protest should remain law-abiding. Canon John Collins, the chairman of CND, and his supporters in the top echelons of CND were strongly against civil disobedience. They felt that the appeal of CND was its simplicity: Ban the Bomb! This "single issue" was to lead to important differences between CND and the DAC that prevented a merger between the two groups. DAC members were not just against the bomb, they were also pacifists wanting to transform society through peaceful means. They were far more active and increasingly took bold, direct, non-violent actions, facing tough police tactics, arrest and imprisonment. The DAC was also strongly internationalist and had important links to the civil rights and anti-nuclear movements in the US.

A more serious source of acrimony arose with the formation of the Committee of 100 in October 1960. Like the DAC, the C100 advocated a far more active approach than that of CND. It soon attracted radicals like Michael Scott, Michael Randle, April Carter and Pat Arrowsmith. A committee of 100 prominent people was to promote civil disobedience against the ever-growing menace of nuclear war. Its hundred dignitaries were distinguished writers, journalists, actors, doctors and scientists. Bertrand Russell's presence was a huge asset — his brilliant speeches attracted the publicity the C100 was after. The DAC and the C100, being natural allies, soon joined forces in a plethora of imaginative, highly publicised demonstrations, sit-ins and rallies, and eventually the two were merged. This represented a huge expansion of potentially disruptive activity. Arrests and prison sentences were to follow, including Bertrand Russell and his wife, Edith. Russell, a veteran peace campaigner, welcomed these, knowing from experience what excellent publicity they provided. CND, aiming to win the support of the opposition Labour Party, stood aloof from these actions. It also insisted on maintaining the single-issue policy, whereas C100 members increasingly took on new concerns such as ecology and the environment, and those like Pat Arrowsmith, who had experienced several prison sentences, advocated prison reform.

The schism between CND, the DAC and the C100, which resulted in a rift between Bertrand Russell and Canon John Collins, affected the movement's political advance. This was confirmed when Hugh Gaitskell reversed the Labour Party's unilateralist stance at the next party conference in 1960, a great blow to CND. The huge rally that the C100 held in Trafalgar Square on Sunday, 17 September 1961, led to 1,314 arrests, with 658 released on bail, the rest spending the night in gaol.

Pat Arrowsmith, DAC, CND and C100 activist

The DAC's concern was that people directly involved should act according to their own conscience. And conscientious objection and pacifism permeated the orientation of the DAC. Whereas CND from the beginning had a lot of Labour Party people in it as well as leading trade unionists, the DAC had a rather different approach. I thought then, and do to this day, that the two complemented and supplemented each other. Both were necessary, and there was quite a good case for having two separate wings to the overall nuclear-disarmament movement . . . Hugh Brock had the foresight to see that the radical side of the movement would vanish if we were part of CND. So we declined to be a subcommittee of CND, as was suggested to us.

(Lord) Hugh Jenkins, founder member CND and chair 1979–81, Labour MP and minister 1964–79, House of Lords 1981–2004

Those of us in politics or on the verge of politics saw that we could only act within constitutional means. We then captured the Labour Party Conference by a motion adopting unilateralism. The great argument in those days, and has been to some extent since, was between multilateralist and the unilateralist disarmament. The unilateralists, of which I was one, said: "We have to *act*, it's not enough talking, we should get rid of our own bomb, only in doing that can we set an example for others to follow." The multilateralists said: "No, we must talk and we must all act together until we get a wider agreement." We only held our resolution for unilateralism for a year, when it was overthrown by Hugh Gaitskell [1960]. Then, of course, the defection of Nye Bevan from our ranks was a considerable blow, and it was then that we realised it was going to be a larger job than we originally thought.

Pat Arrowsmith, organiser for DAC, CND and C100

C100 had in mind a tactic for getting much bigger demonstrations, getting a whole lot of well-known people pledged to take part in sit-downs in central London, which wasn't direct action but rather a deliberate flouting of the law . . . sitting down outside Downing Street, for instance . . . Michael Scott was heavily involved, and [Bertrand] Russell, president of CND, was also president of the C100, which led to major altercations with John Collins. There were very marked splits between the two, and Russell quit the CND presidency. The C100 became much more of a threat to CND because it was much bigger and more potent than the DAC had been. So whatever rifts there had been between the DAC and CND were nothing to the anger and antagonism between CND and the C100, partly because of the personalities involved . . . There were one or two very large civil-disobedience actions. Being very involved with DAC work, I didn't take part in these early actions. Also, I had, and I've still got, some reservations about civil disobedience as such. I've never been in favour of deliberately breaking the law . . . That was the essential difference between the DAC and the C100, although the overlap was much greater than it had been for the DAC and CND.

Peter Sharp, CO, Second World War, CND and C100 member

A lot of CND people were straight down the line, prim and proper, not realising that the act of protesting isn't always nice. The clash that came between CND and the C100 was understandable in a way because the direct action favoured by the C100 seemed a distraction from campaigning against the bomb to some CND members.

Bill Hetherington, CND, C100 and PPU member

By the time I got involved in CND, I very quickly got involved in the C100 as well. On 9 December 1961 I was off on a C100 demonstration. There were demonstrations all over the country and this was the day of the Wethersfield demonstration, for which six C100 activists had been arrested, the five men getting eighteen months and the woman twelve months [Michael Randle, Ian Dixon, Terry Chandler, Trevor Hatton, Pat Pottle and Helen Allegranza, who, after her release, committed suicide]. Ours was a legal march from Oxford to Brize Norton, and those of us who wanted to take the risk sat down at the gates. I shall never forget it because it was the first time I became aware of post-World War II militarism at its height. Talk about "*Arbeit macht frei!*" Over the gate was written "Peace is our Profession". This was at the epicentre with bombers there to take H-bombs to obliterate a city in a second. "*Peace is our Profession*"! If ever I had doubts, I knew where my place was. We sat for a couple of hours; a random handful of us were arrested. I wasn't arrested at that time, but it was a time when I came out as a person committed to civil disobedience and liable to arrest.

Air Commodore Alastair Mackie, CND, Ex-Services CND, Generals for Peace, vice president of CND 1990 to present

I was commanding a squadron of Vulcans, which were able to drop the then very primitive hydrogen bomb. It was explained to us this way: "We must have a strong and effective deterrent to deter the Soviet Union, but if we ever have to use the deterrent, the deterrent has failed." I never could quite live with that because it seemed to me that the corollary is: "If we have something which, if we use it, has failed, then why have it at all?" But I was very busy with this delightful job of running a complicated unit and that was very satisfying as an activity. So I can't say that I was particularly appalled. I just felt uneasy . . .

Pat Arrowsmith, DAC, CND and C100 activist

I was deemed by the authorities to have a leadership role [in a major C100 action: Holy Loch, Polaris base] and I got a prison sentence which, by the standards of those days, was quite a long one, three months, on some criminal offence of Scottish law. So this was not a civil prison. There was quite a furore about this because I'd plainly been singled out. It was on that prison sentence that I engaged in a hunger strike . . . It turned out that there was some marginal civil-defence working done by some of the prisoners, making sandbags against the possibility of nuclear war — of all idiotic things! So I tried to talk to fellow prisoners, communicating my concerns regarding civil defence, and quite a number were against it. So I decided to go on hunger strike until the work was stopped. I went to the acting governor at the time and told her. She was very angry indeed. I had slightly modified my demands and said I wouldn't eat anything until there was consultation with the women about it. I was banged up in solitary and charged with inciting a mutiny under Scottish prison rules . . .

The news of my hunger strike got out and I got floods of supportive letters. I had been on hunger strike for only five days when for the first time I was forcibly fed. What was nasty was that I was never sure when they were going to do it. Up to then I had welcomed a screw coming; now I dreaded the sound of footsteps, which I knew would be for forcible feeding. I wouldn't cooperate with moving from my cell for this, they would have to carry me to the clinic places where it was administered. It was to my advantage that I was a pacifist because, unlike the Price sisters [interned in Northern Ireland], I didn't physically fight against it. When they got me in the chair and opened my mouth, I more or less did what they told me and relaxed and tried to spit it out, so they pushed it down. The nastiest part of being forcibly fed is that you back out again and you either vomit or try to. I didn't realise that it could have gone in my lungs and killed me. It is quite a dangerous procedure, not painful, but very frightening. This meant that I had Members of Parliament coming to see me . . . In the end, I won that hunger strike because the MP Judith Hart persuaded them that the women should be consulted [over the sandbag issue]. This happened and one or two of them had said that I was quite right. My terms had been met so I ended my hunger strike but went on with a work strike for the rest of my sentence.

The Aldermaston march of April 1963, the sixth and the last, drew large crowds, but it lacked the vigour and impact of the earlier marches. Also, the resolution of the Cuban Missile Crisis of October 1962 had shown that the superpowers could achieve peaceful solutions — as Khrushchev had stated, they had "pulled back from the cannon's mouth". The first nuclear hotline — direct contact between American and Soviet leaders — was another step forward. But it was the signing in 1963 of the Partial Test Ban Treaty, which outlawed atmospheric testing, that led to a reduced sense of urgency within CND. The attention of many members then turned to the anti-war campaign against the Vietnam War, which, once more, raised the question of the relevance of the single issue. With the earlier sense of urgency and commitment declining, membership fell in the late 1960s. The signing of the Non-Proliferation Treaty (NPT) in July 1968 by Britain, the United States and the Soviet Union, and moves on the Strategic Arms Limitation Talks (SALT I), signed in 1972, added to the feeling of many in the movement that progress was taking place. There were, however, still energetic anti-Polaris demonstrations in south Cumbria and on Merseyside, as well as Holy Loch and Faslane in Scotland.

Eileen Daffern (Clough), CND executive, Brighton

The peace movement goes in bursts: it suddenly has a surge and then it sinks back. After the Test Ban Treaty in 1963 we felt we had achieved something and people fell away for ten years.

Bill Hetherington, CND, C100 and PPU member

In the 1970s, there wasn't a lot of activity either by the "respectable" CND or the "non-respectable" nuclear disarmers . . . It went into decline partly because of the 1963 agreement between Britain, the United States and the Soviet Union to ban tests in the atmosphere. Also, the Labour government of 1964 didn't ban the bomb. So there was this feeling: what's the point? Therefore it was a very quiescent period on the nuclear side . . . Part of the energy of the first wave had gone into banning the tests: they were banned; you had a victory. But of course the bombs were still there . . .

Maybe another factor in CND's decline was the whole Vietnam issue, which dominated radical people in the period 1965–75. One of the problems for peace people then, and not just CND, was infiltration by people who were effectively *for* the Vietcong. I walked on more than one peace march advertised as such when you found people in front or behind you shouting "Victory to the National Liberation Front of Vietnam", and really it was an anti-American, pro-NLF march rather than a peace march where we had said: "A plague on both your heads, we want both sides to withdraw."

CND did find itself in a predicament by a single-issue campaign. It is interesting to see how often CND tried to put a nuclear twist on any peace issue . . . One of the problems of having a single-issue campaign is when your single issue isn't the flavour of the month . . .

Pat Arrowsmith, DAC, CND and C100 activist

There was a general decision in the end that because the Vietnam War had every possibility for going nuclear, that it was in our [CND] terms of reference, so we did have a position of opposition to the war in Vietnam. But there were a lot of other groups that embraced CND people.

Ruth Osborn, member of Women's International League for Peace and Freedom (WILPF)

The incident which I see as a success was the daily vigil that was organised by an American woman in Grosvenor Square protesting about the Vietnam War. Every day of the week there would be about half a dozen groups of women in the London area who committed themselves to have four or five people there on this vigil. I was one of those who went and held the WILPF banner every Wednesday lunchtime, just four of us, and we did this for three years. The same thing was done in Paris outside the US embassy, in Sweden and, of course, in Washington. This "sit on the stones" approach, day after day, with their embassies hearing it in all those countries, was effective. This was the first time that the United States had to give up a war when it had all the military power but it hadn't won the hearts and minds of their own people and others who wanted peace. I am sure this peace process played a part [in ending the war].

Bill Hetherington, CND, C100 and PPU member

As a British pacifist, I felt a responsibility for what is generally called the Troubles in Northern Ireland. I took responsibility for that, and the PPU from time to time issued statements on this issue, taking the attitude that the issue should be decided by the people themselves, but by agreement and non-violently, not by bullets and bombs, whether by the paramilitaries or the British Army . . . Our view was that Britain should play a minimal role and certainly not a military one . . . We always knew in the hinterland of Northern Ireland there were people who were peace-minded, and these people we also needed to make contact with . . . We came together with other groups in 1973 to form the British Withdrawal from Northern Ireland Campaign [BWNIC], and that was quite distinct from the Troops Out Movement, an overtly Republican organisation. We were neutral; we believed that both sides had rights and traditions and they needed to be respected . . . BWNIC had two major ways of working: we had a leaflet for civilians; we also produced one for soldiers to be given out to British troops who at some stage in their career would be asked to do a tour of Northern Ireland. We went to barracks and garrison towns like Devizes and Aldershot to distribute them . . . Pat Arrowsmith, who was one of our key people, was arrested and charged under the Incitement to Disaffection Act . . . After a trial at the Old Bailey, she was sentenced to 18 months. The leaflet was full of information and warning, but it was held to be incitement. We did modify it, calling it "Some Information for Discontented Soldiers". In the autumn of 1974, 14 supporters were arrested, including myself, and charged, not simply with an offence under the 1954 Act, but with conspiracy to incite HM Forces . . . The result was that we ended up at the Old Bailey in September 1975 . . . The outcome of that trial, which lasted from 29 September until 10 December, was not guilty on all 31 verdicts — a *tremendous* victory.

Denise Innes, member of Mothers for Peace (MFP)

Seven of the women from MFP flew to Dublin for this weekend conference. There were 30 women from the north and 30 from the south in a seminary on the north side of Dublin . . . The seminar was facilitated by a group called "Operation Cooperation North" and they were linked with another group in the north, "Women Together", which has links with MFP . . . Women from the south were from a lot of organisations, including WILPF. The whole atmosphere was one of women wanting reconciliation, of wanting to learn of each other's problems and a genuine warm feeling of wanting to get together . . . The women from the south wanted to go on marches in order to raise the awareness of ordinary people. The women from the north explained that they were "marched out"; they'd done all that and were trying to do something different now in their communities and the communities that weren't involved. Women in the south felt that it was time that they became more aware of what went on in the north. I was surprised to learn that there hadn't been a lot of movement between the women when, geographically, they were so close . . . They talked of their common Irishness — their culture, music and dance — and their hope for the future was the withdrawal of British troops and the UN stepping in with a monitoring force. They were also hopeful that the EU would bring changes.

(Lord) Hugh Jenkins, founder member CND and chair 1979–81, Labour MP and minister 1964–79, House of Lords 1981–2004

When I came to the chair in 1979, we were in a bit of a backlash. It could be said that we failed to get what we wanted from the Labour government, failed to convert them as a whole. We went into '79 at a low and the climb back began then; we couldn't really have gone down much further. It was a bad stage; we all felt a bit down in the mouth. But we gradually got our determination back.

The late 1970s and early 1980s saw a resurgence of CND at both national and local levels — by 1978, 102 local groups had been formed with ever-growing membership applications. This growth reflected the deteriorating international situation and the more aggressive nuclear policies of the Soviet Union and the USA, along with what David Owen called "megaphone diplomacy". At this time, the neutron bomb was being developed in the United States. This was an advanced radiation warhead developed to kill but protect property; it was particularly fearful as it was designed to be used as a tactical weapon in a "limited" form of nuclear war in Europe. European-wide campaigning was successful in helping persuade President Carter to cease production of this weapon. Also by now considerable numbers of the British public had seen the films All Against the Bomb and Peter Watkins's The War Game, which gave a fictional representation of nuclear war. The official publication Protect and Survive, which advised the British public what to do in the event of nuclear war, generated hundreds of new CND members. It was robustly countered by a pamphlet written by the historian E. P. Thompson and others entitled Protest and Survive, which showed the absurdity of the government's advice and the reality of what the use of nuclear missiles in a limited war would do: the complete destruction of western Europe, including Britain. Protest and Survive urged the people of European countries east and west to demand disarmament. This was an important factor leading to the formation of European Nuclear Disarmament (END), which had links with CND.

Another boost at this time was the shift to the Left of the Labour Party made manifest at the Labour Party Conference in 1980, committing the party to unilateral nuclear disarmament. But it was the installation of Cruise missiles in Britain and Pershing missiles based in Europe that was to provoke CND into recovering its momentum, causing the biggest demonstrations against nuclear weapons in history in the UK and in Europe, and a huge increase in British membership from 4,276 in 1979 to 90,000 in 1984, with local membership reaching 250,000. Many members formed and manned the peace camps that started in the 1980s, the all-women's camp at Greenham Common the most famous.

Bill Hetherington, CND, C100 and PPU member

By this second wave of CND — the late 1970s, early 1980s — there was a new generation involved and there never was the same tension with civil disobedience and sit-downs as there had been in the first wave. There was now a kind of "live and let live" feeling . . .

(Lord) Hugh Jenkins, founder member CND and chair 1979–81, Labour MP and minister 1964–79, House of Lords 1981–2004

As Arts Minister [1974–6], I was particularly active in the *War Game* struggle. To get that shown on the BBC was a long and arduous task, and I played a considerable part in it myself: meetings and so on.

Eileen Daffern (Clough), CND executive, Brighton

The first riposte to *Protect and Survive* [1980] was *Protest and Survive* by Edward Thompson, a wonderful pamphlet satirising this and throwing up the whole question of missiles and the need for a nuclear-free Europe. The *outrage* that followed! We were so busy, we organised a petition against it and we had 2,000 people on this great march up the high street of Lewes . . . we had a band playing, and Mary Kaldor and I stood on the bandwagon and gave speeches. The same thing was done in Chichester for West Sussex on the same day. And this happened all over the country.

Christine Kings, CND activist, London

The big demonstration for which I collected money was related to E. P. Thompson's *Protest and Survive*, his response to a government publication *Protect and Survive*, whereby the Home Office gave guidance on how to protect yourself in the event of a nuclear attack. It involved taking the doors off the inside rooms and building yourself a little cubbyhole under the stairs, and having your tins of baked beans and bottled water and waiting for the radiation to disperse before you got on with your life again. I think the Home Office was absolutely shocked at the response. When I first went to CND, it had a membership of around 3,000. We were working out of two tiny attic rooms in Great James Street. There was Bruce Kent, an organiser and somebody who produced the publications, and with me and the other four volunteers, the rooms were absolutely packed.

We had no idea what was going to happen: CND had been in the doldrums; it was the first big demonstration they'd organised in a long while. It had pottered along without any great note taken of it until E. P. Thompson wrote that book. All of a sudden there were 100,000 people on that demonstration and Trafalgar Square was packed, and weeks after the demonstration, postmen were delivering sacks and sacks of mail, people wanting to join CND . . . It's funny how these political movements are suddenly *galvanised* into action. There was something about the moment: the ludicrous advice that had been sent out by the government and the fact that an academic had picked it up and written about it caught the imagination of the press . . . And of course there was Bruce Kent — *Monsignor* Bruce Kent — the fact that CND was headed up by a senior Roman Catholic official gave some legitimacy to the organisation. His public presence was always very professional, he always wore his dog collar and jacket, but he came over as great fun . . .

(Lord) Hugh Jenkins, founder member CND and chair 1979–81, Labour MP and minister 1964–79, House of Lords, 1981–2004

I think we can say that we had a victory there because no government attempts to suggest there is any serious defence against it now. I had a hand in that myself. I put the motion forward in the GLC [Greater London Council] to abolish the Civil Defence Corps. I also took the battle over to Parliament and it was abolished nationally. The inability of any state to defend itself against nuclear war is generally accepted. And people, instead of saying, "Well, if we can't defend ourselves against nuclear weapons, we'd better not have them," are now [1992] relying upon what the government wrongly calls "nuclear defence" — they have dropped "deterrence" as they realise there is nobody to deter, not realising that there is no defence either. No deterrent effect, no defence effect, so the thing becomes steadily more absurd.

Air Commodore Alastair Mackie, CND, Ex-Services CND, Generals for Peace, vice president of CND 1990 to present

After leaving that Vulcan bomber unit, about 1959, I went to the Joint Services Staff College, as a member of the directing staff . . . I did all the homework and then began to take very seriously the rationale of British defence policy. I could make no sense of it. It seemed to me very doubtful indeed whether there had ever been a threat to the United Kingdom from the Soviet Union, and that if there had been and if there was, the way *not* to try and deal with it was with an independent, so-called, nuclear-weapon force. That was wrong . . . At the end of my time with the JSSC, to my great surprise I was posted to the Cabinet Office, to the Joint Intelligence Committee . . . The material from the JIC from all kinds of quarters, not only military and political intelligence but intelligence from the secret departments, is about as good as we're likely to get. I was deputy secretary of the JIC. While much of what I did was quite ordinary routine intelligence work, the thing that fascinated me was the Soviet Studies Section, which the Foreign Office mostly did, but also the secret departments. I read with fascination these assessments by our professional diplomats, our analysts, our intelligence officers of all kinds. It was very interesting that in all I read in two years, I could detect nothing that indicated any Soviet threat to this country whatever . . .

Eileen Daffern (Clough), CND executive, Brighton branch

The energy in the 1980s was absolutely *amazing*. I just lived all the time working for peace. Then we started internationally . . . Now there were always problems with the European Disarmament Movement; I sometimes think there were CIA infiltrations into the European peace movement and I know that others share my belief.

(Lord) Hugh Jenkins, founder member CND and chair 1979–81, Labour MP and minister 1964–79, House of Lords, 1981–2004

There was a resurgence in Europe, a period when END became very active. I thought the European movement was a diversion of effort from our country to Europe, but it may have been sensible given the hostile government then. END, although it didn't sustain itself, was effective in its time and way, and spread the idea of nuclear disarmament and may have had an effect in preventing the idea of nuclear arms becoming as popular and universal as it might have been. Women were also very active in that period in the movement.

Eileen Daffern (Clough), CND executive, Brighton branch

I think my international work was more important than all the peace work I did. My first visit was to Leningrad in 1981 with a group of Manchester trade unionists and Quakers. Going to the Eastern European countries and taking a message of peace invigorated the people because it opened their eyes to the fact that they *did* have allies. The *yearning* of most people! Particularly in the Soviet Union. The Leningraders said, "We lost so many people, 900,000, in the last war, we want peace, why do we want a *war*?" The movement, people to people, grew up, and it grew up in CND as well: people have so much in common, they don't want war. We have had the most *amazing* exchanges with Eastern Europeans. I went to Hungary five times and we brought people from the Hungarian Peace Committee back here. As one woman said, "The Iron Curtain already seems a bit lacier!" With the Sussex Peace Alliance, I went to places like Helsinki, Sweden, to Poland and East Germany, all intent on getting rid of nuclear weapons, and everywhere we went we brought this message of *people to people* . . . These were my memories of so many lost opportunities, because the overtures they had been making at the time of Reagan and Thatcher just fell on deaf ears, but when Gorbachev came in 1987 and talked to the United Nations, there was some hope. He was the one who took up Einstein's point — that we should change our way of thinking.

Canon Paul Oestreicher, Anglican pacifist, CND vice president

I visited Russia and many of the Eastern European countries during the Cold War in my role as Eastern European Secretary of the British Council of Churches and as a member of the Christian Peace Conference . . . I suppose I was one of those — not that many of us — who were genuinely neutral in the Cold War. A lot of people in the West couldn't understand that neutrality and so I was put in the category of a "fellow traveller" to the right-wing people of the West. But on the other side, it was the exact opposite. Although I was not antagonistic to the Eastern bloc, I was sufficiently frank to tell them what I thought. So I was a very inconvenient guest, and in 1968, the Soviet secret police in Prague, who had it in for me, saw to it that I was expelled from the Christian Peace Council's executive committee, thrown out. In a strange way it's a Christian no-man's-land. You find yourself between the fronts, hating this Cold War, hating the propaganda on both sides, telling both sides what you think of them, and being loved by neither . . . But I can't pretend that there wasn't a difference between the West and the East: in the West, you could not be loved but not locked up . . . To say that I was neutral was saying that I was not playing the Cold War game, it doesn't mean that I couldn't tell the difference.

Brigadier Michael Harbottle, Generals for Peace

In 1982, I was in New York for the Second Special Session on Disarmament. I took the opportunity of asking for and getting an interview with Ambassador Anatoly Dobrynin in Washington to discuss with him the possibility of linking our group of generals [for peace] in a meeting with a comparable group from the Warsaw Pact countries, because I'd felt for some time that although it was good having generals from NATO countries meeting regularly, how much better it would be if we were able to sit down with, as it were, the enemy, and to look at the problems that face European security and global security together. Dobrynin was extremely helpful and obviously went back to the Soviet Foreign Ministry. There was a certain amount of suspicion to begin with because they weren't used to that kind of approach, particularly from a group of generals. So it took about 20 months, but our first meeting was in 1984 and we have met every year since and we shall meet again in April this year [1988] for the fifth time. What began as very stereotyped, formal, rather rigid presentations, have now developed into a complete discussion group where very few prepared papers are delivered. We take subjects and we speak from our heads and from our hearts, and we don't sit like most of these meetings with them on that side and us on this side; we are a complete entity.

Bertrand Russell, a veteran of the NCF during the First World War and a great peace campaigner, with Albert Einstein had produced a manifesto demanding that the scientific community be allowed to influence the use to which their creations should be put. During the nuclear-arms race in the bleak years of the Cold War, this had little chance of success. But in 1957, an international scientific body was set up aimed at giving scientists a forum and a voice. Its first meeting was at Pugwash, a small town in Nova Scotia, Canada. As Sir Martin Rees of the British Institute of Astronomy explained, "It was the only medium through which Russian and American scientists and others involved in defence could get together." It was a conduit for serious technical discussion on arms control and a step towards the development of the Partial Test Ban deal and Anti-Ballistic Missile (ABM) treaties, a valuable medium for mutual scientific cooperation and understanding. Pugwash groups were formed in many countries. Professor Joseph Rotblat, a physicist who had worked on the Manhattan Project to develop the A-bomb during the Second World War, was a founder member of Pugwash. He had developed a deep-seated hatred of the monster he had helped to create and he became one of the most outspoken critics of its further development and the philosophy of nuclear deterrence. A range of other anti-nuclear, medical and scientific organisations have since been formed, with strong links between them.

Professor Joseph Rotblat, Director of Research into Nuclear Physics, Liverpool University

We in Pugwash are not an action group, a pressure group, we are simply people who have some knowledge of these matters who come together as individuals; we are not part of any party, or association, each of us speaks for himself or herself. And we discuss matters and come to certain conclusions, and then we try to promulgate them to governments and other bodies, and we hope that our ideas will eventually circulate and influence governments, and we notice from time to time that we do have evidence that this happens. For instance, we have been told that our action to persuade governments to stop nuclear testing was effective and played an important role in the treaty signed in '63 to halt all tests except underground. And recently Mr Gorbachev acknowledged to us that his planning was influenced by our ideas, and this changed the whole world situation. We are not publicity seeking and many people do not know about us, although we've been in existence for 35 years — Pugwash is known mainly as Captain Pugwash, the hero of the comics! But we try in a scientific fashion, quietly, to achieve certain things. At present our project is the desirability and feasibility of NWFW — a Nuclear Weapons Free World.

Dr Ralph Arnold, CO, Second World War, member of Medical Campaign Against Nuclear Weapons (MCANW), the Medical Association for the Prevention of War (MAPW) and the International Physicians for the Prevention of Nuclear War (IPPNW)

Through my activities in MCANW, MAPW and IPPNW, to which they are both affiliated, I have met Russian and Eastern European doctors who were very cautious and reserved in the pre-Gorbachev years; now [1991] they're much more open. It all started with the sharing of information and trying to educate the profession and the public about the effects of nuclear war; needless to say, it's moved into concerns regarding disarmament, generally helping the Third World with the effects of the arms race, and even further into the question of *all* weapons of mass destruction. More recently still, it's quite obvious to us and it's a matter of policy that war is obsolete and is a *total* disaster. And there's the whole environmental dimension as well, which we're addressing. So the agenda has become vastly more widened, and most recently, the MCANW has moved on from mass destruction to the whole basis of war and its psychological and medical implications, and wants to relaunch itself and widen its remit to become like the MAPW. I'm a member of both and the proposal is to unite the two.

Roy Ridgway, CO, Second World War, medical journalist, IPPNW

Russian doctors have changed the Hippocratic oath, adding to it, "As a doctor I will work for the prevention of nuclear war."

Another significant dimension was added to CND in March 1983 when John Stanleigh, who had served in the Second World War, with a small group of other ex-servicemen, started what was to become Ex-Services CND. By September its numbers had grown to 500, and by 1989 the membership neared 1,000 men and women, with contacts in a number of other countries, including the Soviet Union. The vast majority of members were veterans of the Second World War and one member had fought for four years during the First World War. In the 1980s, it also started attracting younger ex-service people who had fought in the Falklands War. Members on the whole did not regret their earlier war service; they became active in the cause of peace because they no longer accepted governments' arguments that nuclear weapons were vital as a deterrence against aggressor states. In 2005, Ex-Services CND was amalgamated with CND.

(Lord) Hugh Jenkins, founder member CND and chair 1979–81, Labour MP and minister 1964–79, House of Lords, 1981–2004

The Labour Party on the whole, to say the least of it, was not enthusiastic about the Falklands War, but the party in Parliament had given support. As far as the Lords was concerned, hardly anybody was against the war. There was this wave of jingoism in the country at the time and everybody was quite affected by it and few were prepared to speak out against it. I was entirely unmoved by this jingoism and felt the whole thing entirely ridiculous, and I said so in the House. I remember causing a bit of an uproar when I described the sinking of the *Belgrano* as "murder on the high seas" — this was not too popular, not only among the hard-bitten Tories, the military men and so forth, but also rather unpopular on our own side. I felt our role in the *Belgrano* business was not an action which I think the British Navy, looking back at it, would regard as the highest achievement in its historical annals. I thought the whole operation was a mistake and I said so in the House at the time, with precious little support. There was some CND opposition to the Falklands War because of the rumours, which went around, that nuclear weapons were being taken into the area. It was denied at the time. I remember asking questions in the House and getting denials . . .

Wade Tidbury, Royal Navy radar operator, HMS *Alacrity*, Falklands War, 1982

Getting back into Plymouth from the Falklands was completely different to how we went in: ships of all kinds sailing out to greet us, sirens blasting, and we went in slower than normal — wallowing in it, really. People were everywhere: on the quayside, on jetties, cranes. Flags everywhere. My girlfriend and family were all there cheering and waving and it was very nice to put my arms around them and give them hugs and be back home again. We pulled up at home to a big sign of welcome outside our house, neighbours rushed out and we had a big celebration party. I remember getting very drunk. And as all this was happening, they put the news on — there had been no film during the war, there had been an embargo — it went very quiet in the house and I started to reflect on what had happened and I didn't feel like the hero I was being treated as. That, in fact, something avoidable and disgusting had happened. In fact, I came back with a lot of questions . . .

I came out of the navy in 1982, I was determined I had to do things differently, but still didn't know the answers to the questions I had about the war and didn't know where to start. I had actually seen the nuclear issue come to the fore; it was something I'd been concerned with in the war. It was certainly the case that nuclear weapons were taken to the Falklands area and, when looking at international treaties, that really annoyed me. Also, it was quite unnecessary as the use of nuclear depth-bombs in a regional war would have been a case of overkill and stupid in a military as well as an ethical sense. It was also related to what was happening at Greenham, all part of the Russians and Americans playing the brinkmanship game, which seemed to have only one conclusion.

I actually went to a CND meeting during my eight weeks' leave before leaving the navy. I went really out of curiosity as they were getting a lot of publicity. Lots of things were said at that meeting and I wasn't entirely convinced by their arguments, but there were certain threads of common sense in what they were saying . . . I became very active in my local CND . . . I felt, and still do, that nuclear weapons, along with biological and chemical, are the biggest threat to human civilisation and the most sensible place to start campaigning . . .

Rev. Kenneth Greet, Methodist minister, CO, Second World War, president of the World Disarmament Campaign

At the end of that conflict came the Falklands memorial service in St Paul's Cathedral. The service was shared between the three of us: Basil Hume, Robert Runcie and myself. Runcie preached and we prayed for those who were mourning in this country *and* for those who'd lost sons in Argentina. And a group of Tory MPs went to town castigating these wet parsons for not properly celebrating the "victory". In fact it *was* a great victory for common sense because, for one, they seriously misjudged public opinion, and the support in the press for the service we'd organised was overwhelming. And I was moved by grieving parents who said, "We're so grateful you remembered the people on the other side."

Air Commodore Alastair Mackie, CND, Ex-Services CND, Generals for Peace, vice president of CND 1990 to present

There is the military branch of CND, Ex-Services CND, which is a much smaller outfit but lends what I have to describe as respectability to the peace movement. It is old soldiers; it is what you might call "short back and sides". It is intensely respectable, it is least suspect, I imagine, by members of the public who take an interest in these things, because it is most unlikely to be, as it were, "Communist permeated". So I have a high regard for that organisation.

Charles Besly, officer, Royal Berkshire Regiment, Second World War, Ex-Services CND

When we do our various parades and CND demonstrations, CND, I'm happy to say, usually put us in the front of the march; that seems to say that we count for something. And as we go along the streets of London, we often get a cheer from the bystanders, which is very warming. I think it must have some slight effect if people think: "Well, these guys have been through it and they're against nuclear weapons; perhaps there's something to be said for that point of view."

Wade Tidbury, Royal Navy radar operator, HMS *Alacrity*, Falklands War, 1982, Ex-Services CND

Ex-Services CND intrigued me. Because I had been through a war situation, I did *feel* like an ex-service person. The members are very efficient and get things done, and those who have been in the military, regardless of their views, are listened to, and that's something I've been able to put to good use in my campaigning. I'd spoken at public meetings and at rallies and got my message across. It has taught me also that a good diplomatic approach is better than all the shouting and screaming.

Commander Robert Green, Royal Navy, Ex-Services CND

I said to Ex-Services CND after I had joined that if they hadn't existed, I would have had to invent them.

William Mutimer, Ex-Services CND

War in some people's eyes is a glamorous thing. But we, as ex-servicemen who have seen the horrors of war, can demonstrate to them, "Look, this is no friendly match, this is killing, maiming, starving." We know that we can show that.

When Cruise was deployed in Britain, and Pershing in Europe, the Soviets withdrew from the Intermediate-range of Nuclear Forces (INF) treaty and Strategic Arms Reduction Talks (START). But the gradual improvement in US-Soviet relations from January 1984, which gathered pace after the appointment of Mikhail Gorbachev, led to a rapid thaw. The INF, START and Strategic Defence Initiative (SDI), or "Star Wars", talks began in January 1985. At the Geneva Summit in November 1985, the breakthrough was obvious when presidents Reagan and Gorbachev agreed that, "A nuclear war cannot be won and must never be fought." The signing of the INF Treaty in December 1987, the first nuclear-disarmament treaty, indicated that both short- and long-range missile systems would be eradicated by 1991. With the vast improvement in East-West relations, membership of CND declined from 110,000 at the beginning of 1985 to 70,000 in 1988.

The changes that occurred in the Soviet Union and Eastern and Central Europe between 1989 and 1990 initially indicated a new era of nuclear disarmament. But with the disintegration of the Soviet Union in December 1991, there were fears of nuclear technology and material being stolen or sold, with the threat of a new form of nuclear proliferation. At home, there were huge concerns within CND about Britain contravening Article VI of the NPT, with Trident, the latest submarine-launched missile, going ahead. Protests continued against nuclear-submarine bases, and work had started tracking

301

convoys transporting nuclear weapons by road to bases in Scotland. Campaigning also continued against the American "Star Wars" programme, and for the maintenance of the ABM Treaty, which had been signed in 1972. The anti-nuclear struggle was far from over.

Air Commodore Alastair Mackie, CND, Ex-Services CND, Generals for Peace, vice president of CND 1990 to present

The peace movement waxes and wanes. The Test Ban Treaty did indeed mark the end of CND's expansion. The INF even more so. We are at the moment [1988] in a phase of contraction . . . One of the disadvantages of the INF has been the leaping by the uninformed public to the conclusion that it's all over and we needn't bother any more . . . but it is a minor manifestation in a long process, a stimulus for us to do more and better to counter any reduction in numbers, to recruit more, to redouble our activities. That is exactly what CND is now doing.

Eileen Daffern (Clough), CND executive, Brighton branch

At the time of the INF Treaty, we were on Ditchling Beacon one night and we had bottles of wine and sandwiches, and all the groups in the various parts lit beacons along the south coast like the Armada. CND produced bottles of wine with an INF label. It was a great moment.

Commander Robert Green, Royal Navy, Ex-Services CND

When I went into my last job in the Royal Navy, which was Staff Intelligence Officer to the C.-in-C. of the fleet, I had my clearance renewed . . . I had earlier been a fly on the wall in the MOD as papers had come across my desk to the admiral as the naval staff debated the replacement of Polaris. I had watched the nuclear lobby go ruthlessly for Trident because of their vested interest, even if it meant terminal damage to the rest of the Royal Navy. I was particularly concerned over the lack of debate about the nuclear-weapons game at that point — at that stage, we could have withdrawn with great honour. We were not in the superpower league; we could have gracefully shown the rest of the world a way out. But we were hooked on this thing. I thought Margaret Thatcher was a nuclear junkie, and if Polaris was heroin then Trident was crack. But she was dazzled by the nuclear boys, who were not just running Polaris but doing their derring-do, Cold War games up in the Barents Sea with this gung-ho feeling, "Let's get on with it, it's a great toy." Among my concerns about lack of decommissioning and environmental implications, I was also concerned with the damage Trident would do to the rest of the fleet. The fleet had already shrunk since Polaris was introduced in 1968 due to the ruthless vested interests of what was known as the "black nuclear mafia". And what was coming next? Trident . . .

It was after Chernobyl that I began to campaign against nuclear power, but I still did not touch nuclear weapons. That was taboo. I rationalised that nuclear power and weapons could be separated, although I was beginning to realise that my fears about Trident were coming to fruition with the beginning of real defence cuts in the navy. And then, of course, you had the collapse of the Soviet Union and the main rationale for Trident went with it, but still I wouldn't speak out against it and was not pushed until the [First] Gulf War.

The Rt Hon. Tony Benn, MP, Bristol

I learned a thing which shocked me to the extent that I could hardly contain my anger. It was related to nuclear weapons, because in 1955 Eisenhower talked about Atoms for Peace. That really excited me. Having been brought up with the Bible, I thought this was the classic case of swords into ploughshares. It so happened that in the late 1960s, I [Minister of Power in 1969] was responsible for nuclear power and I went around speaking about how it was cheap, safe and peaceful. And I discovered that it wasn't cheap and it wasn't safe — Chernobyl and all that — but the thing that *really* shocked me was when I left office,

I discovered from a scientist that all the time I'd been advocating the civil use of nuclear power, our plutonium from our civil power stations was sent to America for their *weapons* programme. So every civil power station in Britain was a bomb factory for the Americans. So I lied to the public quite unknowing that it was actually part of the arms programme. That really shook me, and I learned other things too . . . I hate to say it, but I've come to the view that you couldn't believe a word you were told by the nuclear industry at all.

Rev. Kenneth Greet, Methodist minister, CO, Second World War, president of the World Disarmament Campaign

The whole nuclear-defence industry is the enemy of democracy, its policy conducted by a very tiny cabal of people, and we are assured it must remain secret in the interests of national security. That is a denial of democracy.

Professor Joseph Rotblat, civilian nuclear physicist, founder member of the Pugwash Conference

We have been talking about the elimination of nuclear weapons for a long time, but during the Cold War it was perhaps utopian, but now it has become something to be put on the agenda because the main reason for the building up of these arsenals has gone . . . What *is* the purpose of a British nuclear deterrent?

(Lord) Hugh Jenkins, founder member CND and chair 1979–81, Labour MP and minister 1964–79, House of Lords 1981–2004

We've had failure: we tried to ban the bomb and we haven't succeeded. Far from being banned, the bombs have proliferated all over the world. So we could be regarded as a total failure. On the other hand, it's true to say that compared with our position in the beginning, we're no longer regarded as loonies. People are beginning to see at last that there is sense in what we say, and the idea that nuclear weapons are something different is beginning to be widely accepted. What you could say at the moment of CND is that our impact is to keep the nuclear issue alive and to make people aware of the dangers of the world in which we live. Whether we shall get into power governments who will act in the light of those facts remains to be seen. We haven't been successful so far.

Chie Yuasa, Nagasaki, Japan

As an atomic-bomb survivor, I cannot stand the present situation that there are still many nuclear weapons in the world. It is not peaceful now, and I hope that young people will inform other people of my wish for peace and work for peace . . . I am now, in October 2008, suffering cancer . . . Article 9 of the Japanese Constitution says, "Aspiring sincerely to an international peace based on justice and order, the Japanese people for ever renounce war as a sovereign right of the nation and the threat of force as means of settling international disputes." This article is very important for all of us and I hope that we retain it, although rulers have been trying to change it so that Japan will be able to wage war again in the future.

Kazuyo Yamane, second generation atomic-bomb survivor, Kochi, Japan

Atomic-bomb survivors and their children have not only physical fear but also other kinds of fear, such as marriage and employment. Some atomic-bomb survivors were refused permission to marry because they were exposed to radiation. Even if they married, some women were told not to give birth to a baby by their parents-in-law. My son has a girlfriend, but I hesitate to mention my fear because it may lead to breaking their relationship. The atomic-bomb survivors and their children continue to live with some kind of fear. I sincerely hope that nuclear weapons will never be used again in the future. The best way to live in peace would be to abolish nuclear weapons.

CHAPTER
SIX

1945–90: Cold War (II):
Greenham Common

If by magic they [the Greenham women] disappeared one afternoon, we'd miss them because they became a part of our lives. It's hard to imagine or describe the squalor and adversity that they brought, or that their nuisance factor could become part of your life. But I guess it's like a paralysed arm; after a while you get used to it and it becomes a part of your life.

During the 1980s, peace camps were formed in Britain around the airbases in which nuclear weapons were stored. They included Molesworth, Upper Heyford, Fairford, Welford, Burtonwood and Bridgend. But it was the Greenham Common Women's Peace Camp, near Newbury in Berkshire, that became the most famous. Many of the peace women in the camp belonged to various anti-war organisations and CND, although the camp was independent of these.

It was during the Second World War that a large part of Greenham Common became an RAF station. By 1951, overruling the wishes of local people, the land was purchased by the Ministry of Defence. In 1968, it was leased to the United States and became United States Air Force (USAF) Greenham Common. Its name was later changed to RAF Greenham, although by then it was virtually a self-contained American township with all the facilities necessary for the thousands of American staff and their families living on the base. It was news of the construction of huge missile silos on the base in preparation for the arrival of 96 Cruise missiles that activated a group of women from Wales to set out, in late August 1981, on a march from Cardiff to Greenham Common, After nine days marching over the borders of Wales and across southern England, the "Women for Life on Earth" reached the gates of Greenham and called for a televised debate between themselves and a representative of the government about the nuclear issue. When their demands were ignored, the women set up a camp outside the perimeter of the base.

The numbers of women at Greenham Common varied throughout the life of the camp: women would come and go in cycles, some visiting for just a single day, others staying for days, weeks, months or years. But there was always a hardcore of women scattered around the base in camps at different gates, who lived at Greenham semi-permanently, leaving only for brief periods of respite or for supporting peace activity elsewhere. Despite enduring terrible winters and hundreds of evictions, arrests and harassment from the authorities and some local people, the camp survived the last decade of the Cold War and beyond, providing a powerful icon of women power for the 1980s and the present day.

Ann Pettitt, organiser of the march from Cardiff to Greenham Common

I had been against the evil of the nuclear-arms race and was talking to local groups showing *The War Game* [film] and trying to raise awareness about the arms race and the missiles coming in and the need to try to influence governments' thinking on nuclear deterrence. I was saying that there had to be an interruption in the process and we'd got to get ordinary people to see that *they* could be the interruption . . . Eventually we started to organise a ten days' march with stopovers in towns along the way from Cardiff to Greenham Common in Berkshire . . . Two of the women weren't keen on it being a women's march, but I wanted all women because I wanted to get it into the media, and if we had men as well, that wouldn't happen. I wanted *ordinary* women to come and got to them through women's magazines — *Honey* and *Cosmopolitan, The Guardian*, some peace magazines — and, in Wales, by word of mouth. It astonished me that for most of the women it was the first time they had done anything like this . . . They were from different backgrounds and places and were not stereotypical leftists or feminists. I estimated 50, and that number turned up.

Thalia Campbell (Childs), marcher from Cardiff to Greenham Common

We were like a little tribe moving through the countryside, all day walking and talking together, and at night sleeping on the floor, mostly in village halls . . . We were singing songs as we went along to tunes like "Pack Up Your Troubles in Your Old Kit-Bag" or "Daisy Daisy", but changing the words to things like "Pack up your missiles in your old kit-bag and leave, boys, leave!" . . . As we got nearer the base, it got more and more exciting and more and more tense. And for the last hundred yards I was doing cartwheels and walking on my hands. So it was rather like a circus. We were all in shorts, with brown legs and bare feet, and this is the way we went up to the front gate.

Ann Pettitt, organiser of the march from Cardiff to Greenham Common

As we approached Greenham, we had a big back banner, and a front banner with the tree of life painted on it. We persuaded the police to stay back so that the woman who held the banner led the procession. It was so *moving* as we came up. She had a ramrod stance and was so dignified and serious, and there were tears in our eyes as we approached the main gates . . . Women got up spontaneously and spoke straight from the gut as to why they'd done this five-day march from

311

Cardiff, and how they hoped to stop the missiles coming to Greenham. Lots of people came to see us arrive and many brought tents and food. We got a fire going. It was a lovely night and many of us camped out under the stars for that night, and the next night and the next . . . The MOD eventually gave their reaction: "It is common land, they can stay as long as they like." And we did.

Squadron Leader Ronald Meredith, RAF Commander, Greenham Common Airbase, 1980–3

Some women did chain themselves to the gate, and we had those who chained themselves to the fence in all sorts of odd places. But it didn't present a real problem: we were able to cut more chains than they were able to provide . . . It was a symbolic thing. In terms of the women's movement, you're going back to the Suffragettes — a manifestation of female protest. Fine. They have the right, but it didn't cause us any particular problem. We were quite happy to let them stay there. They did this for the cameras. On the first demonstration, they all chained themselves together and once the photographs were taken, they took them off. There was somebody organising it. I would go so far as to use the term "psychological warfare" — they were exceedingly well trained in the use of the media.

Fran Whittle (Casselden), regular visitor to Greenham Common, 1980s and '90s

Just a small group of us went up from Lewes and took some things with us. It was not organised by CND. It was *tremendously* exciting, like treading on holy ground in a way . . . We went to the main gate; we felt very awkward really because we didn't know what questions to ask, what to do, who to speak to, and we just looked around. The first women we spoke to said, "Well, you just do what you want to." . . . They always said, "We're not making the decisions, it's up to *you*" — that was difficult coming to terms with . . . We did stay the night. The fire had a kind of hierarchy: there were various chairs and you didn't know if you could sit on that chair or on that log in *their* territory. We didn't take any protection, just sat around. We didn't get to sleep, just chatted to whoever happened to be nearby . . .

Jane Dennett (Rowley), Greenham Common, 1980s and '90s

When I first went, I was quite stirred up about the whole nuclear issue . . . I'd come across various other issues: pollution in the sea, the chemical sprays on our food, and I was protesting on all sorts of fronts, and I had to decide what was the most important protest of our time, and it seemed to me that without our planet all the rest were

313

futile. So I decided to focus on the nuclear issue and I had an understanding that it was bigger than just going and standing at a gate . . . So, six months after it started, I went to live there. I decided to sell everything, including my business . . . I was convinced enough to know that's where I wanted to be and I wanted to be there full-time.

Christine Kings, CND/Greenham Common liaison woman

The first time I went there, I was looking at the women all sitting there in their scarves and gloves and wrapped up in their sleeping bags, and they were singing and happy, moving backwards and forwards in unison with the songs and it was *lovely* . . . My colleague and I came back and we were on a high. Neither of us wanted to leave. It was a new sort of demonstration, on a different scale, and it marked a new change of how we were going to demonstrate to people . . .

When I returned during the autumn of 1981 with Bruce Kent, the women were just milling about, lots of little tents everywhere. You almost felt intimidated by the lack of organisation. Bruce and I were invited to sit around the fire with the smoke burning our eyes, there were about 60 women there . . . They told us they wanted to organise a big demonstration in December and they *only* wanted women. A national demonstration! What if it went wrong? People would not distinguish between Greenham Common and CND. So from our point of view, whether the women liked it or not, we had a say in it. The women said, "No, actually you *don't* have a say in it, this is *our* demonstration, we're not doing it with CND."

Bruce could not understand why it was women only, and he represented a large section of CND. He was terribly nice about it, because he's a very nice man. But these women, who were by now living in a very muddy environment with no toilets or water, in cold tents, some had left their families, some had left college to do this, they were not going to be told by *anybody* that it had to involve men. They were finding huge power and confidence as women. Some of them had experienced CND's way of working — how the women were sent out to make the tea and the men got on the platform to do all the talking. So there was *no way* they were going to listen to a man heading CND on how they were going to organise their demonstration ... The meeting broke up with the decision that I would be the link person between CND ... From then on I went to Greenham on a fairly regular basis. I was very happy about this; I wanted to be part of them and to find ways of making the women's peace camp and CND work together, and we did.

Katrina Howse, Greenham Common, 1980s and '90s

In the first year there was a big struggle to get it women only, and there was just one gate, the main Yellow Gate, where I lived. There was lots of excitement, lots of energy, lots of issues and arguments — really, another battle going on within the camp almost constantly, as well as with the military. But there were always enough women to cope.

Charles Besly, Ex-Services CND

I was intrigued with the women's camp; it was a new dimension in anti-nuclear, anti-war, and so I was always supportive, and then [my wife] Kim decided that she wanted to support them. In the early days men were allowed there and I went on one of the early demonstrations. We weren't allowed to sit and blockade the gates, but men were allowed to tend the bonfires and act as legal advisors, and I was very impressed with these women. I thought it was a *tremendous* enterprise with enormous scope for expressing the absurdity of nuclear weapons, which, by that time, I was fully aware of. These women put up with all sorts of indignities and squalid conditions, and they were abused by the press and everyone else. I was *immensely* proud of Kim, and every time she set off in the car, I loaded the back up with firewood, or eggs or vegetables, whatever we happened to have. That's all I could do because it was a women's effort.

Colonel Jarrett McGehee, USAF Commander, Greenham Common Airbase, 1983–6

The women were of all ages and there seemed to be three classes of them. One class consisted of the real anarchists — against everything. Another class were women who really believed in what they were doing, and the third class, they were, you know the sort, "I just don't have anything else in my life, this gives me the camaraderie and bonding I need in my life because I don't have anything else going for me." They didn't seem to mingle with each other and lived at different gates around the perimeter . . .

Jane Dennett (Rowley), Greenham Common, 1980s and '90s

The biggest trauma was regarding my son Peter. He was 18 at the time and in college in Winchester and he came to see Mum. The things the radical feminists said to him were *dreadful*: "Have you come to get your bottle filled?" "Why don't you leave your mother alone?" "It's because of *your* sex that we're in this situation." But he kept coming and managed to talk and make friends with the women, even some of the radical feminists. But he could have been destroyed by it. The hatred was

317

terrible. It was almost as obscene as the weapons. How *can* women hate men so much?

Fran Whittle (Casselden), regular visitor to Greenham Common, 1980s and '90s

I used to think about the women-only aspect a lot when I was there. I never felt entirely comfortable with it . . . I remember at "Embrace the Base" there were one or two men and they had a very difficult time . . . On other occasions, when we were sitting down or attempting to get into the base, then it was right that it was women only. I've been to many demonstrations where men were present and I knew that the ambience was totally different when men were there . . . We were just as strong as men and held our decisions as strongly . . . But I know when I've been on mixed demonstrations it breaks more quickly. The men are more "have a go" more quickly. At Greenham there was more patience, more being prepared to sit it out for longer.

Wing Commander Mick Marsh, RAF Commander, Greenham Common Airbase, 1983–6

It was more difficult dealing with women rather than men in some ways. Obviously, if you've got to physically deal with several hundred people coming at you, you prefer them to be women

318

because not many will use their weight and muscle, although those who did fight fought quite dirty. The difficulty is in the *handling* of them. They operate in double standards and I can't blame them for that. Very often during the demonstrations they'd sit at the gate and stop the traffic coming in. We had large concrete posts which held up the gates, about eighteen inches square, and on one occasion after a demonstration a couple of females climbed up on these and sat there. They were invited to move and refused. And when I asked one of the RAF chaps to remove her, there was an immediate scream from about thirty or forty women, "Don't *touch* her, she may be pregnant." Very difficult . . . we needed to be careful about where you touched them. There would be an immediate scream, and when you've got RAF regiment people who have come from Northern Ireland, where they might have been faced with weapons — difficult. They resented the fact that they had to be there, living in tents, eating from a field kitchen, and not good conditions — they might have welcomed the chance of a good punch-up. There were one or two incidents, but I never had to charge anyone. I think they might on occasions have responded to verbal abuse. There comes a time when you feel you want to respond. If you're actually on the fence for eight hours in darkness and you get things shouted at you, after a while you perhaps respond. I used to get verbal abuse as I went around the perimeter; I was called all sorts of names, OK. But I had to walk away from it; I wasn't too sure there wasn't a tape recorder going to record my reaction. But it was very difficult for young RAF chaps, geared to defend their lives and not used to that kind of thing.

Rev. Kenneth Greet, Methodist minister, CO, Second World War, president of the World Disarmament Campaign,

Motoring in that part of the country, I did go to visit them. I took a little gift of money to sustain their work and was received very warmly indeed by them. In appearance they were a somewhat ragtag collection of women.

William Mutimer, Ex-Services CND

About that time I was a member of Epsom and Ewell CND, and several of the ladies wanted to go but had no transport. So I took them with another chap. I had great sympathy for them. I felt they were absolutely wonderful. I saw in the local paper some years ago that one of the Kingston councillors had written, "My son says they are the green and common women." I wrote back and said, "That's typical Tory rudeness. These women are *courageous* and they are doing it for a principle."

Peter Sharp, CO, Second World War

I never went to Greenham Common Peace Camp; my wife, Joyce, went with the older girls. She wanted to show her concern for children from other countries as well as her own. She did cut-outs of each of our six children and hung them around the base. She chose a name, for example, "Sally", our daughter, with the name of, say, a child from Czechoslovakia on the same cut-out figure. The idea being: "I'm not just here for myself, but for my children and for children in other countries." That was her way of thinking . . . I stayed behind and looked after the smaller ones and the farm. I didn't mind that men weren't accepted there. For me, anything that women do as a group — good luck to them! I've always thought the most important person in a family is the mother. I believe that more women are opposed to war than men. Often men, like me, who are opposed to war are accused, "Oh, you're behaving like the women." But if you think like I do, why not?

Katrina Howse, Greenham Common, 1980s and '90s

Evictions swept *everything* away. The first big one was in September 1982, when the caravans were all swept away, when we were back to living under plastic. There were *hundreds* of police there. After that, the women started building benders and got quite cosy in them. The big eviction of 1983 swept the benders away. The most committed women stayed on, others got put off, but support did come in. The major eviction of 1984 was, on paper, "due to the road widening scheme". But the consultative document that the police, the Ministry of Defence and all the official bodies produced together was headed "The Final Solution to the Problem of the Greenham Common Women". After that, we couldn't even put a tent up for ten weeks! But a group of us came back after that eviction and reclaimed [part] of the old campsite. Just six women in a very small space for ten weeks. We couldn't put tents up; we had constant police presence. They'd stand over us while we slept, and we couldn't even cook. They had fire extinguishers and put out our fires . . . We stuck it out . . . We had no media attention for ten weeks, then it was, "Oh, you've come back!" By 1984, there were several evictions a week. Blue, Orange and Violet gates were set up by then, and in the winter of 1984 there were five evictions a day.

Ann Pettitt, Greenham Common, 1980s

"Embrace the Base" event [12 December 1982] was the best day of my life. I knew that lots of women would come, but as I travelled from Wales it seemed as if the *whole* of the West Country was on the move — the motorway was absolutely *full* of coaches of women waving the colours of the Suffragettes, who had inspired us. Thirty thousand turned up and it was so *extraordinary*, this optimistic spirit of embracing, overwhelming the base. You also brought a little gift which symbolised how important life was to you — you really *embraced* the base and left your gift. There were so many traditional women's things, which showed how *ordinary* women were inspired. The whole of the fence was covered with these statements of what meant most to them: photographs, nappies, flowers; one woman left her wedding dress pinned on the wire, just pinned it up and left. A whole dinner service was clipped to the fence — sacrificed. The women even embroidered the fence — using their art in a subversive way. The feminists were very sniffy about it. I think this showed how feminism had lost touch with ordinary women. Embrace the Base became an icon of Greenham. From that day, 90 per cent of the positive things Greenham achieved and inspired were set up. From then on, it became a movement that inspired women internationally.

Fran Whittle (Casselden), regular visitor to Greenham Common, 1980s and '90s

Some people expressed themselves through their children — there were photographs, cut-outs of their family put up against the fence. They said:

"These are my family," "These are my precious things." There were thousands of ribbons and things of beauty. Lots of poems, lots of writing, *beautiful* banners. Some people had made things at home and brought them there, others had constructed them on the site. So *many*. The fence went around canyons and rocky bits, across streams, it wasn't just flat all the way round, so it was very difficult to stand in some places. We had two coaches from Lewes, about 70 women, from teenagers to some 80 year olds . . . Even though two-thirds of those women never went there again, I think that it would always be a kind of reference point for them . . . I went back there recently [1994] by myself; you could still see tiny traces of little ribbons . . .

Sarah Hipperson (Hanlon), Greenham Common, 1980s and '90s

We were singing and we started keening as we embraced the base. This seemed to be some kind of release that you wouldn't do in your own home, but out in the open, against the fence with this crowd of women, it was natural. Women started keening nervously at the start, but by the time it got round the base, it was a *horrendous* sound, it came from the abdomen and out through the top of the head. There was a sort of abandonment that went with it . . . I was very touched, it was very emotional . . . Inside the base, I think they knew then that they were on to something that was well beyond their ken. That was December 1982, and I believe that's what primed them into using the law a bit stronger, why they started thinking in terms of injuncting women, looking at the land the women were on, looking at the laws, the by-laws that governed the land, putting the lawyers to task . . .

Kim Besly, Greenham Common, 1980s and '90s

Women came from Scotland, Wales, from all over the country and from abroad. There were women from Holland, Denmark, Sweden, Germany, Australia and New Zealand, Canada and the United States. They came from all over the world to take part in embracing the base because they saw how it had sparked a vision of what life *could* be like, *hoped* it would be like . . .

Fran Whittle (Casselden), regular visitor to Greenham Common, 1980s and '90s

The local people who opposed the camp went and pulled a lot of the things off. I often think: "What did they *think* when they pulled off these photographs, these dolls?" You just hoped that maybe it got through to them.

Joanna Englekamp (Wallis), Greenham Common, 1980s

The culture of Greenham had strands from all different directions: there was feminism and other forms of fighting oppression, and there was pacifism and politics. And all that tempered and expressed through this *tremendous* women's creativity, which took all forms. It was an *explosion* of creativity, which was in such stark contrast to the other side of the fence.

Sheila Gow, RAF and USAF secretary, Greenham Common, 1952–91

In December 1982, when 30,000 linked arms around the base, I was taking my mother to hospital and I accidentally hit one of the women. It was very unpleasant because a whole crowd of them came and sat on the bonnet of the car and banged the roof, and dear old Mum didn't make things any better because she told them she'd been through two world wars and believed in defence; they tried to pull her out of the car. So that wasn't very nice, and I had one or two confrontations as I was trying to leave the base where I worked.

Lady Olga Maitland, founder of Families for Defence (FFD)

I had been witnessing, like many people, demonstrations around Greenham Common, and what particularly tipped the balance and the thought that something *must* be done was when I saw the linking of 30,000 hands around Greenham. If you bear in mind that it is a base with a nine-mile perimeter, it was a *colossal* exercise, of such magnitude that I thought: "How is it that there's been no response?" Also it made me realise that the whole anti-nuclear movement was very well organised and *very* powerful.

Sheila Gow, RAF and USAF secretary, Greenham Common, 1952–91

When they had this December thing [Embrace the Base], there were two of them at the bottom of the garden, jeans down. I went out and protested and they were very nasty. And we had cars parked outside here, one of my neighbours' sons went out and let all their tyres down, which was a stupid thing to do because we couldn't get rid of them for a while.

Fran Whittle (Casselden), regular visitor to Greenham Common 1980s and '90s

I did have a thing with a local dog which nearly bit me up the bum once when I was having a pee, but it was dark and late at night and on the verge outside the camp, I wasn't on anyone's property . . . It's sad that it [going to the loo] occupies your mind so much: you're regulating how much you're drinking and worrying about it all the time because you care about the environment, you know it's something the locals don't like and you don't like it too, but what can you *do*? On the Violet Gate on Burybank Road they did have quite a nice little toilet area set up and they were digging proper lavs. On the big demonstration by Orange Gate, they had an *excellent* lav system set up which had been organised by somebody, a good old earth-and-shovel method, which is really the best. But again you very quickly divided into those women who were prepared to do that kind of work and those who weren't.

Christopher Austin, riding-school owner, near Greenham Common, 1980s

The camps themselves are very messy, an eyesore. There is a *huge* amount of rubbish. One reason why the local authority evicts the women periodically is to collect the rubbish. They say to the peace women: "Right, collect all your belongings and scarper," and they do, they go out on to the highway and whatever they leave behind the council takes away. So there is some attempt to keep it clean. But there are no proper ablutions, no proper sanitation. After a major demonstration, the numbers swell and the effects on the common in terms of sanitation were terrific — you were literally stepping in it wherever you went. Also, the firewood belongs to the commoners and the peace women take it and still have fires on the common on regular occasions, which is against the by-laws. But the peace women are against the by-laws on a number of counts and are effectively immune from them, because nobody enforces them against them . . . Also, parts of the common are taken from the use of the locals once peace people stop there. They don't like to walk their dogs because they have to run the gauntlet of the peace camp. The perimeter fence is often in disrepair because they've cut it and, of course, the camps are unsightly. There were one or two complaints about damage to property and one or two wooden fences were pulled down for firewood; they were mainly by people whose houses were close to the peace camps. These find the value of their homes severely restricted because of being so close, and this even in a heightened house market in the mid to late 1980s!

Jane Dennett (Rowley), Greenham Common, 1980s and '90s

Litter was my great burden. I was never without a black litter-bag in my hand going around the base. This was what was levelled at us the whole time: we were dirty, we left litter, we used their gardens or land as lavatories. We were very careful about using cesspits at different parts of the camp and each woman was aware that we were our own worst enemies if we didn't use them . . . I went on the Jimmy Young [radio] show and he was taunting us as to being a menace to the Newbury people, he said that we used their gardens as lavatories, and I said, "We are *very* proud of our shit-pits!"

Brian Baldwin, gardener, Greenham Common, 1986–92

It was our responsibility to keep the grass cut between the fence and the road, and of course, being common land, all sorts of gorse and heather was there, also quite a lot of sucker growths and seedling trees had grown up. We had to cut them down. Two or three of us went out to do this. The women came out — *terrible* — and they stopped us from proceeding, just stood there. In the end, the boss came along and said, "We've got to do it," and we said, "But we can't get past them." So in the end we had to have MOD police protection; they held the women back while we got these sucklings, two or three feet high, down. They just stood there; we couldn't touch them; they'd have you up for assault.

Jane Dennett (Rowley), Greenham Common, 1980s and '90s

Sarah Green was an amazing woman. She had Jay in the bushes. I did midwifery so we were able to have a natural birth, in a bender there. She called him Jay after the birds.

Fran Whittle (Casselden), regular visitor to Greenham Common, 1980s and '90s

There were two sides to the lack of organisation there. Everyone went to Greenham, with their own personal luggage, and they had to deal with the situation there, bringing with them their own feelings and talents. And I think the women who stayed there — although that was an ever-changing situation — who had been there longer, they had knowledge and information maybe that you didn't have . . . But you sometimes felt belittled by them. But to me the continual circulation of newcomers to the camp was its *lifeblood*. Even people who only went for a day helped spread this continual interest in it, and when they made a decision to go, that was *monumental* for them, and throughout their lives it was going to be very important. Only a few could physically live there, keep that up for a

331

very long time, and yet, if there's any definition of a Greenham Woman, anyone who goes and stays there for five minutes is one ... Of course those who lived there permanently were the core, they provided the anchor, but it was the sheer numbers across the whole country that made the difference in the end.

Katrina Howse, Greenham Common, 1980s and '90s

Some women, like Sarah Hipperson, have lived here for years; all have criminal records as long as your arm. We have to go through a lot of fears in ourselves in order to carry on. But there aren't brownie points for so many years. None of us who have lived here full-time are in a hierarchical position. If anything, the longer the time the more the responsibility, but not more power.

Sarah Hipperson (Hanlon), Greenham Common, 1980s and '90s

We owe a great debt of gratitude to different women who came there at different times: the pioneer qualities of the women who marched from Cardiff to Greenham, and another smaller group who were the lesbian women, they developed an aspect of Greenham — the courage they showed to come out and say they were lesbian was a tremendous boost to everything that followed ... We were neither saints nor sinners, but when people refer to these "bloody women", it indicated exactly what *troublesome* people we were. We were troublesome to all sorts of groupings: the military, the Ministry of Defence, the Thames Valley Police, to the people of Newbury . . . There was a little booklet called *At Least Cruise is Clean*. I've got a copy and it is quite revealing who the enemies were in Newbury: the Chamber of Commerce, the construction people and the shopkeepers. There were notices in every pub, "Refuse to serve [Greenham] women", and it was extended to shops and other places. I remember once we were refused service by Tesco on the High Road. The manager was called as the women put their groceries down; he said, "I'm sorry I can't serve you." The women said "Why?" He said, "Because you've got dysentery up there." This woman said, "It's not true." He said, "I don't care, I'm not serving you." So she said to the other woman, "Let's go and touch everything in this store, particularly the meat." Immediately he said, "No, don't do that, you can have them."

Katrina Howse, Greenham Common, 1980s and '90s

To cope with such prejudice, we always make sure that when we go into Newbury we look our best. Obviously those who are prejudiced against us will always be so, however we look. But facing

333

prejudiced people, it's very important for you not to feel dirty; this can be difficult with the mud. I feel that's very important, so if you do meet prejudice there you meet it because they are *prejudiced* people, full stop.

Ann Marsh, wife of Mick Marsh, RAF Commander, Greenham Common Airbase, 1983–6

I could see both sides . . . We used to have long, involved discussions with the Americans. One or two of the wives had given up high-prestige jobs to be with their husbands because they liked England so much. These were deep-thinking, highly qualified women, not the sort you see in the soaps and movies, and they couldn't understand why the women would be moved by the bailiffs one day and back they'd come, not the next *day*, but the next *hour*. They had also heard what the women did when they got in the base . . . So many would say, "They wouldn't get away with it in the States . . ." And I would point out that there was a peace camp outside the White House, "Come *on*, let's be fair about this." I was accused on one occasion of siding with the women. I was invited to a coffee morning and there were two dozen ladies in that house. I was introduced and they turned on me like a ton of bricks, I had questions from all directions . . . They asked why were they *allowed* to be there. I said because it was a free country, that my father was in the last war, that the women are doing what they think is right to protect their children, my children, *your* children, our grandchildren.

Wing Commander Mick Marsh, RAF Commander, Greenham Common Airbase, 1983–6

We did have an offer from a local farmer to spray the women outside the base with chicken manure, which I said had to be refused . . . During one demonstration, it was claimed that the Paras had hit the women with cattle prods and that all sorts of injuries had occurred. My reaction to the press was, "Have you contacted the local hospitals and doctors and found out what injuries were caused?" They did, and no doctor or hospital locally had anything.

Katrina Howse, Greenham Common, 1980s and '90s

I was sitting with a group of women and we had maggots thrown at our heads, which was horrific. A few weeks later they hatched out and, although we had tried to clear them up, we had a plague of flies — almost a bit of biological warfare, isn't it? Another time I was sprayed with green dye. This man came up with a washing-up bottle, I thought at first it could be acid. There were lots of vigilante attacks in the summer of '83. But as recently as February this year [1992], our caravan window was broken. We were attacked by six young men who threw rocks at the two of us there at the time. Most of them were under seventeen, they would have been about seven or eight when the camp was set up . . . We got them arrested, but they were never charged.

Group Captain Stanley Keyte, RAF Commander, Greenham Common Airbase, 1987–9

The Americans would depend on me to keep them out of trouble. From time to time, it was necessary to be quite firm with their troops and prevent them from putting themselves in the wrong. There were cultural differences: a wish on their part to take direct action, to go out there and get the women by the scruff of the neck and eject them when they got into the base . . .

Christopher Austin, riding-school owner, near Greenham Common, 1980s

RAGE — Ratepayers Against Greenham Encampment — was started by a local group who were frustrated at the fact that, in their opinion, the local council was not doing enough as the owner of Greenham Common to get rid of the peace women. It was felt that a lot of public money was going into the peace camp in terms of refuse disposal, supplying free water, social-security benefits, and that something should be done. It was a question of lobbying your district councillors and writing letters to people, this sort of thing rather than any form of direct action. Another group, GWO — Greenham Women Out — was instigated by a retired matron or sister of a Newbury hospital. She was fairly well known for her right-wing views, but was concerned that very young children were there, not having proper housing and sanitation . . . It has to be said that a lot of the local people were in the habit of swearing abuse at the peace women. It was nothing for the local yobs in the early days to wind their car windows down and shout obscenities . . . and there was a certain amount of sport among local yobs baiting the peace women after the pub on a Friday night, "we'll sort them out" sort of thing.

Group Captain Stanley Keyte, RAF Commander, Greenham Common Airbase, 1987–9

Vigilante action happened occasionally. It was difficult because getting the full facts was difficult. Sometimes it would seem like something that had been made up to cause trouble, but it certainly wasn't something that was untrue by any means . . . When these things were investigated by the police, there *was* a basis to them.

337

Jane Dennett (Rowley), Greenham Common, 1980s and '90s

One of my main contributions to Greenham was getting hold of the bolt cutters. Contrary to popular belief, the razor wire they had around the silos is easier to deal with than the other, but of course you have to wear gloves . . . [We proved] if women can do it, then the IRA or other terrorists can do it. So that was the action: to get to the silos and dance on them. We looked like paper cut-out dolls, with police, dogs and sirens going, and we just went on dancing and singing on top . . . we were there for a good quarter of an hour.

Squadron Leader Ronald Meredith, RAF Commander, Greenham Common Airbase, 1980–3

They made it to one of the construction sites, I'm not talking about defending a nuclear-weapons facility, it was really a building site they set up on top of; they were photographed and danced around a bit and waited until some camera people turned up, having more photographs taken. We arrested a couple of them and the rest were allowed to walk out. That particular incursion was the one that went out on all the international media — these women poncing around the top of the place they called a "silo" — much more emotive than a sort of reinforced garage and storage chamber. It was not a silo: there were no missiles on the base; they were not even scheduled in then.

Kim Besly, Greenham Common, 1980s and '90s

Thirty-nine women danced on top of the silos — it was a magical moment to see them dance on the top, waving their arms and singing. Just establishing that there was life on top of the death of the silos.

Jane Dennett (Rowley), Greenham Common, 1980s and '90s

Another time we painted the Blackbird, the stealth bomber, the most unbelievable secret weapon of the Americans to go all over Russia photographing, and it had a membrane instead of a skin, and it couldn't be picked out by the Russian radar. We had an airshow at Newbury and the Americans wanted to show it off. I knew Lady Bader; she came down for fundraising for the Cheshire Homes and asked me not to take any action that day. I persuaded the women not to undertake any action that day, but nothing was promised about that night! So we went in and painted this stealth bomber. This was the only action when we were paid *not* to go to court — well, it was their secret weapon and it had been left unguarded! We had no idea what it was at the time.

Joanna Englekamp (Wallis), Greenham Common, 1980s

The security was pathetic. We didn't have any designs on the active weapons themselves, but if someone had wanted to for terrorist purposes, it would not have been difficult, although they would have had us to argue with! But women went where they wanted.

Christopher Austin, riding-school owner, near Greenham Common, 1980s

What you've effectively got is a huge common with the heart of it as the airbase, but with a great ribbon of common land all around the airbase. So to try to police that was a huge challenge.

Wing Commander Mick Marsh, RAF Commander, Greenham Common Airbase, 1983–6

I don't think the men would have performed *this* incident. On one Hiroshima or Nagasaki day, the women, who were commemorating the dropping of the bomb, ran onto the base. First of all they had no clothes on; secondly they had coated themselves with a mixture of coal ash and rancid butter. They ran on and sat down. They were taken away by the civil police to be charged with indecent exposure. The civil police asked us to hold them and I sent across an RAF coach to hold them in one place. And they actually then urinated in the coach, and threw excrement around. That's the sort of thing that occasionally happened. So we produced an old coach with no seats in it and the driver was protected in a separate compartment. We also blackened out all the windows. They never repeated that. It rankles to this day. I don't think they did the cause of femininity any favours whatsoever.

Sarah Hipperson (Hanlon), Greenham Common, 1980s and '90s

On the 31st May [1983], the technicians arrived from the US. They were specially trained men. That was a very gruesome day: it was announced that they were coming, and we all dressed in black and we had burnt ashes of pictures and symbolic things and we went in keening. We forced our way in and we sprayed ash around all over the place. It was *mourning*, a penitential thing really, and it was incredibly powerful. I was injured there for the first time by an MOD policeman. He took the top of my arms and pressed his fingers in a way that I couldn't lift my arm for ages. But I stayed with it and we were corralled into a space, and another one came up and thumped me right in the back, a

341

huge thump, I just sort of collapsed. I was definitely targeted, now why would they target somebody like me? I come from the same world as they come from. I'm a straight woman, I've got five children; they can't dismiss me in the same way they could dismiss young Pinkie. They knew that I've been a magistrate and that I am a Christian, I was being treated in a way that was supposed to make me run to the hills . . . I was taken down to Newbury and I was the source of a complaint there. I was photographed and really you wouldn't have recognised me. I looked as if I'd gone a few rounds in a boxing ring. I was terribly bruised . . . I was injured another time too, in 1984, when a convoy was coming out and I was up in a tree with others throwing eggs filled with paint at the convoy to mark it so that people seeing it going by knew it was the Cruise-missile convoy from Greenham Common. I was hanging on to this tree and was grabbed and pushed back into space into a gully, about twelve feet, and I narrowly missed a block of concrete. I couldn't move my legs and had to be winched up by the fire brigade; then they put me on a stretcher and took me to the Royal Berkshire Hospital. I retreated for a week, then got on my bike and went back down there again.

Jane Dennett (Rowley), Greenham Common, 1980s and '90s

When they used horses, women learnt that if you stood under their heads or laid down, no horse would step on a human body.

Katrina Howse, Greenham Common, 1980s and '90s

When Helen Thomas was killed, it didn't happen on a convoy, at a convoy deployment, it happened when Helen was going to cross the road at 1p.m., a Saturday afternoon, a bright, clear day, and she was going to post two letters in the postbox at Yellow Gate. It was such an enormous *shock*. She was in a safe area waiting for a police horsebox to pass. It was travelling down to Chichester, not going into the base. But the fact that it was a police horsebox we felt very relevant. There were three witnesses, including a policeman, at the gate. They all saw her standing several feet off the main road. The policeman saw the horsebox pass by her, then he saw her wobble back and forward and then go under the horsebox. It seemed so obvious that the horsebox had come off the road and hit Helen with the wing mirror — they're like iron bars on those horseboxes . . . It was the head injuries that killed her after she'd been hit by the mirror, it wasn't the multiple injuries caused by falling under the horsebox that caused her death . . . In court, we

343

heard the driver say that she'd been standing in the middle of the road; we knew from three witnesses that this was a lie ... They found witnesses to confirm that she was in the middle of the road. The evidence of the other three witnesses [was] dismissed. After one and a half hours, the jury recorded "accidental death". We always knew that there was no justice in this country and they set people up to cover up. But we never expected it with Helen being killed ...

Jane Dennett (Rowley), Greenham Common, 1980s and '90s

After my arrest, when I knew I was going to prison, one of the Newbury police said, "You're not like these others." What he meant was that I was older, married, had been in a respectable business. I said, "I'm *more* like these than they are!" He said, "We could get you off if you give us the name of the leaders." I laughed and said, "There are no leaders, we're all in it together, we are people who have given up everything to make a statement." I went to prison, Holloway.

Joanna Englekamp (Wallis), Greenham Common, 1980s

My first arrest and experience in a prison cell was in Cardiff [after a peace action]. I was very proud of the fact that I was in prison because I'd had this legacy from my grandfather [CO Corder Catchpool], who had spent the First World War in prison and was the hero of the family.

Katrina Howse, Greenham Common, 1980s and '90s

I have been to prison sixteen times, one time for six months. The first was November 1982, when I was arrested for obstruction and got two weeks; that was in Drake Hall, Staffordshire . . . It was a terrible shock going through the barrier, into another world: it's *you*, in *prison!* . . . The percentage of women who've done anything that can be construed as "bad" is tiny. Even those doing life are those who've been battered by husbands and boyfriends and who have turned against them in self-defence. You really have to re-evaluate. You realise that *any* kind of woman can end up in prison. But they're "all bad, all mad, all sad" — in the way they're presented. A very small percentage are really dangerous. I did four months in Bullwood Hall in Essex, and I really felt good about my connection with the women there, felt very solid, very part of the community. But it was a total shock getting up the first morning and looking at this white-tiled washing area and all these women cleaning their teeth. I felt: "Oh God! I'm in prison!" It *seeps* into you. Four months is not long, but, oh, that's your *life*. I've been in

Holloway many, many times, always overcrowded with hundreds of women stuck together . . .

Sarah Hipperson (Hanlon), Greenham Common, 1980s and '90s

I was arrested after a Hiroshima Day protest and put in custody for a month in Holloway. I fasted for 31 days, no food, just water, and that's when I lost quite a bit of weight. At the start of it I had terrible headaches, your body is using the sugar and stuff that is in your body, then you start to feed on yourself, your store. I got out just in time . . .

Group Captain Stanley Keyte, RAF Commander, Greenham Common Airbase, 1987–9

I shall never forget the first time I went to court. I was subpoenaed as a witness by the women. There were 11 defenders and they all said they wanted me there as a witness. I hadn't done this before, so obviously I tried to prepare myself for it, but it was very difficult. When I got to the court, all 11 had been charged with trespass and criminal damage. The basis of their defence was that they had got my permission to damage the fence, and each one took the opportunity of cross-examining me, and that is where all their experience came into play. I was the innocent beginner and they were hardened appearers in court. They were questioning me on things that weren't well known to me. They were bringing up the Hague Conventions, certainly trying to embarrass me and trying to trap me into saying something that certainly wouldn't get them off, but it might be a moral victory for them. It was quite a chastening experience . . .

Sarah Hipperson (Hanlon), Greenham Common, 1980s and '90s

I learned some of the non-violence techniques, which were to sit down and retreat in a non-violent way, just go limp and lie there and don't cooperate, and you make them move you in some way. The essence of it is that you shouldn't have any violent thing going on between you and those moving you. And that's very, *very* difficult. I had to prepare myself before going into non-violent action, most women did. It's a strange feeling, almost like an out-of-body experience; you're going into a higher level of consciousness. So you can ignore to some extent the pain you're suffering, and also ignore the comments, nasty things like being nothing but slags . . . I can remember one time seeing a woman pick up a stone, and about four women rushed round her and said, "We don't do it that way, we're beaten if we do." And I felt: "We can stay here for ever providing we're non-violent, we can cope with evictions, with having our tents taken away, with sleeping outside without any cover, with the bailiffs coming and taking away our possessions, we can cope with being arrested and put in cells and going to court and going to prison, but we can only cope with this because of our non-violence." Non-violence was the ultimate.

Group Captain Stanley Keyte, RAF Commander, Greenham Common Airbase, 1987–9

To say that they were non-violent doesn't quite tell the story . . . Sometimes they would mock the young chaps, making them feel that they were cowards or not proper men . . . The taunting angle they used to their advantage. I think if there had been a mixed camp, there would have been the danger of some physical aspect, which there never was except in the business of restraint. Their protest *was* non-violent — they didn't hurt an individual; they would cause damage, painting things, damaging the fence — but even under those circumstances, heated exchanges could occur and they could be angry being arrested, agitated. They could be quite vicious in their language and demeanour. It could be quite intimidating for someone having to face some of them and arrest them.

Fran Whittle (Casselden), regular visitor to Greenham Common, 1980s and '90s

Everywhere where there are large groups of people, some will do things that you don't agree with . . . I don't think shouting is the thing I like to do anyway . . . I think the silent marching we did with CND was much more effective than shouting . . .

Christine Kings, CND/Greenham Common liaison woman

The arrival of Cruise in November 1983 was not only a big issue for Greenham; it was a big issue for CND. The media coverage was substantial and gave lots of opportunities for intellectuals in the peace movement to write articles and make the point. It gave more of a boost to the women because the missiles were there. But it hardened attitudes much more against them from those who thought we should be America's friends.

Kim Besly, Greenham Common, 1980s and '90s

About mid-'84, all this heavy surveillance, which had started from the time of the arrival of Cruise, went away, and the personnel left migrated to the gates or the "goon boxes" as we called them [guard boxes on stilts] for their surveillance . . . The

349

missiles were still there, and it was just after that that women started reporting that there were certain places around the base where they felt really ill . . . Some said that all energy just drained out from their feet, they could hardly move; others experienced headaches, neck ache, chest ache, accentuated heart beat; some felt their eyes were being pulled out, others had pain in their ears — an enormous variety of effects. Gradually one or two began to say, "The surveillance has gone away, the missiles are still there, they have to be using something else to keep us out — what is it?" That's when I became involved in correlating the investigation into, for want of a better word, zapping.

Sarah Hipperson (Hanlon), Greenham Common, 1980s and '90s

Knowing that I had poured blood over the pillars at the Ministry of Defence, the women approached me and asked if I would do a ritual for them. I said, "Well, I could do an exorcism," so we had a nurse visiting, and she took blood from women, we also burnt some things, and I went home to get some baptismal candles of my children . . . What was interesting was that as soon as I started doing the ritual, the RAF troops in there at the time, and the MOD police, all moved back into a circle and allowed it to happen. This was inside the base, near the silos. One of the MOD was so disturbed by it, he took the candle and broke it. He was ashen-faced; although they wouldn't have understood the Christian element of the exorcism, they would have latched on to the ritual element of it and seen it as witchcraft, and I think they were completely freaked out by it. The ritual sent the darkness out of the base, and the blood represented the loss of life, the spilling of blood, and the women wanted to spill their blood as a counteractive influence; the ashes represented the planet in the way that we were all ashes to ashes, dust to dust, fragile creatures. And this nuclear exercise, this planned threat which came under the policy of Mutually Assured Destruction, was likely to be responsible for the destruction of the planet. When it was finished, I had this feeling that we had cleansed it in some way, even though the missiles were in there, that the missiles wouldn't be fired and would go away.

Wing Commander Mick Marsh, RAF Commander, Greenham Common Airbase, 1983–6

I don't think the weapons were at any stage in any danger. The six shelters, sometimes referred to as the "silos", were very solidly constructed, with thirty-ton doors on each. You surrounded these with a secure fence, alarms, a sterile area, then another fence, alarms, and the guard force outside that. Then, when the incursions started to be a real menace, we surrounded the entire area with two sets of wire in which gaps were left for patrolling with dogs. If they got over the perimeter fence, they'd be faced with these rolls of barbed wire. It was floodlit so you could see them coming and had time to react, and get them to leave or to pick them up. Our radios would get extra people out behind them. So never, in my opinion, was there any risk.

Kim Besly, Greenham Common, 1980s and '90s

We didn't know what this zapping was; we thought it might be electronic and so we set about finding out . . . We realised it could be a side-effect of the proliferation of the communications equipment in the base, so we went to other bases with our instruments and we didn't find anything like the increase in the electromagnetic-field strength that we found at Greenham. We found the women's menstrual cycles were all over the place, adding to which there were older women who had finished the menopause who started bleeding again, and there were young women who had haemorrhaged inexplicably, and there were a number of miscarriages . . . and there was also a range of curious behavioural responses; sometimes the women were overcome with panic and a cold fear — the effects were legion and nobody wanted to believe it, and even the people who might have helped turned their backs on us.

Group Captain Stanley Keyte, RAF Commander, Greenham Common Airbase, 1987–9

I think they really did believe it: they put foil on themselves and a sort of biscuit tin on their heads as a form of protection. It was difficult to prove that it wasn't true. But there was never any basis to it . . . There were lots of aerials on the base, and radios, and the defences around the missiles themselves, so perhaps they drew their conclusions from that.

Katrina Howse, Greenham Common, 1980s and '90s

Zapping really was a huge diversion and an ideal thing for the state: the fear it created put women off from Greenham. They were playing into the state's hands.

Christine Kings, CND/Greenham Common liaison woman

After the missiles had arrived, they wanted to do another big women's event; it was a kind of "Embrace the Base" format whereby women would come from all over the country and they would attach mirrors to the fence so that when you looked at the base you saw all the green trees, the positive things of our world. It would be like getting rid of this horrible barbed wire and

353

reflecting the normal everyday things that we value ... There were a lot of coaches. It was an interesting and lovely idea. But the big demonstration, Embrace the Base, one year earlier — that was the one people will remember. On a personal level, this one wasn't as enjoyable for me; there was the beginning of some tensions in the discussions which had brought this event about, partly to do with the different groups that had attached themselves to Greenham. I don't mean that in a negative way; lots of women's groups wanted to be there. The gates had their own identities and, fair to say, their own politics, and although I wasn't part of that, I detected disagreements about how things could be run: about going into the base, whether more dramatic action should be taken. Also, people wanted to link Greenham with other issues — always a debate on this in the peace movement.

Wing Commander Mick Marsh, RAF Commander, Greenham Common Airbase, 1983–6

During a major demonstration, people would start arriving a few days earlier, and anyone on the outside looking in got a pretty good idea of what was going to happen, and so if you have ladies who were friendly to those inside the base, a word could be got back inside that something was going to happen at twelve o'clock ... The police had means of finding out things, and prior to the demonstrations we'd have meetings with them to plan a reaction. We were not often surprised at what happened.

Katrina Howse, Greenham Common, 1980s and '90s

It was in October 1984 that the first Cruise-missile convoy came out . . . That started action against the convoys and marked a whole new stage. A lot of women at Yellow Gate left at that point, but the group of us left started to develop night-watches every night . . . Then, when they started coming out on a regular basis, we saw what we were up against. We were determined to interrupt, to disrupt it . . . Later they brought out 32 missiles regularly. Two convoys came out, so that was over forty-five support vehicles and eight launchers and four control vehicles. We had to learn a lot about the system and about Salisbury Plain [where the practice occurred]. In 1984/85 we had to go by bus to hunt the convoy and then hunt them over a 60-mile area of Salisbury Plain — just like looking for a needle in a haystack! But we did get to know it well and learnt to track them down. The noise helped; they had this high-pitched generator to fire the missiles, this *awful* high-pitched whine which froze your blood . . . We had more and more success at tracking them down and then got transport of our own, then there was no stopping us . . . It was exhausting work, but we learnt early on that if we got up to the convoy, that high-pitched whining would stop — the potential to fire thirty-two missiles stopped, and often only two women could do that. They poured MOD police in Land Rovers and dogs up there. We had to face the MOD police, the British Army and the USAF personnel, with guns pointed at us, and we felt they would use them . . . We were unstoppable.

Sarah Hipperson (Hanlon), Greenham Common, 1980s and '90s

Each vehicle in the convoy had four Cruise missiles in it, each of these with the potential of fifteen Hiroshima bombs. As the convoy went out of the gate, we would put our hands high and chant, "Blood on your hands, murderers, killers of women and children," and this would go into a keening sound and wailing. Women weeping for the land and the people, directing it against the Cruise-missile convoy. The police got freaked out on this because it was extremely powerful.

Judy McGehee, wife of Colonel Jarrett McGehee, USAF Commander of Greenham Common Airbase, 1983–6

Watching the convoys going out, I felt they were going to war. It was so *eerie*, these great tractor tracks and the women demonstrating, the noise and lighting fires, and trying to stop the convoys getting out. It was frightening; they hadn't frightened me at all until that time . . .

Christine Kings, CND/Greenham Common liaison woman

We set up, through the CND council, a process by which, as these things were coming out of the gate, one of the women would run straight down to the telephone box and ring me at home. I then had a "telephone tree" and would ring half a dozen people who were in different CND groups in the south-east of England, and they in turn would notify others, and within about an hour CND members would be in their cars whizzing around the countryside trying to find these Cruise missiles and obstructing them . . . There were no mobile phones then, just people leaping out into telephone boxes; it was very, very effective. There were lots of skirmishes. They went to Salisbury Plain . . . The women would converge on these things and this was in the middle of the night, nobody else there, only CND members and American soldiers who were not at all sympathetic to this kind of activity. There was one occasion where a number of CND members had been put in a pit and kept there for hours guarded by soldiers — this was very scary . . . It didn't stop people going out, and we had

357

this very good and efficient relationship with Greenham women . . .

Colonel Jarrett McGehee, USAF Commander, Greenham Common Airbase, 1983–6

They certainly seemed to have a good communication system. We referred to it in the US as the "sneaker net" — a group of people who move from camp to camp; that was their courier system, their communication system. As far as we could determine, they didn't have any degree of sophistication in their communication, but sophistication has nothing to do with effectiveness and they were quite effective. In fact, there were times when we would bait them with something somewhere just to see how long it took to make the circuit, and often it would take less than ten minutes. So they had quite an effective communication capability — better than we did, as a matter of fact!

Wing Commander Mick Marsh, RAF Commander, Greenham Common Airbase, 1983–6

They were in a situation where they could win most of the time. They had 24 hours to watch what was happening in the base, which was in their clear view, and prepare their tactics . . . When the convoys went off the base there was no risk, because at no stage did nuclear weapons leave the base on a convoy. They were delivered by air, unloaded right outside the gates of GAMMA [Grickham Alert and Maintenance Area]. The only time they were taken out was when they were withdrawn and taken straight on to an aircraft and away. So nuclear weapons were never at risk . . .

Group Captain Stanley Keyte, RAF Commander, Greenham Common Airbase, 1987–9

The disruption of the Cruise convoys was quite a problem . . . Safety could be an issue because the protesters could be almost suicidal, stepping out in front of a vehicle: that was very difficult. Also they would break windscreens. In fact, the Americans put three layers of cling film on the windscreens, and if they threw paint, they could peel off a layer and see to drive. The vehicles were 40-tonners. Considerable civil police were needed, three police forces involved, a really dramatic business. They tried hard to disrupt them because if they could do so they were proving it was a non-effective weapon. If they could do this, so could others. They got on to the plain and sometimes they penetrated quite close to where the vehicles were camped. In a situation of war then the defence would have been more positive and the nuclear weapons would have been protected in the ultimate way, "lethal force" as the Americans put it.

Wing Commander Mick Marsh, RAF Commander, Greenham Common Airbase, 1983–6

I did have understanding of their viewpoint and why they were there. No one wants to use nuclear weapons, and in fact if you finish up using them, you can say that the policy of having them has failed. As a Vulcan-bomber navigator for five years, I was involved in their potential use, so I'd given the matter great thought. There is no way I wanted to use them, but equally I was in no doubt, and I'm still in no doubt, that they were the thing that kept the Iron Curtain where it was. That without that kind of shield at that time, there was always the chance that the Soviet Union would come further west . . . I'm in no doubt that it was the right decision.

Colonel Jarrett McGehee, USAF Commander, Greenham Common Airbase, 1983–6

If by magic they [the Greenham women] disappeared one afternoon, we'd miss them because they became a part of our lives. It's hard to imagine or describe the squalor and adversity that they brought, or that their nuisance factor could become part of your life. But I guess it's like a paralysed arm; after a while you get used to it and it becomes a part of your life.

Katrina Howse, Greenham Common, 1980s and '90s

I've worked with the best here and I've also seen the worst of what women are capable of. The non-violent direct action has brought out the best in women and in me . . . However bad the worst of the Greenham movement has been, it's infinitely better than what happened at Molesworth mixed camp, where three men living at the camp raped three women who lived there. So I think that even with all the differences between us, and the loss of some expectations about women, I still believe that Greenham, taking the best of it, even with the separation which developed amongst the different gates, has been infinitely better protected because it is all women, and this has done more to change things than the mixed set-up. But you have to deal with reality and learn from it. The whole movement learns.

Fran Whittle (Casselden), regular visitor to Greenham Common, 1980s and '90s

Right at the end, when we visited Blue Gate one very cold winter's day, we stayed a couple of days and did what we could. At the end, we were verbally attacked by one woman who, over the two days I'd been there, I had felt was probably quite mentally disturbed. I think towards the end one did see that, that it had been a tremendous strain

361

on some people. But Greenham was a community and you're going to get all these different types just as you are in any community . . .

Katrina Howse, Greenham Common, 1980s and '90s

We really have worn down the Americans and the British military. It was keeping on the non-violent direct action so much that they had to keep on putting more and more money into the defences and security. The new silo fencing cost well over a million pounds, and of course they'd shoot us if we did get in: Heseltine made this threat. We and others have raised the question of how much money is spent on weapons and we've made it clear that we totally oppose that. We've also stood strong on non-alignment — we're opposed to Soviet, French and American, any weapons. I think we broke through the whole thing. We spoke out against the Soviet Union in Moscow. We have kept the moral integrity of women and could never be seen as one particular political grouping. We have connected up with dissidents in Eastern Europe, spoken up for those in prison, and in that way we have helped break down the Berlin Wall as well.

Brian Baldwin, gardener, Greenham Common, 1986–92

The women certainly kept the security forces on their toes — a good thing. Really, they were a thorn in their side. The costs must have been *colossal*: extra soldiers, all costing more, and the police bill must have been *phenomenal* as they were all on overtime. A waste of public money, and it didn't achieve anything. It didn't stop the Americans or the RAF one iota.

Group Captain Stanley Keyte, RAF Commander, Greenham Common Airbase, 1987–9

As the INF became more a reality, then the situation began to change at Greenham Common. The women thought, "Ah, that's it! We've won. We, the women were going to see the missiles taken out of Greenham Common, and we did it!" . . . When the Russians came to do the inspections, we would drive them around the base in coaches; they acted as if they didn't see the women, pretended not to see them, mostly they carried that on in private too. But a couple did mention them, more on the lines of, "Are there many of them here still?" They didn't show a great deal of interest and made no allusion that they might have caused problems . . . Some of our people felt that there had been a Russian connection with the women due to potential military disruption; I never did . . . I and my colleagues were convinced that what happened was what had been planned to happen — the twin-track policy and the plan to negotiate them away. But the women were convinced this was a victory and had all been worthwhile. From their point of view, it must have been very important to think that.

Fran Whittle (Casselden), regular visitor to Greenham Common, 1980s and '90s

Absolutely, I have no doubt about it whatsoever, that the peace camp was responsible for the removal of Cruise.

Christine Kings, CND/Greenham Common liaison woman

It's difficult to quantify, but I cannot see how the women could *not* have had an impact on the Cold War. They were an embarrassment to the government and the Americans; they kept the issue alive the whole time. There was nothing more that the government and the Americans would have wanted but to keep the whole thing secret, keep it quiet. Greenham just upset that. They were having an international impact; they were giving life to movements all over the world.

Kim Besly, Greenham Common, 1980s and '90s

Greenham was seen as a single issue — anti-Cruise — by the media because of the deployment of Cruise missiles. People who went there understood that it was *much* wider than that.

Joanna Englekamp (Wallis), Greenham Common, 1980s

The camp has always been more than anti-Cruise. It's about women having their own space and doing what needs to be done.

Charles Besly, Ex-Services CND

I think Greenham Common had a *tremendous* stimulus on the peace movement. The women had shown that Establishment figures can be made fools of, and they've also contributed a lot of research to things like Cruise missiles. They've set an example. Had it been left to fellows, I don't think they'd have been so dismissive of the Establishment and pomposity as the women have been. So yes, they've been a marvellous stimulus. They've stimulated *me*, for one!

Christine Kings, CND/Greenham Common liaison woman

In the same way that women refer to the Suffragettes, I think they will refer to Greenham. It was a wonderful example of women coming together to make their point. So many women will have had their consciousness raised, their lives changed by it. Although many young women today may not know of Greenham, their mothers will have had their consciousness raised, and that works its way through generations. For me, I can say, Greenham affected my life; there is no doubt in my mind that my connection with the camp transformed my sense of women's position in society, and the power and the solidarity. I learnt so much about myself and feminism and women's politics, and they changed my world-view of how I see things.

Wing Commander Mick Marsh, RAF Commander, Greenham Common Airbase, 1983–6

I suppose one finished up with a mixture of emotions. I went there with a degree of admiration for them. I left still with a degree of admiration for them, for some of the things that they did and for what they were trying to achieve. They kept me very busy. I regret the double standards I met on some occasions — they wanted to be treated as women, but they didn't want to *act* like women. They wanted us to obey the rules — written and unwritten — but they didn't want to obey them themselves. As I look back on the period, I don't think I would have missed it. There was a lot to be done and we played our part. One of the things the Americans gave us at the end was a plaque: "You helped to make it happen."

Group Captain Stanley Keyte, RAF Commander, Greenham Common Airbase, 1987–9

The whole issue of the common's being a military base was shaken by what the women had managed to achieve. They had a significance because of their persistence and their experience of dealing with these things. They complicated life in terms of the convoys going out and of breaking into the base, but the way they challenged and overturned the by-laws, *that* was impressive. Whatever else they did, that was not trivial. They were an irritation, but, yes, I had a respect for them: for their persistence, determination and single-mindedness and strength of purpose . . . Without question, after 31 years of service, this was the best and most rewarding tour my wife and I have had anywhere, from every point of view. It was sometimes immensely frustrating, but extremely satisfying.

Rev. Kenneth Greet, Methodist minister, CO, Second World War, president of the World Disarmament Campaign

The significant thing is that the word "Greenham" was familiar in Australia, as I discovered. So they did a great thing. People said, "Now, what is this Greenham thing all about?" Here is an example of how a tiny group of rather way-out women, as many would regard them, could send ripples all around the world. It was immensely heartening for those of us who've lived our lives working for small minorities.

Sarah Hipperson (Hanlon), Greenham Common, 1980s and '90s

There is no doubt in my mind, and other women's minds, that Greenham was going to be the most important thing that ever happened to them in their lifetime, in terms of empowerment.

Joanna Englekamp (Wallis), Greenham Common, 1980s

I think that Greenham is perhaps the most important thing that happened to me . . . And it's also crucial to the peace movement. For me, the energy that I put into other aspects of the peace movement came from there — Greenham was where I charged my batteries. I think that the whole women's movement took a lot of different turns after Greenham, but those turns were building on that experience. For my daughters, who were very young when I went there, the camp must be a distant memory. For them it will be something like what I heard about my grandfather [CO Corder Catchpool] in the First and Second World War. They'll know what their roots are and where they're coming from, but what they make of it depends on what the world's like when they're grown up.

CHAPTER
SEVEN

1991–2009: The New World Order

The sea of people in Hyde Park was unimaginable — those two million — the biggest march in English political history . . . On such marches there are always some people who love chanting things and making a furore, but the great majority, it seemed to me, didn't look like red-hot political activists, but were thoughtful, amiable, ordinary, concerned people . . .

Throughout the twentieth century, developments in the anti-war movement have always reflected the changes in world affairs. When the Cold War ended in 1990, followed by the disintegration of the Soviet Union in December 1991, the balance of power that had existed between the superpowers and had introduced a degree of order to international relations gave way to a new unipolar international system dominated by the United States. Although many shared President George H. W. Bush's vision of a new world order founded on peace and justice, others were more pessimistic and sceptical: to them, this was merely a slogan to give legitimacy to narrowly defined American policy preferences: "The New World gives the orders." There was also the realisation that "winning" the

Cold War, although diminishing the threat of world conflict, could be replaced by new forms of warfare, perhaps less manageable. Such fears were confirmed by regional and intrastate conflicts that erupted around the world, especially the Middle East.

When Saddam Hussein invaded the oil-rich state of Kuwait in August 1990, the international response was immediate. By January 1991, troops from more than 30 countries, led by the United States, were poised in Saudi Arabia ready to enforce a UN demand for Saddam to withdraw unconditionally. On 16 January, "Operation Desert Storm" began with massive bombing raids on Baghdad. The ground offensive started on 23 February. It lasted five days. On the eve of 27 February, President George H.W. Bush announced on TV, "Kuwait is liberated."

Kate Hudson, CND vice chair 2001–3, chair 2003 to present

Like many people, I thought the end of the Cold War was going to be a different era, one of peace. I suppose the first writing on the wall that it wasn't going to be the case was when the Warsaw Pact was dissolved and NATO wasn't.

Jamie Shea, head of Policy Planning Unit, NATO

When the Cold War ended, it was a period of mass demoralisation among NATO's staff. We really felt that we'd go the same way as the Warsaw Pact.

371

People worried about job cuts: the Warsaw Pact had gone; NATO would follow, or at least downsize. Nobody knew what the new direction would be; we were victims of our own success. Manfred Werther replaced [Lord] Carrington in 1988 as Secretary General of NATO. He had a hawkish reputation as the German Minister of Defence. Everyone saw his appointment as a sign that NATO would be tough on the Soviets, but he had a whole new set of circumstances that he had neither been trained for nor prepared for . . . The break-up of the Soviet Union led to a brief period where the Soviet cooperation with the US was exemplary, and the support that the Soviet Union gave the United States in the First Gulf War led to the belief that the major powers would not be adversaries but would cooperate, and that would give a great deal of clout in dealing with rogue regimes like Saddam Hussein's. It would produce a new democratic process to guide international relations and the coming-together to solve conflicts.

Bruce Kent, CND chair 1977–9, vice president 1987–90, founder member of the Movement for the Abolition of War (MAW)

I had no faith at all in George Bush Snr's New World Order. I was vigorously campaigning against the First Gulf War. I knew Iraq had gone into

Kuwait, but there were all sorts of negotiating possibilities. In fact Saddam Hussein — no angel — laid out some of them, like clearing out all nuclear weapons from the Middle East, which would have included Israel. But none of these things were acceptable. So there was a war. I couldn't *believe* it. So in a sense we became much more UN-directed because the charter had been violated. After all, Article 42 of the charter doesn't give the Security Council the right to go to war when it feels like it, it has to exhaust every non-violent means of resolving a conflict before it can authorise military action.

Tony Benn, anti-war activist

Ted [Heath] and I both went to see Saddam . . . I had three hours with him. I was driven all around Baghdad until I was dizzy and came to an ordinary street of bungalows and there he was sitting with nine people. There was a revolver in his belt, and at one stage he took it out and I thought I had gone too far! I had a long discussion with him, and what came out of it so clearly was that he felt utterly betrayed by the Americans who had supported him throughout the Iran–Iraq war . . . I said, "If you don't pull out from Kuwait, you will be destroyed by the Americans." He said, "I will be destroyed by the Americans anyway because they are too strong." It was all very interesting; he gave me a different perspective. I was against the invasion.

"Thomas Wadey", British soldier

Our commanding officer told us that Saudi Arabia was under threat from Iraq and that the United States had sent a task force into Saudi Arabia and we were going to do the same. I actually wanted to go; I thought I'd be keeping the peace blue-beret style . . . Then I was sent to Wales for special training. This is when I began to be not entirely happy, when, in lectures, we were introduced to racism towards those of Arab descent: "Be aware, Arabs don't think twice about stealing your belongings and they are full of disease . . ." That kind of thing . . . They were lying from the first moment we were deployed until the time I was meant to go, and afterwards. It was a whole system of degradation of your ability to reason for yourself. When I joined the army, it was made clear that one had to be loyal and have a sense of duty to protect the country, but what they didn't make clear was that you might be asked to obey orders that you thought to be wholly wrong . . . It was very difficult to be honest with myself, but I just couldn't do it. The whole issue was that it wasn't about freeing Kuwait and to do with democracy, it was about the power of control, regaining power in the Middle East by both America and Britain. It was punitive, it was expeditionary, it was imperialistic, it was based on lies . . . The hardest thing of all was that I had to break my duty. And I knew I was going to get a hard time . . .

Eric Hayes, US Marine Corps Reserve, CO, First Gulf War, 1990–1

In college, when my beliefs started to formulate, I became delinquent as a marine ... I began to distance myself from my white colleagues who had begun to see that it was easier to kill darker-skinned people. I heard many racial epithets about Arabs as the [Gulf] conflict built up. They were called "A'rabs", "Raggies", "Camel Jockeys", all to demean and degrade who they were and to make it easier to take their lives. It was part of the psychological training to make killers more efficient ... I thought: "I cannot support this war in the Persian Gulf, it would be a major contradiction of who I have become; when I signed my contract with the military I didn't sign away my capacity to grow and to think and learn ..." The name "Desert Storm" was a rallying point; America was in need of a *big* war, a shot in the arm. With racial divisions, political divisions, the homeless, the poverty, it needed a victory, another focus. A war with a lot of punch, a war with *heroes* — the black hero Colin Powell, the white hero Schwarzkopf — it needed a show of force for those within the country and those outside.

Rev. Kenneth Greet, Methodist minister, CO, Second World War, president of the World Disarmament Campaign

Sanctions weren't given a chance because, in my view, America was *determined* to go to war anyhow. It wasn't a UN war. The UN was misused, and there are a lot of lessons to learn from that . . . The whole moral argument of that war was flawed from the beginning by the fact that the Western nations had armed Saddam Hussein. If you, without let or hindrance, allow money to be made by the sale of infinitely destructive weaponry to ragtag regimes around the world, then what you're doing is selling unholy boomerangs that come back at you.

Sergeant Eric Bollinger, US Marine Corps, Intelligence, 513 Squadron, 5th Marine Expeditionary Brigade

When we stopped in Hawaii [en route to the Gulf], one of the pilots, a Muslim, a very nice guy, very professional, had decided between leaving the United States and arriving in Hawaii that he objected to the war due to the fact that the United States was going to attack an Islamic country. He'd decided that when we pulled into the port in Pearl Harbor that he was going to get off the ship, go to the airport and fly back to the United States, which is what he did. Our command didn't know about it until he showed up in his old unit back in the US, which surprised everyone. That was the first time that I knew of an officer who had decided not to go to the war; he became a conscientious objector. He was smart that he didn't tell anybody what he was going to do because there were other marines who had decided to become conscientious objectors, and they went to the Gulf anyway because they had voiced their opinion and were thrown on an aircraft and flown over there in spite of their beliefs — they belonged to the Marine Corps and they did what the Marine Corps told them.

All members of the British Armed Forces have volunteered for enlistment since May 1963. The problem since then has been how to treat those who became conscientious objectors to military service while serving either full-time or on reserve in their period of engagement, cases which could be considered as "selective conscientious objection". The Ministry of Defence considers that it has a "well-established procedure" for such cases, which are handled by the service concerned. Guidelines are provided for each of the three services. A non-departmental public body, the Advisory Committee on Conscientious Objectors (ACCO), was established in 1970 for appeals from those applications that were rejected by the service authorities.

Andreas Speck, activist and organiser, WRI, London

Right from the beginning, an important part of WRI work has been about conscientious objection to military service and work against conscription . . . Britain is one of the few countries now that recognises the rights of conscientious objection for professional soldiers; it is more advanced than other European countries in this respect. But the problem is that it is only given in armed forces regulations, not in law. Britain doesn't have a constitution so you cannot have a constitutional right; there is no established law, just the regulations of the various armed forces, which are unknown except by a few experts. Military personnel know nothing about them, so someone in the military who might have a conscientious objection will not know that these regulations exist. Even if you look at the MOD website, as I have done, you will not find them. Obviously that is difficult for people who are in the armed forces and develop a conscientious objection, because they don't know about their rights. I assume that most officers don't know about these rights either. It is said that there have been 36 cases since 1971, but I don't trust these statistics . . .

The other problem is that when people don't know about their rights, they will find another way — medical discharge, hardship or other reasons; or they might simply go AWOL and be charged for desertion . . . The argument from the military is that there are no COs; I would always say: "If they don't *know* about it, they will not be *named* as COs: that's why there aren't any!" So it's difficult to get a full picture of what the atmosphere is in the armed forces, or what soldiers really think, or why they want to leave. In Britain, because soldiers don't have the same rights to speak out as US soldiers have, they are always pressured with the Official Secrets Act. So we have few British voices against the war from the soldiers.

"Thomas Wadey", British soldier

I couldn't go to the next person in line and say, "I want to conscientiously object," because we wouldn't even *know* about the term. In practice, you go to the sergeant major and say, "I'm not too happy with this situation, sergeant major, there are a lot of questions I can't get my head around; I need some explanation, I'm not sure I want to go." He said, "Well, I'm sure there are others who feel the same and they'll come back disillusioned with the army and will want to get out soon, but there's not a lot we can do about it at the moment, is there?" Basically he was sympathetic, but he didn't know what he could have done. Even if you went through the *Manual of Military Law* page by page, you would not find the words "conscientious objection".

379

Eric Hayes, US Marine Corps Reserve, CO, First Gulf War, 1990–1

The government handled conscientious objection in various ways: some people who refused to go were given Army Article 15, something very minor; they were put on other duty or eased out of the system. Others were handcuffed, beaten up by senior personnel; others were given a chance to turn themselves in to a holding barrack in North Carolina and systematically put through the process of court martial.

What I wanted to do was to let them know *why* I refused to go, and that my reasons fused with other things going on in the world. That we should all question it. I made arrangements for a press conference at my university; it was well attended, by those for and against the war. This, I heard, went all over the world. Thirteen days after that, at 1.30a.m. in my campus dorm, I was arrested by thirty US Marshals. I was taken to Scott Air Force Base and flown to North Carolina, where I was detained . . . I was a high-profile student, president of one of the biggest organisations on campus. I had no intention of resisting arrest . . . I was treated very carefully due to my high profile: I was never roughed up, they went right by the book. I heard them say when we touched down in Fort Lejeune, "We've got the black honcho" — this being a military term for "big leader". I was taken to the brig and had solitary confinement for 13 days. I was the prize lion they'd captured; they'd come and look at me like a caged beast. The courtroom was packed at my court martial. My beliefs were never discussed, just the intent to desert. The judge gave me five years [served eight months]; he was biased and I think flown back from Saudi Arabia to try my case. The war had started then.

Eldora Spiegelberg, Quaker peace activist, St Louis, MO, USA

There were very many COs in that war [First Gulf War, 1990–1], a number that has never been revealed of those who refused to go or didn't show up. They were imprisoned in Fort Lejeune in North Carolina, and many of them were kept in a special enclave there until the war was over. One or two I know are still there [November 1991].

"Thomas Wadey", British soldier

I'd heard nothing of the peace movement or anti-war protest at this stage; I thought I was doing this all on my own. All these little wild things were going through my head: "Should I chain myself to the railings in Whitehall? Should I go to John Major and tell him he's got to stop?" Listening to the radio on the night war broke, I was devastated and so upset thinking about people being bombed. On my way back, going through Whitehall area, all of a sudden there was this huge crowd of people with placards and I agreed with what they were saying 100 per cent. That's when I met the people who helped me to achieve what I wanted. They helped me go public, that was my choice . . . I was charged with going AWOL . . . It is when you get in touch with organisations such as At Ease and Reservists Against the War that you find that you are not on your own, not an isolated case. When soldiers are told of their rights, it gives them strength and power. Soldiers can organise themselves and they [the authorities] know it, and they have to stamp on it like a great big boot.

Anthony "Tony" Flint, British Army reservist, RAMC, General Hospital, Riyadh, January–March 1991

We were told it had to be done quickly as we were going abroad. On 4 January 1991, I was given injections against yellow fever, meningitis, anthrax, whooping cough and the oral polio. It was unusual to have *five* injections in one go; I'd never known it before. Then within the same week, injections for cholera, tetanus, typhoid, hepatitis B — so in the period of a week, nine injections . . . When we first went out there [Saudi Arabia], we were given tablets to take called NAPs — Nerve Agent Pretreatment. We had to take one every eight hours as an antidote to any nerve agent that might be used, we were told. In a couple of days, we all realised that we were suffering side effects. In my case, I was getting nausea and diarrhoea, others were vomiting, and as time went on some were showing signs of depression and aggression as well. Some of the girls were having problems with their periods. One in particular had a period for two solid months. We were told to take them for our own protection, and we took them because at first we thought they were safe . . . Later we were given another set of injections: another anthrax, whooping cough and the plague injection; we were also taking the NAPs tablets and once a week anti-malaria tablets. I remember writing to my wife and telling her about the pain and ill-effects I was suffering.

Commander Robert Green, RN, Ex-Services CND

After the first Scud attack on Tel Aviv, all the Israelis had to do was to wheel out their nuclear weapons so that the US satellite could spot them. Total panic: Bush to Shamir: "I'll do *anything* to stop you, what do you want?" "$10 million please, and then we'll go from there." Thirty-eight more Scuds were fired at Israel. The Israelis were cowering in their bunkers wearing gas masks, and they must have been wondering where their nuclear weapons had got to. This really vindicated what I thought: that Israel's bomb had not done its job — it was a liability, not an asset . . . In the midst of all this, there was the IRA attack on the Gulf War Cabinet with mortar bombs on Whitehall. Where was Polaris? Not a facetious question any more because the terrorist threat is the biggest threat this country faces, and it was demonstrated graphically by that. I was told, sniffily, by an MOD civil servant when I asked him that question, that Polaris "was not designed for this". So, what *is* it designed for? What *is* its use now? Where *is* it targeted? So for me the whole deterrence doctrine had collapsed, it was a myth. I felt a sense of betrayal for the Royal Navy and felt that we had to stop Trident from ultimately destroying it. So, that was my run-in to the [First] Gulf War, and that's what was needed to break me out from my brainwashing taboo. It was very traumatic. And I did feel when I came finally to stand at the foot of Nelson's Column — of all places — in Trafalgar Square, 12 January 1991, that I was committing high treason, and I fully expected a snatch squad from MI5 to come out and take me to the Tower . . . I joined Ex-Services CND as I deliberately wanted to keep some attachment to my military service because I believed in the Royal Navy and the military.

Mary Campbell, International Gulf Peace Camp, Iraq and Jordan, 1990–1

The purpose of the peace camp was simply to make a little oasis of peace between the two warring factions, that was our objective . . . The camp was called Judayyidat Arar; it was on the border between Saudi Arabia and Iraq, and it was a permanent camp for pilgrims on their way to Mecca — these enormous farm buildings enclosed in wire fencing. Water was brought there by big tanks. Outside were young Iraqi soldiers in military posts. There was a great mix of people there, which I glory in. There wasn't much publicity about the camp in the media and we had no contacts at all with the British government or Foreign Office; we were *persona non grata*, an embarrassment . . . The first sign of war was when the bombers started going over very low. We were in our sleeping bags and knew they were going to bomb Baghdad. It was very emotional, that part; having been in Baghdad earlier, we had seen a lot of the people who were going to be on the receiving end . . . There was a sort of depression, an anti-climax when war started, we felt very flat. We had watches during the night for anyone coming or any other activity, but what could we have done? Had we been bombed, we had no trenches dug, not even the tools, and there were 73 of us. Then word came that we would be evacuated . . . It was rather sad, so little accomplished . . .

Janet Cameron, British civilian doctor, International Gulf Peace Camp, Iraq and Jordan, 1990–1

After the war started, we were taken away to Baghdad by the Iraqi soldiers. We were put into the Rashid Hotel. I was up on the seventh floor looking out at this dark-grey sky with all the red lines of tracer fire going up, and it looked absolutely like the *Space Invaders*. We also went round some of the hospitals and saw some of the casualties. I went to the Orthopaedic Hospital; the windows were out, it was still freezing at night, there was no water or electricity, and they were beginning to run short of anaesthetics — this was 30 January. God help us! We shouldn't have done this. It wasn't necessary and it didn't do anybody any good and had nothing whatsoever to do with freeing Kuwait . . . I'm a doctor and I was just standing there . . . their own doctors were standing there saying, "We haven't got the supplies . . ."

Mary Campbell, International Gulf Peace Camp, Iraq and Jordan, 1990–1

We were taken to see the bomb damage, including the powdered-milk factory. The Americans claimed it had been used for chemical warfare, but there was no sign of that. I'm willing to place a large bet on the fact that it was what it claimed to be, a dried-milk factory built by the French in 1970, the only one of its kind in the Middle East. We saw evidence of milk churns scattered all over the place, packets of dried milk, and there were also some full boxes that had escaped the bombing. It had been a direct hit all right.

Sergeant Eric Bollinger, US Marine Corps, Intelligence, 513 Squadron, 5th Marine Expeditionary Brigade, Saudi Arabia

We thought the milk factory and the air-raid bunker that were bombed were intelligence bunkers, but that was because the CIA and higher intelligence had passed that down to us. In retrospect, I would say that they were not intelligence bunkers, and that the baby-milk factory was what they said it was and that in these cases our intelligence did fail, they miscalculated.

Anthony "Tony" Flint, British Army reservist, RAMC, General Hospital, Riyadh, January — March 1991

One of my jobs was counselling the battle-shock casualties, for which I'd had no previous training . . . I remember one particular chap I counselled who was the platoon commander of what has become known as the "Friendly Fire incident", when an American anti-tank aircraft fired on some British troops, killing nine of them. We had the rest of the platoon brought in. The platoon commander described what the pilot had done as "pure bloody incompetence". His recognition should have been a lot better as all the Allied forces were marked and could be seen from the air; they were also a different shape from the Iraqis . . . The pilot came down twice, his weapons were laser-guided, the chaps inside had no chance. We had the survivors in hospital for three or four days before they were sent back to England. I hear that one or two are still [1995] suffering psychiatric treatment.

Sergeant Roy Selstrom, Army War Graves Unit, Saudi Arabia, First Gulf War

We arrived [where the Friendly Fire incident had happened] and set up the collection point. I remember opening the first bag, putting my hands in, and I pulled out a foot, no boots, there were these two bones coming up from the ankle and the rolled-down piece of sock — that's all there was . . . I'm looking at those two bones and the piece of sock . . . and looking at the toenails, and it's not even registering with me. Where's the rest of the body? Just this foot and associated parts, a hand, the top of a shoulder — all these bits and bobs in this one bag . . . I was looking for a *body* to process . . . I'd been told there were nine bodies, but six of them were just . . . you know . . . I picked a head up on its own . . . I carried on like that for a while and then we came across three whole bodies which were perfect, nothing wrong with them, they had heads, arms, legs. We got the first one, and put him up on the trestle table, he was lying there . . . I couldn't understand . . . you know for the last hour I'd been digging through heads, arms, legs, I couldn't understand how these three were *perfect* . . . I told myself, "Get a grip!" . . . Just stood there and thought — "What's going on? This is *reality*." We'd dealt with all these traffic accidents, gunshot wounds, the other bodies before the land war had started, and then these nine — we'd fallen right into the deep end: six bodies which were nothing, just parts in bin bags and three totally whole. It was so hard to pick a head up, all burnt and that . . . and then these three that just looked as if they were asleep . . . My mind was trying to make the connection — these bits, heads, arms, legs, torsos, it was just like a fucking big jigsaw bag . . . We were in shock.

It was hard after that to crack on . . . everyone withdrew into themselves, they were very quiet . . . we were in war — and had seen the full force of what war can do to the human body — just rip it to bits . . .

Sergeant Eric Bollinger, US Marine Corps, Intelligence, 513 Squadron, 5th Marine Expeditionary Brigade, Saudi Arabia

It became rather crazy once the ground war started. The best way I can describe it is that it was like a feeding frenzy with sharks . . . The leash was cut loose towards the end of the war within the target area. One of the things that bothered me the most was when the Iraqi forces were retreating out of Kuwait City, there was a major traffic jam along the highway outside Kuwait City going north. The marine pilots that I worked with saw a target-enriched environment and would do anything they possibly could to get out there and drop bombs on the target. They were dropping cluster bombs and all sorts of things on people who had no kind of defensive capability whatsoever. I had refused at that point to even debrief some of those pilots because they were so crazy with bloodlust . . . Marine Corps Harriers have cameras fitted in the nose, and the pilots would come in for their debriefing and some would run to their video machines, plug the flight tape in and they would all sit around and excitedly point out all the different targets they were hitting, and reverse it back and go through it real slow, watching the vehicles and people running and all kinds of other stuff. I would just leave the room. One of the things I said after the war was over that it was pretty sad that we went in and destroyed a Third World country in six months and got out with our conscience still intact . . .

Laurence Manton, journalist, *Soldier* magazine, Kuwait/Iraq

We arrived at the Mutla Ridge, and what the Americans had done was to seal off the Baghdad side of the ridge and all the helicopter gunships came in and started machine-gunning the convoy of escaping Iraqi vehicles. It was quite astonishing. What had happened was that when they started getting attacked, the Iraqis ran off to the left into the minefields and were blown to bits there; and those that ran into the open desert on the right were pursued by the American helicopter gunships and blown to bits . . . it was *surreal*. I remember saying to my photographer, "Photograph everything, we'll never see anything like this ever again . . . look, look! A foot!" And there was a bare foot standing in the middle of this road. There was a minibus with the door open, a guy by the door. I went over: "You all right?" He must have got out at the time of the blast, caught with an arm through the window, and there he stood, dead . . . The Iraqis had looted Kuwait City to such an extent that they'd thrown away their ammunition and taken everything they could. So there was this Iraqi Army lorry with the tail-flap down, and spilling out of it was all these bunches of plastic flowers — a

391

spectacular sight. I turned round and there was an Iraqi gasmask bag, and sticking out of it were the two feet of a doll — it looked like the doll was in its own body-bag . . . Flowers and dolls . . . it was unbelievable!

Eldora Spiegelberg, Quaker peace activist, St Louis, MO, USA

Many Americans are glad to have what they call the "Vietnam Syndrome" erased. They want to believe that the Vietnam War was a disgrace because of those pacifists who opposed it and how our brave men were very much wronged when they came back, and for years we considered it a blot on our history. Now [1991] they want to say that *this* war certainly proved that our forces are superior and can take on the whole world and we are second to none in ability to not only win a war, but to see the whole international community and the United Nations on our side.

Sergeant Roy Selstrom, Army War Graves Unit, Saudi Arabia, First Gulf War

We got back to Al Jubail and that night, that's when it hit me. I'd changed. I was having problems: I was crying and shaking, I just couldn't stop crying; I was high, I was low. But crying all the time, even when chatting to people. It was getting me annoyed . . . Then it was claustrophobic:

I was locked in a room which was coming in towards me, and everything was moving out of focus at the same time. It was frightening. I was getting lots of panic attacks and anxiety attacks — I know what they are now, I didn't at the time. I thought I was going mad: shivering, sweating, cold, crying, my hands shaking all the time. I was freaked out . . . headaches, people going in and out of focus. I was having hallucinations. March 8 1991, I went sick . . . a report was taken of my symptoms, I just sat there crying my heart out . . . It was surreal, I couldn't put my finger on when the breakdown had occurred . . .

Anthony "Tony" Flint, British Army reservist, RAMC, General Hospital, Riyadh, January–March 1991

I never felt right after I returned home; I was very very snappy, had fits of depression and found it very hard to readjust . . . Gradually things got worse and worse; then in April 1994, I had a complete nervous breakdown. Lots of veterans have the same symptoms: difficulties in breathing, short-term memory loss, weight loss, aches and pains in the joints, headaches . . . I'm amazed at the way all of us have been left to suffer, and frightened as well because we're passing things over to our wives and children, and some of the lads find their children have birth defects. How many generations is it going to affect? I was quite willing to be killed by a bomb or bullet as a medic soldier to make people well, but to come back and go through what I'm going through, and my family too, and being told that it's got nothing to do with my service to the country is absolutely deplorable.

Brian Haw, Parliament Square, Peace Campaign, Westminster, London 2001 to present

At this time [2001] there was the "March of Tears" by the Gulf War veterans. Whether you agree with them going in '90-'91, at least these men put their lives on the line, didn't they? Not like all the people in Parliament. They received no respect, no recognition. I took my hat off and joined them. There was one man who was bent over, a big powerful man he would have been, he could barely walk, and we had to keep stopping so he could get his breath. He would have been one of those suffering from what was called "Gulf War Syndrome", which is from our war material of depleted uranium. Many have been suffering since that war. We marched to the Cenotaph.

Anthony "Tony" Flint, British Army reservist, RAMC, General Hospital, Riyadh, January — March 1991

The war was basically a technological war . . . We went in there for the oil and for the governments to try out their new weapons systems in a war situation. This is a very different view from what we got from the media — Saddam Hussein had to be stopped or else it would spread. I thought it my duty as a reservist to do something about it. Now my whole attitude to it has altered.

At the time of the First Gulf War an intrastate conflict was building up in the Balkans, and by the spring of 1992 Yugoslavia had disintegrated. The process started in 1991 when the European Community recognised Slovenia and Croatia as independent states. In 1992, after President Izetbegović declared the independence of Bosnia, UN peacekeepers began to work in Croatia and Bosnia. Their purpose was to alleviate suffering of the people and try, through peaceful means, to bring an end to the terrible civil war that was coming to a close in Croatia but raging in Bosnia. The Bosnian War lasted until the Dayton Agreement was signed on 21 November 1995. On 24 March 1999, just over three years after the Bosnian conflict had ended, NATO launched an intensive bombing campaign on Kosovo and Serbia to prevent, it was argued, a humanitarian disaster being inflicted on the Kosovan Albanians similar to that experienced earlier by Bosnians.

Gordon Rushmer, war artist, Bosnia

Generally, you record the aftermath of war: that's the time you see the effects of war and that's what you record . . . I was then working with the Dutch Marines, and the colonel took me to this village of

Ahmići and explained what had happened there, how the Muslim civilians had been killed and how he and the Dutch boys had come in afterwards. It was gutted. It was mid-winter, snow, cold, winds — I caught it at its bleakest. Time had passed, but nothing had happened since the massacre, the place was just a ruin. But only the Muslim houses had been devastated, they'd had the star and crescent painted on them, the Croat homes were still standing. The houses — Muslim and Croat — were intermingled, it had been quite an integrated community . . . It brought home very quickly just how cruel people are: they'd not only raped and slit throats, but they'd called on the services of an impaler as well — that took my breath away! They stuck people on iron pikes or pieces of wood, and the "good" impalers arrange it so that their victims stay alive longer . . . a ghastly business . . . So, a baptism of fire. I didn't see the dead, but in this whole place you could *feel* it, and there was still the smell of burnt wood . . . These people were still squabbling over wars fought in the 1300s! I was not allowed to stand and sketch; it was still far too dangerous, so I took a lot of photographs. I saw the destroyed mosque of Ahmići — that's where the people were burnt alive. It's now an icon. Its toppled minaret has been used in many programmes on the Balkan wars; it is a very strong symbol. I just *had* to paint it to get it out of my system.

Martin Bell, BBC senior war correspondent, Bosnia

The main problem was that we were allowed to show very little, as the BBC didn't like to upset the viewers. The trick was to preempt to some extent what the objectives were going to be and push the envelope as far as you could. In Ahmići, I had used the vivid image of a burnt clenched fist. My equivalent in the second mortar attack in Sarajevo was a shot of blood spilling down a storm drain. Apart from wide shots of bodies covered with white sheets, you had to put in something to show what it was about. It was very difficult as we were hampered by the BBC guidelines, which were very restrictive at the time, and still are, in my view. War *is* an upsetting business . . .

Kate Hudson, CND vice chair 2001–3, chair 2003 to present

It was in the late 1990s that I began to get involved around two issues: one was the expansion of NATO in 1999, with the Czech Republic, Poland and Hungary in March of that year — I think that was a wake-up call to a lot of people, that the nuclear issue was very much there — then, ten days later, the NATO assault on Yugoslavia [Kosovo].

Jamie Shea, NATO spokesman on Kosovo, 1999

What I recall from the meeting of 23 March of the NATO ambassadors was how quick it was. You'd always believe that a decision to start a war, which it was in effect, would be a very difficult decision, that ambassadors would be up all night . . . but it didn't happen that way. Javier Solana [Secretary General of NATO] called a meeting and said that he had consulted with the various capitals and that everyone had agreed that Milosevic had not complied with the NATO conditions. NATO's credibility therefore meant that we could not make empty threats, we had to take action, and they were going to General Wesley Clark to make air strikes within 24 hours. Did anyone have any objection? Nobody said a word. And the way I recall the meeting was that within five minutes, it was over. So, in other words, one of the most momentous meetings was also one of the shortest. But it certainly did a lot of good to NATO's credibility because we had so many long, inconclusive meetings over Bosnia, where our hesitations clearly undermined our credibility and purpose with the media.

General Sir Michael Rose, Commander of the UN Protection Force in Bosnia, 1994–5

General Wesley Clark said, "We're going to disrupt, destroy, devastate and degrade the Serb military machine." No such thing was done; none of the objectives were achieved. For eleven and a half weeks of this intensive bombing campaign, ten thousand Albanians were killed and a million were driven from their homes. Hardly any damage was done to the Serb military machine, and it was a moral failure on the part of the West not to put troops on the ground and observers on the ground and to be engaged on the ground. All of which could have been done and which could have stopped the fighting. But of course they were caught in the belief that they had solved the problems of Bosnia by bombing. It was a tragedy for the people of Kosovo that they should think like that . . . You can't face complex humanitarian or even military problems by the use of air power alone. That message has finally got through, but that was not the message that NATO was sending in 1994–5 and through to the end of the Kosovan war.

Eve-Ann Prentice, senior journalist, *The Times*, Kosovo and Serbia, 1999

About a hundred journalists travelled down a motorway which had been bombed very heavily by now . . . We got to Nis; there was a market right in the middle of the city and it had been market day and it was as if an army of Al Capones had hit town and opened up with machine-gun fire. At this time there were reports and rumours that NATO had been using cluster bombs, and this was very evident there, not only because of the damage but because you could see the cases. So we started collecting these. These are bombs that, when they explode, they have a whole lot of bomblets in them and these are full of fragments of hot metal and nails and God knows what, and it's just like the effect of sub-machine guns spraying all over the place. Everywhere there were dead and dying people who'd been buying in the marketplace. It was pretty gruesome. I counted 33 bodies. Other journalists saw loads more in the hospital. This was very important because we were able to prove the Allied use of these weapons when NATO had specifically denied it. They said in Brussels that what they had meant to say was: "We're only using them where permitted under the Geneva Convention, which is against troops in open battlefields . . ." This was Friday, 7 May 1999.

400

Andreas Speck, activist and organiser, WRI, London

When the Cold War ended, the "peace dividend" was very short-lived and there was a new justification for war: humanitarian intervention. For example, the 1999 bombs in Kosovo and Serbia. WRI used a slogan for our demonstrations: "NATO in the skies, Milosevic on the ground." I was in Germany at the time; this was a clear statement to distance ourselves from the bombings as well as from Milosevic.

Gordon Rushmer, war artist, Kosovo, 1999

A couple of days after I'd travelled this road up to the border, a bus came south from Serbia into Kosovo full of [Serb] families going to visit the graves of their killed relatives. It went over a manhole cover under which a bomb had been planted, and apparently two fellows on the hill waited until the bus went over this manhole cover and the bus went up. It was a devastating explosion. The hospital in Podiavo, then in charge of Albanians, refused to take any of the wounded, so the Brits had to organise an evacuation by helicopters down to the hospital in Pristina. That horrified me, even the doctors and nurses refused . . . that's real *hate*, isn't it? But that's *war*. I'm always saying to myself: "That's war, people hate, people fight . . ."

401

Lindsey German, convenor, STWC, London

I think a lot of people had been politicised by the Balkan wars. The war in Kosovo was quite a popular war, because people thought: "This is saving the lives of refugees — a perfectly reasonable thing." Those who opposed it were very tough politically. They understood that it wasn't just a humanitarian issue, that there was an element of imperialism, and that's where I was coming from too.

Eve-Ann Prentice, senior journalist, *The Times*, Kosovo and Serbia, 1999

For Tony Blair to suggest that Kosovo is a shining example of success of Western humanitarian intervention, well, I'd like to challenge him to send his family to stay there. It's very, *very* frustrating to hear about the "success" of Kosovo; the media bears a huge responsibility for this, and they're not brave enough to take on the Establishment that has propagated this black and white view of it.

Concerns about an increasingly unstable world were heightened dramatically following the attacks of 11 September 2001 on America. It is too soon to assess the full impact of 9/11 on the United States and the world, but in effect it marked the real beginning of the twenty-first century. The attacks on the World Trade Center in New York, the Pentagon in Washington and the failed attempt that ended

402

in a crashed plane in a Pennsylvanian field, galvanised Americans behind President George W. Bush's "War on Terror", which was initially welcomed in other parts of the world too. The first campaign in the War on Terror was directed by the United States against the Taliban militants in Afghanistan. Although a separate regime, the Taliban had supported al-Qaida and provided sanctuary for its leader, Osama bin Laden, making itself, it was argued, a prime target. The Taliban were soon routed, in the short term, mainly by American military strength, supported by a limited "coalition of the willing". The attack on Afghanistan led to a resurgence of the anti-war movement that had started to gather strength with the First Gulf War and the Balkan conflicts. This is when the Stop the War Coalition was founded. It was an alliance of activists from Labour's Left, many of the major trade unions, Plaid Cymru, the Greens, the Communist Party and the Socialist Workers Party.

Dianne Lee, peace campaigner, St Louis, MO, USA

After 9/11 of course everybody was completely shocked, devastated. I'll never forget that day. No, I'll *never* forget that day and how horrible it was. But I think even more horrible were the days that followed, and hearing the hatred and calls for vengeance here in the United States. I worked with a man from Algeria. His children were in public school and his daughter, who had just started wearing the veil, had it ripped off by a group of

403

jeering boys. We have a large refugee population in St Louis and many of the women wear the veil. They tend to shop in Soulard Market, and a group of us went to the market and walked it continuously in order to be a presence accompanying anyone who wanted us to help them . . . The first few days after the attack, the government was saying that we were on a heightened alert, but "Go *shop*! That's how you can support your country!" Ads in the media told us: "Go buy that washing machine. Go buy that car. Be patriotic — shop!" It was disgusting . . .

Bill Quick, lawyer, St Louis, MO, USA

Watching it, my first thought was, "Oh my God, we're going to be going into war against somebody!" That would be the American response. In the days after 9/11, when it was decided that Osama bin Laden and al-Qaida were behind it, and that Osama bin Laden had been sheltered and supported by the Taliban regime in Afghanistan, it seemed perfectly acceptable and appropriate to go into Afghanistan to take the Taliban out and pursue Osama bin Laden.

Kate Hudson, CND vice chair 2001–3, chair 2003 to present

9/11 was the main thing at the annual conference 2001 . . . This is when I was elected vice chair. In my speech, I started off by saying: "One deplores this criminal action, and the perpetrators should be brought to justice. But I deplore it in the same way as I deplore state terrorism which results in the deaths of civilians, and acts such as the bombing of Hiroshima and Nagasaki." Then I said that the appropriate response was not to bomb Afghanistan and kill more innocent civilians, that the international community should seek out and bring suspected perpetrators to trial. That war was not the answer. That was the position that was taken up by the CND conference 2001 . . . The first demonstration against the war in Afghanistan was held by CND, it was a vigil in Downing Street . . . At around that time, STWC was set up. CND was never affiliated to it, we are not part of STWC, but we began to cooperate with it on various things.

Lindsey German, convenor, STWC, London

I suppose that my route into STWC was 9/11. I remember that clearly, everybody does! And you know it is going to change the world. The day after 9/11 they immediately started talking of the war [in Afghanistan] and linking al-Qaida with the Taliban. The second day after the attack, they started talking about Iraq . . . We all thought: "This is going to be something *big*, and we've got to do something." Lots of people said: "No, you can't do anything. Nobody will sympathise with you; this is such a terrible attack you'll look as if you're defending the terrorists." We organised a small meeting first of the Socialist Workers Party; a couple of hundred people came and quite a few were peace activists . . . We decided as a result that we'd go for a really big meeting. It was the end of September and it was held in Friends House in Euston. When we got there, we'd not only filled the big hall — about 13 or 14 hundred people — but also filled the small hall, and then we had 500 people outside that couldn't get into either hall. So we had an outdoor meeting too. It was really *incredible*. The next week we had an organisational meeting. There was huge controversy going on at that meeting . . . But out of this meeting came STWC.

Bruce Kent, CND chair 1977–9, vice president 1987–90, founder member of MAW

In one sense, to be cruel, I think 9/11 was God's gift to the right wing in the States, because they could then declare a war which has no limits, no defined enemy, and no end in sight, and you can spend money hand over fist for this "War on Terror". The attack was a barbaric act, I don't justify it at all, it was a perversion of the Muslim faith, but it was a crime of major murder. The war in Afghanistan was a great mistake that violated the UN Charter; it was an opportunity which could have internationalised us, an opportunity that was thrown away just as the human rights in this country have been thrown away. I think we're losing a terrible lot of the things we were so proud of in this country because we have been galloped into this.

Canon Paul Oestreicher, Anglican pacifist, CND vice president

I think actually that 9/11 has made less difference to the world than a lot of other things in history. Clearly, the trauma that other nations have experienced throughout the twentieth century is a trauma that the American people have never experienced — war never touched America. They were involved, but only at some distance from their own shores, and the fact that the only superpower we have at present was attacked on its own soil traumatised Americans. In any case, they don't have a very high threshold when it comes to accepting the unacceptable — the stiff upper lip, which is part of British life, is no part of American life. Everything is taken in such a way that many Brits would see as hysterical. So it's not surprising that America has vastly overreacted to what was of course technologically a very successful attack . . . The fact that the president then declared war on the attackers was probably one of the biggest mistakes ever made.

The attack on Afghanistan was just the first phase of a wider and much more aggressive American strategy that attacked Islamic terrorism in states wherever it had been, or would be, endorsed. In January 2002, the stakes were raised by President George W. Bush's rhetoric with slogans about "crusades" and an "Axis of Evil", which included the "rogue" states of Iran, Iraq and North Korea. The US National Security Strategy of September 2002, which advocated a policy of unilateralist, pre-emptive war, had a dire impact in the field of international human rights. An Amnesty International report of 2004 maintained that human rights and international humanitarian law were under their most sustained attack in 50 years.

Although the British government, led by Prime Minister Tony Blair, stood firmly behind President Bush, other western European governments perceived events differently. Their differences came to a head over the Iraq War of 2003. This was ostensibly over the issue of weapons of mass destruction, which Saddam Hussein was accused of harbouring, and the claim by the United States that he was involved in the 11 September attacks. France, Germany and Russia together played an active role in thwarting Anglo — US efforts to achieve a UN resolution authorising action. Peace activists were not surprised by the events leading up to the Second Gulf War. Many had visited Iraq during the 13 years that followed the 1990–1 war, witnessing the disastrous effects of sanctions on the lives of Iraqis — by 1996, half a million children were estimated to have died as a result. They had also seen the damage caused by illegal air strikes, mainly by the Americans and British, on Iraqi infrastructure during this period. This seemed a sure sign that Iraq was being softened up for another conflict. It soon became clear, in the way

408

Saddam's name was linked to al-Qaida, that Iraq was indeed the main target. All these factors fed into a groundswell of popular protest culminating in the vast marches of 15 February 2003 in European capitals, the United States and cities worldwide. In the UK, 10,000 marched in Belfast, 50,000 demonstrated outside the Labour spring conference in Glasgow, where Tony Blair made a belligerent address, and 2,000,000 people took to the streets in London to protest — a record number for any British protest.

In partnership with CND and the Muslim Association of Britain, the march was organised by the STWC, which became the major focus for an escalating mood that extended way beyond the usual left-wing activists. The event's hardcore were those who had opposed military action in Kuwait in 1990–1, Kosovo in 1999 and Afghanistan in 2001. But the march also attracted a vast, diverse swathe of the public, many of whom had never marched or protested before. They took to the streets and marched, not always from firm ideological positions or pacifism, but from a rising anger and fear that a war fought outside any true international agreement would make an already unstable world even more hazardous.

On Tuesday, 18 March, just over a month later, the British prime minister, Tony Blair, urged a packed, divided and sombre House of Commons that it had to "give a lead, to show that we will stand up for what we know to be right, to show that we will confront the tyrannies and dictatorships and terrorists who put our way of life at risk . . . A dirty radiological bomb is a real and present danger to this country . . ." On the evening of 20 March 2003, the war went ahead — the most unpopular war in Britain's recent history

409

— the legality of it doubtful. The official British legal advice was that existing UN Security Council Resolutions provided the necessary cover. The battle, launched by the mightiest military force in the world, took just three weeks to topple Saddam Hussein. On 14 April, Tony Blair informed Parliament: "We are near the end of the conflict, but the challenge of the peace is now beginning."

Tony Benn, president of STWC, anti-war activist

Before the 2003 war, I went to see Saddam a second time: that was televised and broadcast in full. I just went to ask him questions. I said, "Do you have weapons of mass destruction?" He said, "No." I didn't know whether to believe him or not, but it was perfectly true. I said, "Do you have links with al-Qaida?" He said, "No." I knew that was true because Osama bin Laden called on the Iraqis to overthrow Saddam because he was a secularist and not a religious leader. So it all turned out to be correct . . . It was an opportunity to hear the man we were going to topple . . . I went to avert a war, I'm glad I went . . .

Lindsey German, convenor, STWC, London

The group of people who came together, most of them had a left-wing background, but we never put that as a condition for joining STWC. What STWC did was to bring together people who disagreed about a lot of questions, but did see that this was going to be one of the greatest mobilising forces over the next few years. It has been pretty non-sectarian; what we've been able to do is rise above the real sectarian politics which give the Left such a bad name.

Andreas Speck, activist and organiser, WRI, London

The [2003] war in Iraq had a long time frame when all the lies came out. Stop the War Campaign said the important thing was mobilising marches from A to B, but they didn't really look into — yes, but what if we don't succeed? I don't think demonstrations alone will succeed.

Tony Benn, president of STWC, anti-war activist

STWC is a very interesting movement because it's completely non-sectarian. It has been open to churches and people of all opinions around the issue of that war. I think it has been the most powerful political movement of my life because it really has helped to change opinion in Britain and America against the war.

Kate Hudson, CND vice chair 2001–3, chair 2003 to present

Throughout 2002, we continued to have demonstrations. I had become an officer of STWC in 2002 . . . I proposed that CND was a joint organiser for the massive mobilisation against the war in Iraq September 2002. The MAB was involved for the first time as well. But the existing leadership of CND thought that we shouldn't be jointly organised, and there was tension in the leadership about the extent to which CND should be involved with anti-war campaigning. Every time there has been a war that has been relevant to CND, most people take the position that they want to do something, but there's always a small number of people who think we should only do things on nuclear weapons. My concern was about the *breadth* of the anti-war movement. I've always felt it important that the anti-war campaign should involve all different perspectives and people from different walks of life, CND is drawn from a particular section of British society: largely middle class, largely white, many Christians and faith people, many pacifists, liberals, some lefties — a broad church. I felt that it was important that its constituency, all of whom would have been against the war in Iraq anyway, should become involved in the movement so that it didn't become a sort of ultra-leftist thing . . . I thought that if CND didn't play a role in that it would be marginalised and taken out of the anti-war framework . . . it was this approach to the anti-war movement that made me change my mind about standing for the chair in 2003 . . . I was hoping that CND would bring the nuclear issue into the framework of all those new activists who were worked up about the war . . . We were significant in shaping the tenor of things, which we wouldn't have done otherwise. We had more members, more money than STWC, plus the fact that we were a household name and held in high regard. So STWC were always keen to keep that relationship.

Tina Richards, state organiser of Military Families Speak Out, Salem, MO, USA

When President Bush gave his State of the Union address in 2002, and watching both sides of the aisle, Democrats and Republicans, stand up and applaud this man who had just spoken of an "Axis of Evil", I thought: "Oh my God, do they not *understand!*" I was so amazed at where he was taking our country. This was *not* the opportunity I had seen after 9/11 — that we were uniting for peace. He was using words like those used in the Crusades centuries ago — "good" and "evil". So I recognised early on the lead-up to war and tried to tell my son, Cloy, a marine, that no matter what the media were saying, it was obvious that they were all lying. I had been involved in a support group called "Marine Moms Online", formed after

413

9/11. Afghanistan was going on and we were sending support packages there. With all the lead-up to the Iraq war, I used to protest how it was obvious they were lying and was told to shut up or get out. Eventually I was kicked out, having been told that I was a traitor to my son, that I might just as well go out and shoot him. By the time Cloy was deployed in 2003, in a war which I knew was based on lies, I was an emotional wreck.

I remember watching the start of the war and all the newspapers, "Shock and *awe*, shock and *awe*!", and everyone seemed happy that all those innocent people were being killed. It was such a *sad* time. No one else in the community had a son in Iraq. I was isolated, at that time . . . I felt I was the only person in the United States that felt this way . . .

Tony Benn, president of STWC, anti-war activist

At the time of the Vietnam War, [Harold] Wilson would *not* send troops to Vietnam. He came to the Cabinet once and said he'd just had dinner in Washington and Lyndon Johnson drank a toast: "To our closest dissociate." He was so *angry* with Wilson, who wouldn't even send a Scots Band — Lyndon Johnson would have settled for any British soldier in uniform to help him. Then of course in the Iraq War, Blair did everything that he was told. I still believe if Blair had said to Bush, "I'm not going along with this," Bush would have found it very difficult to take on Iraq alone, because he would have remembered Vietnam. He needed us, not for our troops, but for the political cover it gave him. This so-called "special relationship" is really a *colonial* relationship because another thing I discovered [as a minister] is that we don't have our own nuclear weapons, the Americans lend us the technology; as a result, in return, they expect complete access to *all* our intelligence information . . . I found there was an integration of the officialdom in London and Washington which leaves ministers in a completely false position because we're not deciding the things we say, we're deciding what the Americans have told us to decide.

Laurence Manton, journalist, *Soldier* magazine, Kuwait

I had heard of an expression for when wrong decisions are taken — "that way is madness" — and that was my view when I heard we were going to war in 2003. I think that it was a commonly held view, and I remember that *Focus*, the MOD's newspaper, carried some anti-war letters from staff at the start of the Second Gulf War. A lot of people were aggrieved that *Focus* had printed these letters from civil servants who had disagreed with the war. But the answer came back from the top of MOD, "People are entitled to their opinions."

Lindsey German, convenor, STWC, London

In the run-up to February 15, we went to the Social Forum in Florence, Italy, where all the European Left and social movements came together. And on the last day, we had a meeting to organise an international day of action for February 15, 2003, and it did happen all around the world — a great *dynamic* thing. About a week before the march, we knew it was going to be huge: we had the *Daily Mirror* doing their own placards, the route was published in the *Evening Standard* — a thing you don't normally get for demonstrations, not unless it's the right-wing Countryside Alliance. And we had David Gentleman's placards, such famous pieces of work — the blood spots became a symbol of so many of them. I remember saying to one of my colleagues before the march: "This is going to be such a big demonstration," and him saying, "Yes, I think we're going to get a million."

Kate Hudson, CND vice chair 2001–3, chair 2003 to present

I think the link between the organised sections of the Muslim community with other components of British society, like the Left or the peace movement, was absolutely historic. It was the first time that the Muslim community became involved in that way with British non-Muslim organisations, and I think that was exceptionally significant and has led to a real opening-up . . . The connection with the Muslims has also brought in working-class supporters.

Maggie Shevlane (Vitalis), advanced-skills teacher, Sandgate, Kent

As a student, I had been on the anti-Vietnam War march, and I had been taken on the Aldermaston marches by my father, but since 1968 I hadn't been on anything. I went on that march on 15 February 2003 because I felt very strongly that it was wrong to invade Iraq. There was no justification for this war: there was no direct threat against British interests; the idea of Saddam Hussein being able to send missiles within 45 minutes to Britain was absurd. I felt also that people were being conned into thinking that he had a connection with 9/11 and al-Qaida. But that was the justification for going "shoulder to shoulder" with Bush — an utterly stupid man. It didn't make any sense whatsoever. I went to say it was not in *my* name, my *husband's* name, my *family's* name!

Bruce Kent, CND chair 1977–9, vice president 1987–90, founder member of MAW

I was very accustomed in the '80s to being in Hyde Park on the platform and watching 100,000 to

417

200,000 people in that park, and it was absolutely inspiring. I used to say, "Hold up your banners!" and these banners would go up like flowers coming out of a garden — wonderful! But that February they exceeded that by far, by far, *by far*, and I was very briefly on that platform and there were people as far as you could see. I think there was such a *massive* sense of betrayal in the country, people were outraged, having seen the outcome of the first Gulf War, they thought: "God, they can't do this thing again!"

Tony Benn, president of STWC, anti-war activist

Somebody wrote an article saying it was just Trots having a day out. Well, if there are two million Trots in Britain, we've misunderstood public opinion substantially!

Maggie Shevlane (Vitalis), advanced-skills teacher, Sandgate, Kent

Whatever political affiliation you had, whether you were rich or poor, working class, middle class or upper class; it was multicultural, there were elderly people, people with young families, with pushchairs, men carrying children on their shoulders — they were all there and it was quite *tremendous* to see . . . they were there to have their voices heard.

David Gentleman, artist, illustrator and designer

The sea of people in Hyde Park was *unimaginable* — those two million — the biggest march in English political history . . . On such marches there are always some people who love chanting things and making a furore, but the great majority, it seemed to me, didn't look like red-hot political activists, but were thoughtful, amiable, ordinary, concerned people . . . It was before the war started and I'm sure that's why it was the biggest march, because people at that point had some hope that war — what was clearly going to be a total debacle and bungle — could still have been averted. Which of course it wasn't.

Kate Hudson, CND vice chair 2001–3, chair 2003 to present

The point I made was that, prior to this, we were particularly proud that the largest demonstration in Britain had been the anti-Cruise demonstrations in the 1980s, of 300–400,000 or more. The reason people had supported these was through fear and self-preservation, those personal things — we were frightened that we were going to die. With the anti-Iraq demonstration, there was no kind of personal reason to be there, virtually nobody had been to Iraq, or knew any Iraqis, we weren't going to be directly affected by the war, there were no compelling reasons to have that kind of demonstration. But it did take place in this quite extraordinary way. One element is the humanitarian instinct, not wanting innocent people to be killed. But I also think there was a great sense of moral outrage by ordinary people about the government lying — the way Blair behaved — that was a massive mobilisation.

Bill Hetherington, PPU activist

The PPU has always had a very firm policy in terms of joint activity. We will never formally join in terms of letting our name be put on a manifesto, whether for a march or demonstration or whatever, if the manifesto implies that war is OK. It's amazing how many people can't accept that: "You're against the Iraq War as much as we are, why can't you accept that?" We say, "Yes, we're against the war, but we're not *for* something else." Because they want to get respectable people on, they'll put something on that implies it's all right, it represents a "just war", for example. The huge argument that many have had over the legality of the Iraq War: "Was it sanctioned by a UN resolution?" As if, from a moral point of view, that made any difference. On the big march of 15 February, there were PPU people there and the PPU ran a stall alongside selling *Peace News*.

Brigadier Jeff Mason, Commanding Officer, Commando Logistic Regiment, Royal Marines, Operation Telic, Iraq, January — May 2003

You have all the television screens tuned into News 24 and there was a big wide TV screen in the main galley while we were in the administrative area in Kuwait. So clearly everybody could see the major protest in the UK and outside the UK too. And a number of papers were vehemently anti-the-war, and the troops were reading them. That really was the only issue. I got them together to talk them through why we were there, and to put aside any doubt and any issue going on: we had a job to do and we were going to *do* it. Of course as soon as we crossed the line to departure, then everything was for "our boys" and the media was on side.

Lindsey German, convenor, STWC, London

People thought: "If two million people marched, then surely someone should *listen*." They didn't ... I think the BBC's role was absolutely *disgraceful*. They barely covered the hundreds of protests that took place on the day that war started. Essentially, the media coverage when war began was as if a military coup had taken place. The only people whose opinions they valued were loads of high-up military personnel, or military experts and defence secretaries, essentially to

421

justify the war: "How are they doing? How far have they got? Where are they on day five?" and so on. I think that was a big psychological shock to people . . . People still say to me: "Well, we didn't stop the war so wasn't the campaign a failure?" I don't regard it as a failure. I say: "You have to look at it, historically. How long did it take the Suffragettes to get what they wanted? How long did it take the civil rights movement?"

David Gentleman, artist, illustrator and designer

And there's been an increasing sense of déjà vu with the following marches, but I also think it's been worth going on and making a point. It hasn't been fruitless. Blair looked unstoppable and now [2008] Blair has become a kind of ineffectual joke figure.

Maggie Shevlane (Vitalis), advanced-skills teacher, Sandgate, Kent

The march didn't work. But I'm proud of the fact that I went on it, and I feel that it's very sad in terms of our democracy that we weren't listened to, and that the aftermath of that war proved that we *should* have been listened to.

Bruce Kent, CND chair 1977–9, vice president 1987–90, founder member of MAW

Parliament was quite out of step with public opinion. It was bad for politics, a disaster from beginning to end. No plan what to do with Iraq once they'd militarily knocked it over. Of course the two greatest powers in the world and a few others could knock it over, but they couldn't build it up again.

Andreas Speck, activist and organiser, WRI, London

After the 15 February demonstration, when the war started, we were trying to focus more on saying: "Yes, demonstrations are important, but we need to focus more on non-violent resistance." This wasn't welcomed by STWC. We were trying to mobilise for blockades of military bases . . . We were saying that the military bases in Britain are used for the war in Iraq, so planes are taking off from Fairford to bomb Iraq, and we could shut down Fairford if we wanted to. If, of the two million people who were in London on 15 February, only 1 per cent would have gone to Fairford to blockade or enter the base, they wouldn't have been able to use it. In STWC there was nobody saying: "OK, what's next?" The next thing was to get another march. So the big problem was that we knew the demonstrations would not stop the war, that although 70–80 per cent of the people were against the war, they [the government] can sit out demonstrations. But if we had done more mobilisation against the bases, on the one hand we would have had more direct confrontation with the soldiers, which might have increased resistance from them; and on the other hand, it would have been much more difficult for them to function, especially Fairford, an important base where the B52 bombers take off to bomb Iraq. If they couldn't use Fairford, then it would have been a logistical problem.

Reg Keys, founder member of MFAW

We are not a group of pacifists or anti-war protesters, but against the war in Iraq, 2003. Because of the deliberate misleading of Parliament about weapons of mass destruction, the way the whole case for war was made, it soon became abundantly clear that it was a war of options, not necessity. This is when a fair section of the families of the bereaved came together as a group to form MFAW. We give support to each other, go to meetings together and give one voice in an attempt to bring the government to account for what was going on in Iraq. Not only was the whole basis of the war based on falsehood, WMD, but also about the lack of kit, the circumstances in which these young people were dying, meant that somebody had to speak out, and we felt that as military families we were the ones to speak out. Our members are from a broad range of backgrounds, from a cleaner to a company director. What we have in common is a strong sense of right and wrong, what should be done and shouldn't be done. It has been frowned upon by many people. It is not in the British tradition to question the army.

Rose Gentle, founder member of MFAW, Pollock, Glasgow

My son Gordon was killed in Basra by a roadside bomb. It was announced on TV that a British soldier had been killed and it showed the body of a soldier lying on the ground. I thought, "That looks like my son." Later they told me it was Gordon . . . Gordon was a 19-year-old lad, he had no idea where Iraq was, he thought he was going for peacekeeping. He went out there after just twenty-four weeks' training and was killed in just under three weeks. I knew he could be killed or injured when he joined up, but he wasn't killed by weapons of mass destruction, which is why he was sent . . .

Kate Hudson, CND vice chair 2001–03, chair 2003 to present

Some of the MFAW have come on demonstrations, mothers and sisters as well as men. They

425

speak at demonstrations and we've been together in Downing Street and at the Cenotaph. They are clearly against the war in Iraq, but would never do anything disrespectful towards the army, but are very opposed to government policy. That has helped to create a good culture within STWC; it already existed in CND, where we have Ex-Services CND and one of our vice presidents is a retired Air Commodore [Alastair Mackie]. Perhaps an anti-army stance could have developed in STWC, but it didn't happen because the influence of the Military Families helped people understand *why* young men join the army, this is very often through poverty, to get jobs and training opportunities, not killing people but helping people. I think it's very important that there hasn't been hostility towards the troops.

Martin Bell, former senior BBC war correspondent, founder member of MAW

I know a lot of senior soldiers and they were nearly all opposed to the war within a few weeks of it starting . . . I know families of soldiers who went on the peace march; one was the wife of a major general. This war was not widely supported by the army, but of course the army is a "can-do" organisation. It doesn't say, "Well, we're not too keen on this war, prime minister . . ." If it does, then it gets into the political domain and of course its funds are going to be cut. So there was distrust of the government from all sides at this time, which has been cumulative and it is more acute now [2009] that we know more about those MPs' expenses.

Brian Haw, Parliament Square, Peace Campaign, Westminster, London, 2001 to present

What did I say to Tony Blair?

Forty-five minutes Mr Blair.
Forty-five minutes Mr Bliar.
Dodgy dossier.
Plagiarised thesis.
Forty-five minutes sexy lie.
Because of that all the innocents had to die.

Monstrous! Foul! He was a barrister, a lawyer: *shame* on him, he abused the law.

Tony Benn, president of STWC, anti-war activist

The Hutton and Butler reports were cover-ups. Recently I've invented an imaginary character called "Lord Button" who is a composite of the two, and he's brought out of retirement whenever there's a crisis and proves conclusively that the government had nothing whatever to do with it.

427

Kate Hudson, CND vice chair 2001–3, chair 2003 to present

In the autumn of 2002, with Mark Thomas, the activist comedian, we challenged the legality of going to war on the basis of UN Resolution 1441. The court ruled that it was non-justifiable and wasn't in the interests of the British people to have this ruled upon, so we were ruled out . . . it has since transpired that the Attorney General at one point shared our view. It subsequently became very important again because the issue was coming out, it was realised that the war was not legal.

Bruce Kent, CND chair 1977–9, vice president 1987–90, founder member of MAW

There were some COs in the Second Gulf War: not many, but a few. Particularly that young RAF doctor [Malcolm Kendall-Smith] who did one tour and then came back and said he wouldn't go again, I think he was court-martialled. So a handful, but not a great number, unlike the United States, where a number of people fled to Canada and elsewhere because of their refusal to take part in that war . . . People who say "no" are brave.

Bill Hetherington, PPU activist, ACCO representative

When people ask me what I am involved in today [2009] and I say conscientious objection, they say, "Isn't that a bit old hat? Isn't that an historical thing?" I have to tell them that it *is* a current issue . . . and that it is still an issue within Britain with volunteers to the armed forces of all ranks as well as reservists . . . There is a formal procedure, but there is no reason why any member of the armed forces knows that it exists.

Brigadier Jeff Mason, Commanding Officer, Commando Logistic Regiment, Royal Marines, Operation Telic, Iraq, January — May 2003

You make a natural assumption that if somebody is a volunteer — we're all regulars, we were not conscripted — then why would you want to join an organisation in the first place unless you wanted to serve in that organisation? Of course perceptions change and certainly, in the build-up to the Iraq war, we in the military had never come across such anti-war feeling at home, and it was difficult to get that across to the soldiers, sailors and marines under my command. But I would never have dreamt that somebody would come up to me and say, "Actually I don't believe that I should be taking part in this conflict." But I had never been

429

trained what to do in that situation. Just thinking off the top of my head: you'd have to have a debate with that individual about why, as a regular, he couldn't take part in the conflict. I suppose there must be a system to deal with him or her, but I have to say I'd be at a slight loss with someone who had voluntarily joined the service knowing what they could perhaps have to do.

I do remember in 1982 going down to the Falklands, on HMS *Intrepid*, that there were a number of individuals in the ship's company who were new and hadn't been with the ship before — and these would be senior ratings, chief petty officers as well. And when we sailed down they said, "We didn't join the navy to go to war." Which was of course quite true because in the twenty years before '82, the navy essentially had been a peacetime organisation and had not fought a general war. Perhaps these wouldn't have been classified as conscientious objectors, but they were certainly raising a concern that what they were about to do, they didn't want to do it. War had always been a spectre that might happen and actually it *was* going to happen. I think one of them was flown off. I don't know what happened but he couldn't do his job, wouldn't do his job? I'm not sure . . .

I personally wouldn't treat an individual with contempt or suspicion if they had said that. I would think that a) there was something wrong with them or b) they had a sudden change in why they had joined so there must be something wrong or something that's causing them to do that. You have to be quite strong to hold up your hand and say, "I'm not going to do this any longer." In an organisation whose fundamental existence is to achieve an end state of success through physical violence, and for someone who is a volunteer in that organisation to suddenly say, "I don't want to do this," pulls you up short. So you have to get some professional advice. I've never had it happen to me, fortunately.

Malcolm Kendall-Smith, a medical officer in the RAF with the rank of flight lieutenant, was the first British officer to face criminal charges for challenging the legality of war against Iraq. He did not claim conscientious-objector status; his argument was that the war was manifestly unlawful. A court martial, held in Aldershot from 11 to 13 April 2006, found Kendall-Smith guilty of five charges of disobeying orders. He was sentenced to eight months' imprisonment. He was also ordered to pay £20,000 towards his defence costs; these were covered by legal aid. He was discharged from the RAF.

Kendall-Smith's case was followed by the similar case of Trooper Benjamin "Ben" Griffin, who also took his stand on the illegality of the Second Gulf War, rather than on the exercise of conscientious objection. Griffin was a British SAS soldier who served a three-month tour in Baghdad alongside American forces, including Delta Force personnel. He refused to leave for a second tour, citing the illegality of the invasion as well as the illegal tactics of the United States troops and policies of the coalition forces, which he had witnessed first-hand. Griffin, unlike Kendall-Smith, was not court-martialled.

Malcolm Kendall-Smith, statement made after the court-martial sentence had been passed

I have been convicted and sentenced, a very distressing experience. But I still believe I was right to make the stand that I did and refuse to follow orders to deploy to Iraq — orders I believe were illegal. I am resigned to what may happen to me in the next few months. I shall remain resilient and true to my beliefs which, I believe, are shared by so many others.

Iraq was the only reason I could not follow the order to deploy. As a commissioned officer, I am required to consider every order given to me. Further, I am required to consider the legality of such an order not only as to its effect on domestic but also international law. I was subjected, as was the entire population, to propaganda depicting force against Iraq to be lawful. I have studied in very great depth the various commentaries and briefing notes, including one prepared by the Attorney General, and in particular the main note to the PM dated 7 March 2003. I have satisfied myself that the actions of the armed forces with the deployment of troops were an illegal act — as indeed was the conflict. To comply with an order that I believe unlawful places me in breach of domestic and international law, something I am not prepared to do.

The invasion and occupation of Iraq is a campaign of imperial military conquest and falls into the category of criminal acts. I would have had criminal responsibility vicariously if I had gone to Iraq. I still have two great loves in life — medicine and the RAF. To take the decision that I did caused great sadness, but I had no other choice.

Ben Griffin, interview with defence correspondent Sean Rayment of the *Sunday Telegraph*, 12 March 2006

The Americans had this catch-all approach to lifting suspects. The tactics were draconian and completely ineffective. The Americans were doing things like chucking farmers into Abu Ghraib or handing them over to the Iraqi authorities, knowing full well they were going to be tortured ... I can remember coming in off one operation which took place outside Baghdad, where we had detained some civilians who were clearly not insurgents, they were innocent people. I couldn't understand why they had done this, so I said to my troop commander "would we have behaved in the same way in the Balkans or Northern Ireland?" He shrugged his shoulders and said, "this is Iraq", and I thought "and that makes it all right?" As far as I was concerned that meant that because these people were a different colour or a different religion, they didn't count as much. You cannot invade a country pretending to promote democracy and behave like that.

Andreas Speck, activist and organiser, WRI, London

Conscientious objection is usually a middle-class movement — to be able to articulate, to know about philosophical questions, theories and so on — it is not to say that uneducated people don't resist, but they don't use these kinds of terms. So, generally, I would say that in all countries, people who are COs are very much middle class. We see today that the military needs more qualified people, part of the professionalisation of the military, which means they need to conscript the middle classes more; when this happens you see more of the CO movement. That's why it's growing in certain parts of the world, America for instance . . .

Leon "Bud" Deraps, ex-US Navy, Second World War, Veterans for Peace campaigner, St Louis, MO, USA

My grandson, Leon, named after me, grew up in Columbia, a very small Missouri town, less than 500 population, like all rural Missouri, very conservative, very religious. The recruiters are in the schools there just as they are in all the minority schools all over the country; they're even in Mexico now! My son in the late 1960s volunteered for the Marines and served four years. However, he didn't get to go over to Vietnam, didn't go through what many of the veterans went through and are still suffering from. Leon, the youngest of his six children, was seeing this recruiter in the school all the time, and he decided to join the Marines just like his daddy did. He signed up, aged 17 years and went in when he was 18, just after he graduated from high school.

I saw him before he went to boot camp and urged him to change his mind. But then I saw him when he came back and gee, look at this picture here before he went into the service — a smiling, happy kid. Now look at *this* — dead eyes, mouth turned down. What they go through! They are drained of all emotion and all they learn is kill, kill, *kill*. Every military march has cadences. Here's just one:

> Throw-some-candy-in-the schoolyard
> Watch-the-children-gather-round
> Load-a-belt-in-your-M60
> Mow-them-little-bastards-down.

An ex-drill sergeant wrote this one: "We're going to rape-pillage-and-burn, rape-pillage-and-burn . . ." This is what they march to for 16 weeks.

435

When the Iraq War took off, I had started warning my son and his wife just what was happening to our troops, and they forbade me to say anything more — they just didn't want to hear anything about it. They were determined that he should go. So they proudly sent him off and I'm sure that he was a very good marine. They made him a lance corporal right out of boot camp, and he went straight out there as a humvee [High Mobility Multipurpose Wheeled Vehicle] driver in Falluja. In about three months, a roadside bomb hit his vehicle. He and another marine were killed and three others were seriously injured.

Now at the funeral in that little town, in a small cemetery way off the road, 500 people showed up to see him buried. But at that funeral, my family were saying what a noble cause he died for and they were still supporting the war. During that year, 2004, their beliefs and mine had separated, and they didn't want any contact with me. Even when he went over and came back in a coffin, even at that funeral, they felt alienated from me. They felt that my visit to Iraq at the time of sanctions in the 1990s, to work on a sewage and water plant for the Iraqi people, was shameful. That I had been supporting the enemy that had killed their boy. I have nothing but love and support for them because I grieve too . . .

Tina Richards, state organiser of Military Families Speak Out, Salem, MO, USA

His experience in Iraq has changed Cloy totally. From being a happy, family-loving kid, he went into alcohol, drugs and violence, very unstable. He's been identified as suffering with survivors' guilt, and post-traumatic stress disorder, he has threatened killing himself and, if provoked, the fear is that he might kill or seriously injure somebody else. He has turned totally against the war in Iraq, but would never be a conscientious objector and would probably serve in Afghanistan if he felt that wasn't all lies. But he realises now that the Iraq War was an illegal and immoral war and he belongs to the Anti-Iraq War Group and has started to talk about the terrible things he saw and did in Iraq, especially to women and children. But he isn't against all wars, no.

Reg Keys, founder member of MFAW

Tom was in the first wave sent out in 2003. He had been out there from February to June '03 and was due home in eight days' time. He was sent to a police station with just five colleagues to discuss refurbishment with contractors when a mob attacked the police station and Tom and his colleagues were killed. That's all we were told. Over the coming months we began to find out in more detail, and the more we found out, the more angry the families became . . . When Tom was killed he had no distress flare, no red-phosphorus flare, grenades, smoke grenade, morphine. There was a standing order that all sections in the Al Amara base must have two effective forms of communication; my son didn't have one . . . Whatever happened they couldn't call for help. The only communication they had was a 30-year-old radio, vehicle-borne, which evidently didn't work in the First Gulf War . . . There was also a standing order that they should have 150 rounds of ammunition; they only had 50 against a mob about 400–500 strong with rocket-propelled grenades and AK47 rifles . . . I've read the post-mortem details of three of them; I spent two hours with the pathologist, Nick Hunt; I know every wound on Tom's body. So I know how my son met his death just four days short of his twenty-first birthday and eight days before coming home . . . Clearly people were at fault here, what else had they covered up? . . . You had 20,000 well-equipped troops in Northern Ireland when Tom was there, but just 8,000 in Iraq, that far-off land with a totally different culture — it was futile, futile . . .

David Gentleman, artist, illustrator and designer

The moment came when the toll of people known to have died because of the war in Iraq had reached one hundred thousand. STWC wanted to make this point. I was thinking about it, how a thousand seems a lot, but how one hundred thousand is an unimaginable kind of figure. And I wondered if you could, by printing a thousand sheets of card, each with a hundred drops of blood on it — blood being a very emotive symbol — and laying them out, then you would be able to see in one eyeful how many lives of individuals it took to make up one hundred thousand. My job was to make them fit . . . eventually it was a perfect job. This was 12 February . . . It was to last just one day. It started early in the morning and the exact position was worked out by Nicholas Wood and his architect friend . . . I've got a wonderful photograph taken by Jess Hurd which gives the detail of individual blood spots in the foreground, back to the skyline of the Palace of Westminister, Big Ben, and the buildings of Parliament and the skyline of the House of Lords. It made a telling juxtaposition because without Parliament's supine agreement to the whole thing, those one hundred thousand would not be dead. I think the idea of making the unimaginable abstraction of one hundred thousand — just six digits on a sheet of paper — into one hundred thousand drops of blood, was taking it into a new way of understanding a number. The number has gone way beyond that now . . .

Brian Haw, Parliament Square, Peace Campaign, Westminster, London 2001 to present

For five and a half years, I was sleeping on the pavement with a piece of plastic tarpaulin over my face — no framework. And in the wintertime you get the ice and the snow, and in the summer you get all the condensation — not very nice. And completely and utterly vulnerable, and somebody can be putting their boot in you as they go by, you just have to trust . . . I've been attacked: my nose was broken by an American, and by an Israeli. Was he violent! Nobody else has knocked me down on that pavement, but he did. The police? I'm on crutches; that's the result of police attacking me on 5 May, Bank Holiday Monday, 2008 . . . How long do I intend to stay? Another 30 seconds, I hope. Do you know, I'm so utterly pissed off for being here. It's so bloody *horrible*. I drag myself out of that tent on the pavement in pain. It's horrible. What keeps me going? What the flaming hell keeps someone going in Palestine, in Iraq or Afghanistan where there is no fucking hope because they're all dying! And what are we doing about it, folks? What is happening? Where is law? Hope? "Salaam. Shalom. Peace. Justice. Peace *now*" — that's what I call out on my megaphone . . .

Tony Benn, president of STWC, anti-war activist

In the summer of '45, coming back on a troopship from the Middle East, where I'd been sent after qualifying as a pilot, I heard the words of the Charter of the UN, which are written in my mind: "We the people of the United Nations are determined to save succeeding generations from the scourge of war which twice in our lifetime has caused untold suffering to mankind." Those words are a pledge my generation gave to the future generation, and we tore it up when we went into Afghanistan and Iraq.

Reflections Across a Century of Protest

The reality is that deep in their hearts an awful lot of Establishment people don't believe that there will ever be a world without nuclear weapons and they don't believe that there could ever be a world in which war becomes eccentric, not a mainstream thing. And they talk about "Utopia" and suchlike. Well, Utopia will only happen when we make it happen . . .

ON WAR

Stephen Winsten, CO, First World War

There comes a time in history when a thing that's noble suddenly becomes ignoble, shameful. And that's a time when you try to stop that kind of thing. It happened in 1914 with the war. That to me was an ignoble thing. And I'm proud of the fact that Wilfred Owen, Isaac Rosenberg and Siegfried Sassoon and Edmund Blunden showed it up as the obscene thing it was with their poems . . . No more glorification of war: show it for what it is.

442

George Dutch, CO, First World War

As the war dragged on, people were more and more coming round to see that the war would achieve nothing. It didn't. The Great War was a disaster, and the "great peace" of Versailles was a disaster. The wars that we've had since are only breeding more wars. The Great War bred the Second World War, and that the Korean and Vietnamese wars, and they're breeding more wars all the time and all over the world . . . None of the peoples of the world want war or bloodshed, nuclear weapons, or anything of the sort. They only get them because they're told they're for defence. But of course they're not; they're for *attack*. You can't defend with bombs. You throw them at the enemy; you don't hold them for yourself. There's no such thing as defence in modern warfare. It's all about those who can get in first and do the most damage.

Tony Benn, president of STWC, anti-war activist

When I went to Hiroshima in 2008, it was the most moving experience of my life, and the thing I shall never ever forget is that I saw on the steps a little mark and I said, "What is that?" And they said, "That was where a child was sitting and it was vaporised," and next to it was a metal lunch box, twisted into a hideous shape, and the child

443

had completely disappeared. And I went to the Hibashi Hospital to meet the survivors ... The whole thing connects in my mind as the crime of war. I look at my grandchildren; they're the first generation in human history with the means to destroy the human race. Theirs is also the first generation which has the resources, the know-how and the money to solve the problem. If the money wasted on nuclear weapons were diverted, it would make a huge difference. So these ideas became my core beliefs, and out of that came the various campaigns that I've been involved with.

Laurence Manton, journalist, *Soldier* magazine, worked in Northern Ireland, Bosnia and Kuwait/Iraq

There's very little conventional warfare these days [2006] of the kind where you'd send tanks and troops in and attack the enemy, and kill them or take them prisoner. Now you have artillery that sends over rockets, and you send in the aircraft and bomb them, and cluster bombs go everywhere and wipe out an area the size of a football pitch. Then the troops go in and mop up. And now it's a war against terrorist insurgents and you're fighting an enemy that looks the same as the peaceful ones in a country, and I don't think that's a war you can win.

Reg Keys, founder member of MFAW

If you watch the adverts for army recruitment, they portray soldiers as high-tech cyberwarriors, with push-button technology, who call in air strikes and assistance in the blink of an eye, but it isn't the case. We've had recent cases [2009] of soldiers dying in the middle of minefields because they didn't have maps of them. You have Chinook helicopters coming in to rescue them in the middle of the minefield and setting off further explosions. You had the soldiers outside the minefield discharging their rifles to gain attention because they hadn't got batteries for their radios. If you are going to ask a soldier to put his life on the line for his country, the least the soldier can expect in return is the equipment to do so. Anything less is a betrayal of the oath of allegiance the soldier signs. Gone are the days of the First World War, which my critics tend to hark back to, where you were told to go over the top and run into machine-gun fire and that's it, there's no recompense. Those days are gone. We're in the *twenty-first century* and life cannot be taken so cheaply, with such futility . . .

Rev. Kenneth Greet, Methodist minister, CO, Second World War, president of the World Disarmament Campaign

Like all Christian leaders, I find myself wrestling with the Christian doctrine of the Just War. It is, I think, significant that every time there's a new conflict in which this country is involved, say, the Falklands, then the First Gulf War, Church leaders find it more and more difficult to describe war as "just". The reason is that the doctrine of Just War has been a doctrine of limitation. That is to say, the Church has never officially said all wars are admissible and Christians can participate. They always sought a way to lay down certain conditions, so that in its present form, the doctrine of a Just War insists that such a war must be declared by a legal authority; that it must regard the doctrine of proportionality, and only use that amount of force that is necessary to secure your ends; that the means used should be consistent with man's nature as a rational being; that there should be no direct attack on non-military objectives. The more you add up these clauses, the more it becomes apparent that there's *no way* in which modern warfare, with its almost infinite capacity for destruction, can rest upon the old doctrine of Just War. So Church leaders are searching around for other means to justify participation in warfare. And with the introduction of nuclear weapons, most thinking Christians today would have to describe themselves as "nuclear pacifists" . . . So we're in a very interesting stage in the ecclesiastic Christian Church's argument about war and what should be the attitude both of Churches and individual members of Churches to war . . .

ON COLLATERAL DAMAGE

Bruce Kent, CND chair 1977–9, vice president 1987–90, founder member of MAW

Looking at these wars on television, they look like video games, these guided missiles going along with these little target squares around them and picking off a lorry on a bridge. Nowadays drones are being directed from Arizona in the States; they can pick off a man on a camel in Yemen if they want to. All that has made war more awful and more detached . . . One hundred years ago, nine out of ten war casualties were military; today [2008], nine out of ten of those who die in war are civilians. You can't talk any more about "collateral damage" . . .

Martin Bell, former senior BBC war correspondent, founder member of MAW

I've now spent half a century in the unquiet corners of the world . . . There have been many changes in warfare since I first started war-reporting half a century ago. First of all, the weaponry is so much more destructive. Second, there is increasingly a lack of any distinction between soldiers and civilians as targets. I would say, anecdotally, most of the more recent wars I've been in civilians are about 90 per cent of the casualties. By and large soldiers are better able to take care of themselves, and the civilians, especially the very old and the very young, cannot. So there is another reason why wars have become more futile: because they are fought among civilians and actually for the allegiance of civilians, they are hearts-and-minds campaigns, and you do not change people's minds with high explosives . . . Also, there has been an increasing proliferation of civil wars, wars of collapsed states and what General Sir Rupert Smith calls "wars among the people".

Don McCullin, world renowned photo-journalist, West/East Pakistan (Bangladesh) Civil War, 1971

. . . I went into this flooded schoolroom which they had designated as a hospital. I could hear crying and there was a girl sitting at the foot of her mother's bed — more like a table really. They'd propped her up and she was frothing all kinds of foam stuff from the nose and mouth. She was in the last throes of dying because someone had given her the wrong medicine. Her daughter was absolutely . . . in meltdown . . . screaming. I took a picture. You know sometimes people say to me, "Do you ever hide behind a camera?" What they mean is, "Do you emotionally hide?" Which you do. You think, "Do the job. Don't think. Do the job." This sad woman died and they were going to take her to the Dead Tent area. But the children threw themselves down on the floor and were banging their faces and punching the floor with their fists. I was breaking up! I thought, "God, this is nothing to do with photography. Nothing to do with journalism. It's to do with . . . these people don't deserve this. They're just peasant farmers." It was all I could do to get through those next few moments.

So I photographed the woman lying down and the children crying all over her. And the father was holding the baby which was trying to bite his knuckles from hunger. Then, when it was all over, I think I was crying. The father said to me, "What should I do?" I put my hand in my pocket and did something which could be despicable because whatever you do at this stage couldn't be right anyway. So I gave him a great bundle of filthy old Indian money and I said a stupid thing, "Go to Calcutta" (get away) — the first thing that came into my mind. "Feed your family. Feed your family." I was buying him off in my own emotional way . . . I was almost playing the knave. I felt so two-faced and so bad. And I thought, "You know you have got a

449

really amazing picture here" but at the same time, "What a terrible way to earn a living."

Janet Cameron, British civilian doctor, International Gulf Peace Camp, Iraq and Jordan, 1990–1

It's always innocent people that get blown up or suffer; you never get the governments: they're sitting in bunkers. During that war [Iraq, 2003] I thought: "If only you could give the politicians of both sides the rifles and stick them out in the desert and let them get on with it, I wouldn't have felt too bad about that!" I always fall back on telling people about the Battle of the North Inch in Perth. At the time of James the First of Scotland, there were these two clans and they were forever slaughtering each other, raiding the cattle, carrying off the women and generally creating mayhem and devastating two fairly prosperous areas of the Highlands. Finally the king had enough and said, "Right, you want to be warriors, I want 30 men from each side." So he got the thirty from each side and he stuck them in a ten-foot stockade in a large park in Perth called the North Inch. He then said, "Get on with it," and they started fighting. And they bloody well fought, and the king and his court sat and watched, and the king pointed out that this was war, would they kindly look at it and see if they *liked* it. It went on until there was just one man left on one side and six or seven in the other clan. That was the end of the feud. That settled it.

Tony Benn, president of STWC, anti-war activist

War is the murder of men, women and children; it's rape; it's torture; it's plunder. That is what war is, and it is presented in quite a different way in the media. I've never been able to distinguish in my own mind the difference between a stealth bomber and a suicide bomber — both kill innocent people for political purposes.

Sergeant Eric Bollinger, US Marine Corps, 513 Squadron, 5th Marine Expeditionary Brigade, Saudi Arabia, First Gulf War

I was all excited when I first went over there because I was envisioning something glorious and reflecting back on how soldiers must have felt when they entered World War I . . . But I saw war for what it was. It really shattered my preconceived illusions, that it is not as clean and neat as the generals, and the press they manipulate, would like us to think. It's a messy affair that winds up doing a lot of damage to people who have no relation to the combat — like the civilians in Iraq who are having to endure all the hardships with us having taken out their water plants and other infrastructure.

451

So I have a very different perception of war than I had before. Today I'm very much active in human rights. I run an Amnesty International chapter here on campus and people say, "Well, isn't that a big switch in ideology, going from being a marine to being a human-rights worker?" I tell them that if they had seen some of the things that I had seen in the Persian Gulf, 1991, then they would understand.

Reg Keys, founder member of MFAW

When I look back on that night of "shock and awe" bombing of Baghdad, killing hundreds if not thousands of innocent people, was it not an act of terrorism by men in suits? I think it was. Iraq was a country on its knees with a soft underbelly after years of sanctions. Now [2009] it is back to a tribal system with women of a lower order.

Brian Haw, Parliament Square, Peace Campaign, Westminster, London 2001 to present

On 7 February 2007, General Dannant was voted by 18 per cent of Channel 4 viewers the most politically inspiring person in the country; Tony Blair had 8 per cent, David Cameron had 6 per cent, the Archbishop of York 12 per cent. And Brian Haw of Parliament Square had 54 per cent. Why did the people vote for me? Love your neighbour as yourself and love your neighbour's child as your own, no matter what their country, colour of skin, race or religion. That's Christianity, Mr Blair, Mr Bush, Mr Brown. That's humanity, sanity, that's the path of peace . . .

ON THE ROOTS OF WAR

Colin Ward, anarchist

It's funny that in the popular imagination anarchists were associated with bombs and bomb-throwing and so on. But if you totalled up the whole history of political assassinations, you would find that the amount done by anarchists was about .000 per cent. The anarchists' reply of course is that it's the governments who wield the bombs which people have actually got to worry about. And nowhere more than in the post-war period has this been more evidenced: that it's governments which possess nuclear weapons, it's governments which possess war planes and so on. There is a very strong intellectual argument for the anarchists' case that all wars are wars of governments against people.

Reg Keys, founder member of MFAW

These men — Blair and Bush — are nothing short of war criminals responsible for hundreds and thousands of deaths and total misery in the Iraq War. The MFAW has been pushing for an independent public inquiry and there has been a gathering voice from anti-war MPs . . . I've recently had an invitation to go to Portcullis House, London, for a meeting where they are going to draw the terms of reference the inquiry will encompass . . . I was galvanised into my campaign to enter politics for the May 2005 election, standing against Blair in Sedgefield, when I won 10.7 per cent of the votes . . . When I look at the public outcry against MPs' expenses today [2009] — claiming £2,000 to clear a moat, claiming for chandeliers, the second homes, TV, sinks and all sorts — and when those lads arrived in Iraq, some of them didn't even have a pair of desert boots! I feel so disgusted with this; I want to bring them to account and I'm tempted to take a foray into doing it again — to give them a good kick in the ballot box . . .

Martin Bell, former senior BBC war correspondent, founder member of MAW

It is good that the original decision to hold the public inquiry [into the Second Gulf War] behind closed doors has been reversed — you can't do that any more. These wars are fought in our name. It had to come. I'm amazed it has taken so long — six or seven years after the event by the time it gets going. Let's see what the evidence is, and if the evidence is delivered in public, then we can judge.

Brigadier Jeff Mason, Royal Marines

It's an interesting debate that anti-war demonstrations should be focused on the government, not on the military. We don't decide to go to war; it's the higher authority that makes that decision. All too often people confuse the military with the government, and the same fury that's put out to the military should be focused on the government. We are only an instrument and tool of that government's policy, not the decision-makers.

Martin Bell, former senior BBC war correspondent, founder member of MAW

Another change I've noted in warfare is that the present wars in Iraq and Afghanistan is the first time that our young men and women are sent to war by politicians who, not a single one of them, have any experience of war, none have them have even worn a uniform or served in any regiment or any armed force whatsoever, so they are more inclined to believe that wars can deliver political outcomes, which they can't.

Gordon Rushmer, war artist, Bosnia, Kosovo, Afghanistan and Iraq

Some wars are necessary I am sure, some things need to be put right, but we don't always tackle it the way we should. I *despise* politicians; there are very few now [2007] that I've got any time for at all, and I'm talking of British and Americans more than others. They seem to waltz into situations without any thought of what the knock-on effects are going to be, and they're not around long enough to worry about the after-effects, like in Iraq — that'll roll on for years and years. That is a real tragedy . . .

Maggie Shevlane (Vitalis), advanced skills teacher, Sandgate, Kent

If they're going to take us into war, they must say what the reasons are, be upfront and don't *lie*. It was through lying to the people and Parliament that Parliament became muted and we were not a proper democracy. What's happening now [2009], with the MPs' expenses scandal, in a way is fantastic because it has shaken the status quo and suddenly the British people, who are not very political, are beginning to see how things work. They don't like it and they are saying so. So that's *true* democracy. Maybe today if we went on another march we'd be listened to! But in February 2003, we were just dismissed: "You don't really know anything. *We* make the decisions. *We're* in charge."

Air Commodore Alastair Mackie, RAF, Ex-Services CND, Generals for Peace, vice president of CND 1990 to present

I think our prospects of destroying ourselves are very great. I'm thinking now of Arnold Toynbee, whom I have a great respect for. Just before he died, as a very old man, he saw no hope ... He saw sovereign nationhood as a total evil. As long as we think in terms of patriotism of this country and that, as long as we have huge impersonal institutions which we have no control over, as long as weapon systems, and all the human aspirations and evil that go with weapons, as long as all this depends on what we call sovereignty, as long as we think in those terms, so long will we be warlike.

Jerry Hanson, Vietnam veteran, member of Veterans For Peace, Marengo, IL, USA

On campus we had several demonstrations and vigils for the First Gulf War. As a professor I was sympathetic to the students, because I didn't want to go to the Vietnam War but felt it my duty to do that. My message when speaking out against the war was a lot about the horrors of war, and that one shouldn't be so easily convinced to go to war. But another message was that you really have to be patient with people who *support* the war, because once war begins the integration process starts: people's children get drafted through no fault of their own, or they join the military in times of peace and don't understand the implication, and then in a short period of time, they are expected to convene on the battlefield, and parents automatically want to defend their interests and if that means bombing the hell out of people, so be it. They want their sons and daughters home safely. It occurred to me that a whole lot of consensus for the military was that sort of sentiment: "Whatever it takes, we want them back . . ." You have to make people understand why you're against the war, but you have to understand why some people are drawn into a blind sort of patriotism and go along with the appalling cheerleading . . . The government promised to bring people back, and they did, but people don't care how many Iraqis died in those bunkers in the sand. Integration in a military state means you identify with the state, even reluctantly — that sense of duty of obedience that I didn't question when I went into the Vietnam War — a penetration of nationalism into the very soul of a person.

Mervyn Taggart, absolutist CO, Second World War

I've never really felt any great pride in my country. That's perhaps rather a dreadful thing to say. I feel that the value of nationalism and patriotism is only in so far as it contributes to a composite whole to the culture and progress of mankind. But certainly not that my country's any better than any other. This is the danger of patriotism, that it leads very often to a sense of national superiority, which is an element in war and certainly was a major element in the crimes of the Nazi regime and the war that they unleashed on the world.

Jennifer Morel, pacifist

The world is my country. I look forward to the day where there'll be no frontiers. That's my ideal world. The men and women of the world are my brothers and sisters. That's the way I look at it. And there's no class, colour or creed anywhere, no divisions at all. If I have any patriotism then it's to the world and to the people in it, not to one country.

Bruce Kent, CND chair 1977–9, vice president 1987–90, founder member of MAW

I always say that security has now moved from the castle perception of the world to the boarding house. With the castle, you have a big big wall, and you have cannonballs and you keep them smart and shiny, you've got boiling oil in the pot and a drawbridge that works. You don't want a war with

459

another castle, but by God if it comes about, you're ready and they're not going to get over your walls. That's the way people used to think about nation states — big castles with big cannonballs. Today we live in what I call the run-down boarding house. Some of us live in the rich west end and others in destitution in the east end. But we all have the same water, the same decayed electrical system, we've got woodworm in the joists and no fire escapes. And the idea of one end fighting the other is simply absurd, because all the problems affect everybody in the boarding house. Security is now a *global* concept.

Canon Paul Oestreicher, Anglican pacifist, CND vice president

The famous dictum: power corrupts and absolute power corrupts absolutely — this on a collective scale is the cause of war. And of course social injustice can be used to justify war, and the leaders of al-Qaida of course recruit from the dissatisfied. But on the whole they're recruiting young intellectuals, brilliant people who can organise, they are not those who have no bread. Poverty is wrong, full stop. Absolute poverty is sinful when others have more than they need. But the idea — as many argue — that if we beat poverty we'll have peace is not something that I subscribe to.

Harold Bing, absolutist CO, First World War

If you ask people about their attitude to war today [1974], they say they're against it, of course. But it doesn't mean that if it comes they'll resist it. I think that if we had another war, we'd have far more COs than we had in the Second World War, but I think the majority of people in this country are inclined to say, "Well, if the government decides then we'll have to accept it." . . . Once a law has been passed, they accept it; this is the attitude of the English people.

Jennifer Morel, pacifist

To my mind, the working classes of the world are brought in to do the fighting because they are the majority. If they were to say, "No, we're not going to war," then probably you wouldn't have war . . .

ON THE COST OF WAR

Reg Keys, founder member of MFAW

I accept the risk which goes along with being a soldier. But they're *professional* soldiers trying to do a professional job. The least one can expect is that they're given the basic tools for their trade. My son died without the tools of his trade . . . The government has always said that a soldier doesn't have the "right to life" under Article 2 of the European Human Rights Act [EHRA]. Also, the Health and Safety Act does not apply to soldiers outside Britain's territorial waters, only within. A case has recently [2009] been brought by a mother whose son died of heatstroke in Iraq. It was upheld. The government appealed and this was turned down. Now, under Article 2 of the EHRA, the right to life does relate to the soldier. At present it is going to the House of Lords. That could open a floodgate for the families to take the government to court for a breach of human rights against the children they've lost.

Martin Bell, former senior BBC war correspondent, founder member of MAW

I know that last time when I asked Combat Stress, the Armed Forces mental-health society, they had 8,000 men on their books — men, hardly any women then — and it must be more than that now. Most of them were veterans of the Falklands War, but the first wave was coming through from Iraq and Afghanistan. When you consider that our soldiers, especially the infantry, are involved day by day in the most intensive fighting since the Korean War, there are going to be a lot of cases coming at us, bruised minds. I think we're beyond palliative care here and various new therapies are being tried. There's now a realisation in the MOD that this is a very, very serious problem. One of the statistics that struck me was that two hundred and fifty men were killed in the Falklands, but more than that number of men have taken their own lives. That indicates the scale of the problem. There are now people in the government who understand, but I still think we suffer from having a lack of military experience among the government.

Reg Keys, founder member of MFAW

What a lot of soldiers turn a blind eye to is depleted uranium. It is used in ammunition, it's used in warheads, and when I asked, "why do you use it?" the answer was, "You get more bang for your bucks." It does leave contamination. There's a high level of deformity amongst babies in Iraq. Maybe we should start looking at this and getting our soldiers tested when they get back. I can't help but think with the bombs we rained on Iraq that it must be a badly contaminated land now . . .

James Gilbert, Vietnam veteran, St Louis, MO, USA

When I got out of the army, I didn't have any money so I didn't have a lot of clothes, and I went back to college wearing my field jacket to school. I'd been away for two years in the war and didn't know too much about what was going on at home. One day, I remember seeing this woman, out of the corner of my eye; she came racing at me screaming, "Baby-killer!" Oh . . . *wow!* . . . I never did any of that stuff, although I knew guys who did, and given the context of their lives, I know *why* they did it. And I don't think we can hold them responsible. It's easy when you live in a sanitised, sterile kind of environment and judge, but it seems to me that the judgement is made when you go to war, because part and parcel of that is the atrocities — you can't have a war without atrocities. It isn't the guy doing it, it's the *society* that's supporting all of this. If you think what it's like to be out in an unfriendly jungle for 30 days, not to know who your allies are, when those coming up with hand grenades are literally kids, and you're getting shot at, and you don't want to be here, and maybe the people at home don't like the war — you're mad, you're crazy, you've become an animal, you *have* to be an animal to get by. You *can't* survive as a sensitive human being, you cannot.

Bruce Kent, CND chair 1977–9, vice president 1987–90, founder member of MAW

And if you link militarism with other social needs like poverty, health, education and climate change, and see the interconnectedness of these things, then war doesn't just kill on the battlefield, it kills all the time by stealing from the people things they can actually use. One of my laments so far is that we haven't got major anti-poverty agencies to take on this enormous drain of militarism as seriously as they should. We're spending today about a trillion and a quarter dollars: that is a thousand billion plus. But the connections are not made because people haven't woken up to the fact that militarism is part of the problem. Military vehicles and aeroplanes use gallons and gallons of high-octane fuel, even if there isn't a war, and they occupy acres and acres of land for their affairs. Even without war, there are going to be accidents; there are something like 17 nuclear-reactor submarines on the ocean beds of the world. So all these problems are interwoven.

Bill Ramsey, war-tax resister, peace activist, St Louis, MO, USA

If we're going to get to the heart of war, we've got to change the way our society takes a huge percentage of the world's energy resources and we look to that as a long-term solution — how do we save food and resources and not waste them?

James Allen, member of Veterans Against War, social worker, St Louis, MO, USA

As a social worker, I'm absolutely scandalised that we talk about the "victims of war", but the victims of war include not just those who are actively engaged in the conflict. In a city like St Louis and

465

other American cities, the victims of war are the poor, the elderly, all of those who rely on health and welfare services. If you look at the US Budget over a period of time and compare the difference between the defence and welfare service, you will find great increases in the former. Where do these increases come from? They come at the expense of the welfare services. So, when we are talking about the victims of war, we have to think not just of those who are engaged in the actual waging of war, but those who are affected because of the way the money is being spent. Every time there is an increased expenditure on war, it is being taken away from others in need. As a social worker, I cannot support this. I am also a war-tax resister; that is I recognise my obligation to pay taxes to something other than war, but withhold a portion of my federal taxes that I have worked out go to the defence budget.

Leslie Hardie, CO, Second World War

Violence is concerned with power and greed; people seek their own advantage to the detriment of others in the world. The financial people who swindled pensioners out of their pensions showed violence towards these people.

Tony Benn, president of STWC, anti-war activist

With the Iraq War, the Americans are spending $400 million a day while people are dying of starvation in places like Ethiopia, Somalia and Haiti. So, the second crime of war is not just the crime of killing people, it is the crime of diverting resources that would meet the world's needs.

Lesley Abdela, gender expert, women in post-conflict reconstruction areas

In the modern world, we're facing horrendous challenges right now: epidemics like HIV/Aids, all the things that are going to come out of climate change — the floods and famines. Women will be in the front line of these, because they're the ones so often displaced, they're the ones who end up being trafficked, they're the ones who will bring up the next generation. It's not an optional luxury; it all ties up with conflict. The more we get climate-change problems, we'll get more conflict, because people will fight over water, fight over resources, and if we're going to solve these problems, then we're going to have to draw our leadership from the full talent pool — women and men.

ON THE LURE OF WAR

Canon Paul Oestreicher, Anglican pacifist, CND vice president

War is actually enjoyed by a lot of people, the adrenalin runs and nations are buoyed up by it . . .

Ernest Goldring, CO, Second World War

The war for some people brought a great deal of excitement, a great deal of compensation in lives which were in other ways dull, monotonous and boring; great opportunities for displaying courage and bravery and recognition, so that in some ways it brought the best out of people as well as the worst. The experiences we heard about in the East End of London in the bombing, the courage of the people there was absolutely terrific, and the uncomplaining way they faced up to the world when they came out of the shelters, not knowing whether they'd got a home to go back to . . . I think there is no doubt that war has a unifying effect . . . A great community spirit develops, a great willingness to help, support and comfort, things which in peacetime people seem very reluctant to get involved in. There is that side to it.

Colin Ward, anarchist

There was a phrase used in the First World War by a writer called Randolph Bourne who talked about how in wartime the state and the nation become what, unfortunately, they can't actually become in peacetime. He spoke of the nation "lumbering into the great peacefulness of being at war". It's a phrase which has always stayed in my mind because there is truth in this. I'm sure that plenty of people in the war thought their destinies were being solved for them; they didn't have to think for themselves and act for themselves. And of course as you will know very well, people do cherish the sense that they perceive of national unity and common initiatives in wartime. And the [Second World] war was, in that sense, a peaceful period.

Janet Cameron, British civilian doctor, International Gulf Peace Camp, Iraq and Jordan, 1990–1

Let's face it, there's something about warfare that goes very deep into the human psyche. People *like* fighting. There's nothing like a good battle to get folk interested. I think the peace movement misses out on this — that they ought to go and mobilise those who are not totally respectable, totally pacifist, but want to go out there and do something active . . .

469

John Petts, CO, 224 PFA, 6th Airborne Division, Germany, 1945

One thing I did learn about human nature watching violence occur was to discover that war and violence is only possible to the angry, the acquiescent and the sick. We know about the angry — those who are full of righteous anger and have to go and do something about it when faced by wrong; that is understandable. We know about the acquiescent — the people who, when conscripted, doggedly trail their feet and go along with it because there's nothing else to do — they haven't got the force of personality or moral courage to resist orders and be out of step with their community and their time. But the third, the sick, are those people who have violence *in* them. Don't ask me who they are, just pick up any newspaper any day and follow the criminal cases in the courts. And the terrible realisation is that never do all those sick people have such an opportunity to destroy, smash, harm and hurt as in the case of war. And so I have seen men doing things to men and women by members of all sides. I have seen British soldiers doing things I wouldn't wish to describe or put on record. A man can kill another man in anger or because he's commanded to because of the war, but if you're sick you go up to his body after you have killed him and, picking up a spade or a rifle the wrong way, you smash, and smash, and smash his face to a pulp until someone pulls you away. That's what I mean by sickness. That's what I mean by sadism at the level of madness. That's *war*.

Lesley Abdela, gender expert, women in post-conflict reconstruction areas

I think there's absolutely nothing to be said in favour of fighting wars. But one would be lying if you didn't say that sometimes as a result of wars in history, good changes have come about. There is a dilemma: war is ghastly, but it's also exciting, you see a light in men's eyes, and I know a number of media friends who get a buzz, you feel very alive, you live every day so much more, and you don't have so much time for trivial things back home. So I would do everything I could to prevent a war. I would like to be in a world where you can cause the same amount of changes without needing to go to war, because it's futile, it's pointless. And you know it's pointless when, later on after the war, you see people who were at war with one another sitting down together and having coffee, and you see places where you can say, "I remember that place ten years ago, people were murdering each other, so what was the point? We could have sorted it out over a game of backgammon, for heaven's sake!" If only politicians and people at the top could be more trusting and open . . . Surely we can find other ways of changing things without causing so much misery and so much horror and waste.

Don McCullin, world renowned war photo-journalist, 80 conflict-zones

Quite frankly I'm ashamed of it all really — I mean all of the things I've seen in my life, all the blood, all the burnt children. I'm absolutely disgusted with the whole business and if you say to me, "Well, why did you stay doing it for thirty years?" I suspect I was suffering a kind of mental breakdown in a way...I was actually nothing less than a kind of war junkie really. I recognize this today. But at that time all I could do was to go to war. If I wasn't in a war, I was at home, unhappy...I'm somebody that went through all that, but at the same time there were moments when I was excited about it. Which was totally wrong.

Reg Keys, founder member of MFAW

I think at one time since 2003 there was a dip in recruitment, but it's picking up again now. The strange thing with young men, flushed with the exuberance of youth, is that they *want* to go to war, they see themselves as immortal. Maybe they play computer games and when you get hit you can just reset the machine and you're standing up again. But when you're hit by an AK47, you don't get up again . . .

ON PACIFISM

Bruce Kent, CND chair 1977–9, vice president 1987–90, founder member of MAW

Pacifism? I still eschew the term, not that I have any personal feelings about it, but for the man or woman in the street, a pacifist is someone who sits down and lets wicked people do wicked things and doesn't interfere. It's not the fault of pacifists, it's the way it's been written, and sometimes you have to say that the coinage of language is so damaged that it's not going to be redeemed. I never use the word about myself. I wish we could find a little simple word for the priority of non-violence. But I believe the absolute priority of non-violence does not exclude the fact that if I was in here alone with you and some thug came in with a baseball bat and wanted to beat you with it, I would seize the thing as best I could and try to stop him. Then to push it a bit further and say: well, suppose you were paralytic and you had a gun, would you shoot him, not in the leg, that wouldn't stop him, but in the heart, would you do that? I'd say, yes I would.

Paul Townsend, CO, FAU, Second World War

It was fairly easy for us to be pacifists, but would I, if I was a Serb or Croat or Bosnian Muslim of a certain age, have the courage to stand aside? . . . I mean, how easy it was to go before a comparatively tolerant tribunal and then be allowed to do the most useful things in a unit of Friends!

Vic Newcomb, CO, 224 PFA, 6th Airborne Division, France and Germany, 1944–5

I never liked the term "pacifist"; it seems to imply a totally irresponsible acceptance of what comes along. I don't think that's what the anti-war movement or the COs were about. We were in opposition to planning the use of war for national purposes, and we actively promoted another approach to international problems, a better way.

James Bramwell, CO, 224 PFA, 6th Airborne Division, France and Germany, 1944–5

There must have been so many combatants whose heart wasn't in the war, but it was a job they had to do. It is the dilemma of all those who are not professional soldiers, the amateurs. This was so movingly expressed by the poets of the First World War . . . The war of 1939–45 was not a subject for poetry any more. The "pity" that Owen talked about was moral already and so one didn't feel inspired in that war to tell the world what it was about. It already *knew*. It was a different world.

Mervyn Taggart, absolutist CO, Second World War

I've always found it easier to talk peace to people in the military, particularly with officers . . . They are far more realistic than the philosophers we tend to be surrounded by in the peace movement. They know what war's like, and they've gone into the forces often to keep the peace and see this as a way of protecting a country and deterring aggressors. The weakness of the peace movement is that it concentrates on a philosophy which hasn't really been very successful so far. But I've always had some very wonderful experiences with military men who have understood my point of view very much better than even those in the Quaker Church.

Martin Bell, former senior BBC war correspondent, founder member of MAW

I think that some of the best advocates and ambassadors of peace are military people — people with knowledge of war because they have seen for themselves how it fails to deliver what politicians, who have no experience of war, expect of it.

Lesley Abdela, gender expert, women in post-conflict reconstruction areas

When I first went to Bosnia as a journalist for just a few weeks during the war there, I had a mindset that was pejorative towards the military — I really didn't like the idea of military machines and militarism. What changed my mind was that one day in the Bihac enclave, which had been under siege for two years, suddenly some planes came screaming over, and all the Bosnians I was with looked up, smiled with relief and shouted, "NATO. NATO!" They felt *safe* then, and I saw that when you had a disciplined military protecting people, it can be a force for good. Now of course things can go wrong — Srebrenica, for instance — horribly wrong, but if you've got well-disciplined troops of any nationality and they're protecting people and behaving properly, then my respect for them has grown a lot. Before then, I was very biased against anything militaristic.

Marjorie Asquith (Whittles), CO, FAU, Second World War

The thing is that soldiers *are* brave, and I can't help thinking there must be some other way of using that spirit. It would be nice if there were a volunteer force in every country. It could be armed in case of having to defend itself against something really violent. But it could be trained as disaster teams, and there would be opportunity for members to put their lives on the line. I still think there are enough people who want to do that. They would be sent to any part of the world where they'd be needed — it would be peacemaking and not just peacekeeping. People do need a bit of an adventure and perhaps to take some risks. Regiments could be kept and honours awarded, say in an Armenian earthquake. They could be "robust pacifists". Soldiers sent out to kill in the Second World War turned out to be very good at looking after refugees and doing other peaceable things . . .

Lindsey German, convenor, STWC, London

I am not a pacifist, no. I don't agree with pacifism as such, and as an ideology I don't think it's very coherent. But, although as a socialist I'd say there are wars that it's right to fight — the Vietnam war against the Americans, or the Spanish Civil War — as I get older, I think war is so terrible now that, while I think there are certain wars that you *can* justify, and I do believe that people have to stand up for themselves and fight back, the weapons are so terrible that we have to find a way of developing a world without war. I don't believe the pacifist route is the way to go with this. But I do think there are no winners in war, and the people who suffer are increasingly civilians and women and children. If you look at modern-day wars, the

477

numbers of birth defects, the number of cancers, the depleted uranium that is used, all those kinds of things are obviously apparent. The number of mentally ill soldiers through both the weapons of war they work with, and the general experience of being in the army, are huge. So it's a very big question.

Vic Newcomb, CO, 224 PFA, 6th Airborne Division, France and Germany, 1944–5

I worked in Africa for ten years and have friends who regard themselves as part of liberation movements of Africa. But however much I say there is another way and you should be actively pursuing the way of non-violent resistance, or civil disobedience, or persuasion to achieve what is denied you, I find it impossible to condemn them when they say, "No, we have got to take to the bush and justice will only come out of the barrel of a gun." Their belief that armed conflict is the only way is very different from the kind of military build-up that most advanced nations take refuge in to defend their own interests.

Canon Paul Oestreicher, Anglican pacifist, CND vice president

Although I am a pacifist, I have never shied away from violent situations or people. I agree with my successor at Coventry Cathedral, Andrew White, who [speaking from his ministry in Baghdad, 2006] says, "I don't waste my time talking to liberal people, they're not the problem, it's the nasty people I spend my time with."

(Lord) Hugh Jenkins, founder member CND and chair 1979–81, Labour MP and minister 1964–79, House of Lords 1981–2004

I regard myself as a nuclear-pacifist. I took part in the Second World War with a bit of a struggle. I eventually decided that Fascism had to be defeated. But during the course of the war I became convinced that it had to be the last war because we were going to destroy ourselves. That conviction crystallised when the bomb was dropped on Hiroshima. I've never been hostile to pacifism, but at the same time I was not one of them. I am not a pacifist now, but if I am sure that today almost any war can end in a nuclear war, and if I am a nuclear-pacifist, perhaps I *am*.

Eric Turner, CO, Second World War

I still feel against war and violence, yes. But I am less innocent about it. I can see a place in the world for an instrument of force such as the UN forces which attempt to arrest certain kinds of political behaviour before too much damage is done . . . I know that for many Quakers that falls short of what our peace witness ought to be, but that is the point I have reached. I still think it leaves my central pacifist position intact. But it's easy to say that when you're 72. My sympathies are with the young people who still have to consider what they must do if war came — a different kettle of fish.

Theo Cadoux, CO, Second World War

No, I am no longer a pacifist. I am not sure how long I remained one, but it took some time for it to sink in. As you get older, you get less sympathetic to one's fellow men, feeling that a lot of what they suffer is their own fault. And so much more aware of the depths of wickedness that appear to exist in other people. There is no doubt there was enough to know at that time about the behaviour of the Nazis towards the Jews and others in concentration camps. But one persuaded oneself at that time they could be brought round to another point of view if only you had a chance to talk to them — that everyone had good in them that could be brought out. But the longer I live, the more convinced I become that some people are wicked and unredeemable. When I see some of the things that are done all over the world by groups of raiders and guerrillas and suchlike, I feel I would have no compunction, if I were in a position to do so, to stop them by forcible means and, if necessary, kill them.

Reginald Bottini, CO, Second World War

I now incline towards complete pacifism on the grounds that the level of destruction today is so much greater, and that I can see no cause, no ideology, no oppression which would justify opposition to it by the slaughter of countless millions.

Janet Cameron, British civilian doctor, International Gulf Peace Camp, Iraq and Jordan, 1990–1

I think I'm less of a pacifist than before I went out to Iraq [1990–1]. If I lie down and let people walk over me, what happens to the children? You have this problem with people who have families: you can always accept it for yourself, but it's a little different when you have a family to consider. Then you have everybody else's families to consider, and then you go right back to the argument: oh, you can only fight in self-defence. And what constitutes self-defence? Sometimes it's easy to draw a line and be absolutist about it, but not for me.

Rev. Donald Soper, Methodist minister and peace activist

For me, increasingly, the concept of the pacifist position is the only one that will work. But it's got to be a *political* matter as well . . . If you create a programme that depends on the preparation for war, then the situation today requires a massive transfer of power administration away from the preparation for war, and so long as the economy depends on millions of people employed in the production of weapons, you're in a cleft stick.

Spencer Cox, CO, Second World War, USA

If nobody keeps the idea of non-violence and pacifism alive then society has lost a great deal. I also think that pacifists are put in an unfair position by being asked to defend their position when somebody like Hitler comes along. If we had had our way originally, then the power Hitler gained would not have *existed*. It's unfair for pacifists to be put on the defensive when the world is not of their making.

Bishop Freddie Temple, CO, FAU, Second World War

Very often I would spend my holidays with Uncle William Temple [Archbishop of Canterbury, 1942–4], who, although pro-military, also made the interesting point that there must be pacifists among us. He used to say, "England is worth fighting for, but only if there are sufficient pacifists in it."

ON LOOKING AHEAD

482

Tony Parker, CO, Second World War

Oh yes, I had very high hopes of the UN at the end of the war; I think everybody did. Everybody, not just pacifists, would like a world without war and would like universal brotherhood and would like a more sensible way of conducting human affairs, so I wouldn't be unusual in having high hopes of the United Nations. They were disappointed, but then I suppose in a sense that's to be expected.

Eileen Daffern (Clough), CND executive, Brighton branch

The most revolutionary statement I've read is the charter of the UN. It's never had a chance. They talk about a New World Order and forming a new organisation, but we've got one and we've got to make it work . . .

Kate Hudson, CND vice chair 2001–3, chair 2003 to present

I think it's right to talk about the wider anti-war movement, not only those who organise the marches, but beyond that: the new organisations, the old ones, the pacifists' organisations like War Resisters' International, the Lib Dems, and other new groups coming from different angles against war. They are organising things in their own way and being brought together under this big

483

umbrella [STWC] for the demonstrations. We've never been able to get a demonstration of that size again. To some extent it was because 15 February [2003] happened *before* the war had started and people were trying to stop it. It wasn't a protest demonstration; it was trying to persuade the government not to do it. But I think, after the occupation, that the mobilisation has held up pretty well and it has continued to be active against the Afghanistan War, the possible attack on Iran and the main issue of getting the troops out of Iraq . . . I think it's hard to quantify these things, but I think the anti-Iraq war demonstrations are part of the troop withdrawal we've recently seen, they had a positive impact. Also, everyone today knows what weapons of mass destruction are — WMD has become such popular and common parlance . . . So the issue really moved forward.

Lindsey German, convenor, STWC, London

What is very interesting is how important women are in the movement today . . . If you think of me as convenor of STWC, and the current chair of CND is a woman, and the past chair of CND was a woman, you see that we've got lots of women at national level. But what we find is that women locally are very often the backbone of the campaign. The Muslim women are *incredibly* important to it; you get young women in their hijabs who are supposed to be, by common

484

consent, mostly passive. They're exactly the opposite to that: they're tremendous, absolutely *tremendous*. So the whole question of women and the anti-war movement is a very interesting one. We've had a couple of generations now where women have been politically active and conscious about doing things as women, and I suppose the reason why women are so well represented is partly that this is a campaign which has coincided with that, and it's all coming to fruition now.

Rev. Donald Soper, Methodist minister and peace activist

I'm more and more convinced that just as the temperature got rid of the dinosaurs, the whole concept of armed violence is in danger of getting rid of us . . . But one of the characteristics of the Christian way is this indomitable hope that if you cannot see the prospect of the better world, you've got to hope for it and put your trust in it, even when that trust seems intellectually or morally insubstantial. I think, morally, we're in a recession . . . I still believe that we're not good enough for the society we want to see and won't be until we have an elevation of the quality of personal responsibility and goodness. That's what I object to in the capitalist society, which believes it doesn't much matter how good you are; in fact, the more selfish you are, the more likely you are to succeed. I think that's the pity, the most dreadful thing.

485

Bruce Kent, CND chair 1977–9, vice president 1987–90, founder member of MAW

The reality is that deep in their hearts an awful lot of Establishment people don't believe that there will ever be a world without nuclear weapons and they don't believe that there could ever be a world in which war becomes eccentric, not a mainstream thing. And they talk about "Utopia" and suchlike. Well, Utopia will only happen when we *make* it happen. It's culture change that I'm aiming for.

Denis Allen, absolutist CO, Second World War

When I joined the Quakers, I was interviewed by a couple of elderly Friends and asked if I believed in the Second Coming. I said I believed in the ultimate arrival of the Kingdom of Heaven on earth. Now [1990], I have to say I don't. I think the earthly kingdom will always be imperfect because we are all imperfect. But I'm optimistic in the light of my German friends who told me, "We have to be wiser." I think that's possible, providing the wisdom is genuine wisdom and not just technical efficiency — *that* is very scarifying.

Kenneth Wray, absolutist CO, Second World War

The situation regarding peace today [1980] is very different. Whereas before the [1939–45] war you felt you could make an impression somewhere, that what you did registered, today everything has become so vast that your efforts, parallel to those you made before the war, would be quite fruitless and useless. It's nice to join marches, Aldermaston or somewhere, but they don't have any effect, simply because everything is so *big* — they can be ignored. Until you are bigger than they are, you will be ignored. And God help that you will never be bigger than they are. You've got to keep the small unit, the one, the freedom and humanity. It's only the individual that can keep that. I am sure of that . . . The growth of state power is so terrible that I feel the individual can do nothing except stand up against it every time it comes up.

Ronald Huzzard, CO, Second World War

The abolition of slavery is a good case in point; there was only a very small minority prepared to make a stand against the slave trade. The whole pressure of democratic rights in this country has come from people who took a stand and were persecuted: the trade unions development, the Tolpuddle Martyrs, the Suffragettes — how many years were they in advance of their time? And so I felt this about war when I was faced with the choice early in 1940. And like Martin Luther, I decided: "Here I stand, I can do no other."

Lindsey German, convenor, STWC, London

I've always had the view that if you look at the history of progress, of change — it does come not just from the movement, or from political parties and so on — but it comes from what people *do*. I always say at meetings, "We don't get change from American presidents, however much you might think he's [Barack Obama] a good thing." But change always comes from what people like us *do*, and that's the most important thing. You can go back as far as you want — the Peasants' Revolt or whatever . . . So I think we've drawn on that tradition and it gives us a fantastic amount of experience and also an historical sense. Otherwise, if it's only one damned thing after another, then you start thinking, "Oh, we've had a demonstration and that didn't work, then another demonstration and that didn't work," without understanding that you are changing ideas and changing methods of working. I mean, the way young people do things nowadays, the technology is ABC for anybody under 30: the texting, the emailing, and this is obviously having an impact on the way people organise. A tremendous wealth of experience is coming together and that's what a movement is . . .

Mervyn Taggart, absolutist CO, Second World War

I don't think that human beings will ever reach their true level of achievement and development until every human being has some say in decision-making at all levels. And I think that this, in some way I can't fully understand, has a great bearing on the question of war and injustice on the mass scale we're experiencing today.

Don McCullin, world renowned war photojournalist, 80 conflict-zones

I started becoming aware of the power of photography in the 1960s. I suddenly thought to myself: "For the first time in your life you have a purpose. Use it. You could turn the minds of certain people and situations." I think looking back, that it was me being slightly naïve. Because I've looked back and seen repetitious events taking place in the world that have got worse and worse. I've never thought in all honesty, that anything I've ever done photographically has changed anything. My work may have helped certain people's attitudes, but it certainly hasn't turned anything completely around the other way. I'll give you an example. A friend of mine, Eddie Adams, who took the famous photograph of the police chief in Saigon shooting the man in the head — the war raged on for another seven years after that. Take all the appalling atrocities that have taken place in Sierra Leone where you have drug-crazed youths chopping off the hands and limbs of children and babies. And then Rwanda . . . So I ask myself, "Have I done any good?" Have I changed anything? And quite frankly, I really don't believe I've changed anything at all . . .

But the way I have tried to conduct my photography is that I want you to *look* at my photographs. I don't want you to reject them and say, "No, I can't look at those pictures. They are atrocity pictures." Of course they *are*. But I want to become the *voices* of the people in those pictures. And I want to seduce you into actually hanging on a bit longer when you look at them. So you do go away with some — not immediate memory — but that you go away with some conscious obligation. The complacency is always going to be there, but you have to *fight* that complacency . . .

Bruce Kent, CND chair 1977–9, vice president 1987–90, founder member of MAW

In this country we founded a movement called the Movement for the Abolition of War. It started in 2001 and Joseph Rotblat was our president. When he got his Nobel Prize in 1994, he said, "The time has come for us, not just of getting rid of individual weapons systems, but to talk about the *abolition* of war." So this is a big thing for me, to try to get people to realise how unnecessary, apart from being barbaric, war is, and to put mechanisms in place to make war an unthinkable thing to do by way of resolving conflict. So I think that a wider view of ending war has entered into the focus of the peace movement in the way it wasn't in the 1980s. Then we were up against Cruise missiles and Polaris submarines, and hotspots, and people weren't thinking any more except to defuse this row between the two superpowers.

Tony Benn, president of STWC, anti-war activist

Every generation has to fight the same battles again. There's no permanent victory and no permanent defeat and there are two flames burning in the human heart: the flame of anger against injustice and the flame of hope of a better world. And my job is to go out and fan both flames.

Eileen Daffern (Clough), CND executive, Brighton branch

I think we're optimists or pessimists by nature, and I think my genes have made me an optimist. I think everyone working in the peace movement must be an optimist . . . I'm now ninety-five, I've seen in nearly a hundred years human nature change . . . I *believe* in change, and given the opportunity, given that we don't holocaust ourselves out with nuclear weapons, we *will* be a better race . . . But I think that history moves very, very slowly. When you go to the Grand Canyon and stand on the south rim and the guide points to the mile down to the Colorado River at the bottom and then points to a centimetre from the top — that's the time man and woman have been on earth, and that gives you perspective . . . We're still in a state of barbarism . . . It gives me a reason why we're so incredibly stupid and our politicians are the worst that I can remember . . . But without hope, what's the point of living?

List of Contributors

CONTRIBUTORS: SOUND ARCHIVE

Each contributor's surname is followed by their maiden name (where appropriate), date of interview and the reference number (in brackets) from the Sound Archive, Imperial War Museum, where the testimony is kept. Japanese names are given in western style, surname at end.

Abdela, Lesley, 2008 (31557)
Allen, Denis, 1990 (11522)
Allen, James, 2006 (29886)
Arnold, Dr Ralph, 1991 (12102)
Arrowsmith, Pat, 1995 (12525)
Asquith (Whittles), Marjorie, 1989 (10650)
Austin, Christopher, 1992 (12901)
Baldwin, Brian, 1993 (13084)
Barnsley, Tom, 1988 (10144)
Baty, Private James, 2001 (21192)
Beavor, Douglas, 1980 (4788)
Bell, Martin, 2001 and 2009 (22155)
Benn, (The Rt Hon.) Tony, 2008 (31686)
Besly, Charles, 1992 (12746)

Besly, Kim, 1992 (12685)
Bing, Dorothy, 1974 (555)
Bing, Harold, 1974 (358)
Bollinger, Eric, 1994 (14195)
Bottini, Reginald, 1980 (4660)
Bracey, Bertha, 1980 (4646)
Bramwell, James, 1986 (9542)
Brocklesby, Bert, 1988 (10122)
Brockway, Fenner, 1974 (476)
Brough, Bill, 1991 (12103)
Burbridge, Harry, 1989 (10773)
Cadbury (Rowntree), Tessa, 1994 (14205)
Cadbury, Michael, 1987 (10051)
Cadbury (Wilson), Rachel, 1987 (10038)
Cadoux, Theo, 1989 (10738)
Cameron, Janet, 1991 (12227)
Cammaerts, Lt Colonel Francis, 1985, (11238)
Campbell, Mary, 1991 (12222)
Campbell (Childs), Thalia, 1992 (12698)
Carter, Sydney, 1986 (9218)
Cox, Spencer, 1994 (14206)
Daffern (Clough), Eileen, 2008 (31687)
Daniel, Jack, 1986 (9399)
Dennett (Rowley), Jane, 2001 (21017)
Deraps, Leon "Bud", 2006 (29692)
Douglas-Home, William, 1988 (10354)
Dunn, Ted, 1988 (10355)
Dutch, George, 1974 (356)
Eddington, Paul, 1986 (9328)
Englekamp (Wallis), Joanna, 1992 (12700)
Flint, Tony, 1995 (15368)

494

Fox, Lloyd, 1988 (10173)
Gandhi, Arun, 1998 (18633)
Gardiner, Gerald, 1988 (10456)
Gentle, Rose, 2009 (32733)
Gentleman, David, 2008 (31507)
German, Lindsey, 2009 (32727)
Gibson, Tony, 1991 (12267)
Gilbert, James, 1991 (12394)
Goldring, Ernest, 1980 (4658)
Goodlif, Phylis, 1989 (10774)
Gow, Sheila, 1992 (12940)
Grant, Donald, 1975 (711)
Greaves (Catchpool), Jean, 1996 (16835)
Green, Royal Navy Commander Robert, 1993 (13271)
Greet, Rev. Kenneth, 1992 (12705)
Haley, Tom, 1988 (10143)
Hanson, Jerry, 1991 (12396)
Harbottle, Brigadier Michael, 1988, (10145)
Hardie, Leslie, 1991 (12179)
Harris, Michael, 1986 (9325)
Haw, Brian, 2008 (32520)
Hayes, Denis, 1981 (4828)
Hayes, Eric, 1994 (14200)
Hayler, Mark, 1974 (357)
Heard, William, 1980 (4760)
Hetherington, Bill, 2009 (32521)
Hipperson (Hanlon), Sarah, 2000 (20900)
Hoare, Joseph, 1974 (556)
Horsfield, Alec, 1997 (17516)
Howse, Katrina, 1992 (12904)
Hudson, Kate, 2009 (32734)

Morel, Jennifer, 1980 (4692)
Morris, David, 1987 (9811)
Morrish, David, 1988 (10116)
Morrison, Sybil, 1974 (331)
Mutimer, William, 1994 (14229)
Nesbitt, Cathleen, 1976 (733)
Newcomb, Vic, 1986 (9400)
Nicholls, Bernard, 1980 (4631)
Nicholls (Steynor), Doris, 1980 (4634)
Norman, Frank, 1980 (4652)
Oestreicher, Canon Paul, 2006 (29424)
Osborne, Ruth, 1995 (15372)
Page (Watson), Nora, 1980 (4659)
Parker, Tony, 1986 (9233)
Parsons, George, 1987 (9789)
Pease (Wedgewood), Helen, 1976 (821)
Pettitt, Ann, 1992 (12745)
Petts, John, 1987 (9732)
Powell, Hugo, 1988 (10351)
Prentice, Eve-Ann, 2005 (27750)
Quick, Bill, 2006 (29886)
Radley, Philip, 1974 (642)
Ramsey, Bill, 1994 (14203)
Randle, Michael, 1992 (12919)
Rée, Captain Harry, 1985 (8720)
Richards, Tina, 2006 (29877)
Ridgway, Roy, 1987 (10350)
Rose, General Sir Michael, 2002 (22726)
Rotblat, Professor Joseph, 1992 (12588)
Rowlands, David, 1993 (13631)
Rowntree, Michael, 1989 (10883)

Rushmer, Gordon, 2007 (30249)

Selstrom, Sergeant Roy, 2005 (27459)

Sharp, Peter, 2008 (30340)

Shea, Dr Jamie, 2008 (32525)

Shevlane, Maggie, 2009 (32736)

Sinclair-Loutit (de Renzy Martin), Angela, 1987 (10040)

Solomon, Myrtle, 1981 (4846)

Soper, (Baron) Rev. Donald, 1992 (12790)

Speck, Andreas, 2009 (32726)

Spiegelberg, Eldora, 1991 (12389)

Spray, Bill, 1988 (10551)

Sugden, Molly, 2002 (22598)

Swann, Donald, 1985 (9133)

Taggart, Mervyn, 1980 (4657)

Taylor, Dr Alan, 1993 (13649)

Temple, Bishop Freddie, 1991 (12035)

Tennant, Nancy, 1997 (17554)

Tidbury, Wade, 1993 (13085)

Townsend, Paul, 1993 (13411)

Trory, Ernest, 1980 (4693)

Turner, Eric, 1988 (12225)

Verney, Bishop Stephen, 1987 (9832)

Wallace, A.H., 1964 BBC TV *Great War* series (4254)

Ward, Colin, 1986 (9327)

White, Evelyn, 1988 (10142)

Whittle (Casselden), Fran, 1994 (13876)

Wigham (Derbyshire), Kathleen, 1980 (4671)

Winsten, Stephen, 1976 (784)

Wray, Kenneth, 1980 (4696)

Yamane, Kazuyo, 1992 (12791)

CONTRIBUTORS: DOCUMENTS

Each surname is followed by the reference number (in brackets) in the Documents Department of the Imperial War Museum, where the account is filed.

Barnard, Clifford, memoir (00/9 IWM)
Bartlet, Dr J .E. A. (87/25/1)
Harrison, William (99/84/1)
Harvey, John (76/99/1)
Hayler, Mark (74/56/1)
Macauley, John (97/10/1)
Milne, A. A. (Spec misc J3, XX02)
Radford, John (87/63/1)
Redgrave, Lionel (88/11/1)
Serraillier, Ian (94/10/1)
Skirth, J. R. (99/53/1)
Walters, Nigel (97/40/1)
Yamane, Kazuyo, private papers (Kazuyo Yamane, Kazunori Yamane and Chie Yuasa)

CONTRIBUTORS: PRINTED BOOKS

The surname is followed by the reference number (in brackets) in the Printed Books Department of the Imperial War Museum, where the account is filed.

Barnard, Clifford, memoir (00/9 IWM)

OTHER SOURCES

McCullin, Don, filmed interview, Stu McKenzie and Lyn Smith, 2009, held by IWMs Film and Video Archive.

Rayment, Sean, " 'I Didn't Join the British Army to Conduct American Foreign Policy' ", *The Sunday Telegraph* (12 March 2006).

Sengupta, Kim, "Prisoner of Conscience: RAF Doctor Who Refused Iraq Service is Jailed", *The Independent* (14 April 2006).